NOMA 2.O

Vegetable
Forest
Ocean

NOMA 2.0

René Redzepi,
Mette Søberg, and
Junichi Takahashi

with Nate French

Photographs by
Ditte Isager

Artisan | New York

Library of Congress Cataloging-in-
Publication Data is on file.

ISBN 978-1-64829-172-2

Design by Gretel
A.A. Trabucco-Campos and
Dylan Mulvaney

Project Management
Claire Banks

Artisan books are available at special
discounts when purchased in bulk for
premiums and sales promotions as well
as for fund-raising or educational use.
Special editions or book excerpts also can
be created to specification. For details,
contact the Special Sales Director at
the address below, or send an e-mail to
specialmarkets@workman.com.

For speaking engagements,
contact speakersbureau@workman.com.

Published by Artisan
A division of Workman Publishing Co., Inc.
225 Varick Street
New York, NY 10014-4381
artisanbooks.com

Artisan is a registered trademark of
Workman Publishing Co., Inc.

Printed in Italy on responsibly
sourced paper

First printing, October 2022

10 9 8 7 6 5 4 3 2 1

How to Use This Book

The purpose of this book is to show you what's been going on at Noma 2.0 in a meaningful way. While there is no substitute for sitting at a table conversing with the people who cook your food—and then eating the dishes—photography and language is the next best thing.

The photographs here almost speak for themselves, but not quite, which is why informative text accompanies them. You'll see, however, that this text is not a recipe. The lists of ingredients do not include measurements, because what's relevant here are the ingredients themselves, those elements reflective of the flow of each season—Vegetable, Forest, Ocean—and the creative perspectives our team brings to them.

These elements are divided into components. Some components are used to build even more complex components; others are used on their own in the dish. The ingredients marked with an asterisk (*) belong to the set of essentials we design for each season, such as oils, garums, and broths. Recipes for those components, including specific measurements and instructions, can be found in the Gastronomique section (pages 330–351).

The narrative descriptions are not literal instructions. Rather than explain all the steps needed to make the dish, they are meant to illuminate a bit more than the photographs might reveal—what's under a layer of mushroom soil, what's stuffed into a delicate zucchini blossom, what's beneath the cluster of tiny blossoms and bee pollen.

For a deeper dive into the Noma kitchen, scan the QR code to access the full technical recipes of each dish, complete with measurements and methods.

Reflection on Twenty Years   René Redzepi

I had barely announced the decision to close Noma and rebuild it in a derelict corner of Copenhagen when I was seized by doubt. There was plenty that I hadn't thought through, like where to find the money, or how to transplant a restaurant without losing the hard-won trust of our guests. But the question that did terrify me, as I surveyed the graffiti-covered patch of land that would become our new home, was this: What if we move here and do things exactly like we did them before?

This book is about the new Noma, its people and spaces and, of course, the food. But it's also about the invisible structures we set up to sustain creativity, innovation, and surprise. Part of what drove this move was the determination not to let previous success poison our creative minds. The need to rekindle our appetite for new things. The urge to stay alert to fresh opportunities. From the architecture to the seasonality of our menus, everything at the new Noma helps keep our minds open.

But before we moved in, we moved out—into the world, with pop-up restaurants in far-flung locations. I wanted us to go someplace so far from our own culture that we would look at everything with fresh eyes. The Noma pop-up in Japan fed our passion for fermentation and our ongoing search for umami. In Australia we marveled at the unique native species—have you ever tasted a succulent wild gubinge fruit? Mexico taught us about fire, and how to build heat in cooking through the use of chiles.

Out of our travels grew the idea to divide the year into three distinct menus, determined by the bounty of each season. When the leaves fall from the trees, we go to the forest in search of wild plants, mushrooms, and game. When the soil is frozen and nothing grows, we turn to the oceans, where the fish are fat and pristine, their bellies full of roe. And when everything turns green again, we become a vegetarian restaurant, serving up everything edible from the plant kingdom.

It's a way of aligning our menu with the flow of ingredients. And each one—vegetable, forest, ocean—contains microseasons with ingredients that say, Hey, you thought this was a good idea, but let me tell you something else. A week of rain might nix your cherished asparagus dish. A day of strong winds can ground the boats you relied on to catch the turbot that was destined to be your main course. An early frost burns off the chanterelles that were going to make your game season sing.

Devising an entirely new menu three times a year puts us under enormous pressure. I am writing these words in late winter. Soon, we need to plan our next vegetarian season, but the ground outside is like a block of cement. Somehow, we need to dream up dishes around plants that won't make an appearance in nature for months.

We also make it a rule not to repeat ourselves—we have too many guests who dine with us year after year. But it's not as if nature obliges us with a new species of deer each fall, or a crop of entirely different plants the next summer. It's up to us to find ever new perspectives on familiar ingredients.

It took time for us to get used to the new menu rhythm. Now we know that the transitions between seasons are our moment to work on larger ideas and techniques. In the run-up to our first vegetarian season, we spent months obsessing over a plant-based shawarma that would be meaty and rich. Right now, we are testing a Nordic version of tofu, grinding biodynamic legumes into milk, adding niacin, and then steaming the mixture until it sets. The test kitchen turns into a laboratory. It can take hundreds of tests to perfect a bean or walnut tofu—half a degree up and a

Opposite: René Redzepi and the preservice meeting. **Above left:** The calm before the work begins. **Above right:** Each season's menu is served on its own set of handmade pottery.

Clockwise from left: A cadre of chefs in service, with head chef Kenneth Foong on the pass; the lounge, a place to gather after the meal; a stand of echinacea in the meadow outside.

Clockwise from left: A path through the garden to reach the front door; a shellfish study for the Ocean season; nature is art.

little less salt can mean a world of difference. But from a single idea, an array of others can sprout. Once you nail a fava bean tofu, you might serve it ice cold, with asparagus juice; or hot, with reindeer ragout; or sweet, with strawberry coulis. You might make a version that is light like a custard.

Much of the time, the team in the test kitchen isn't cooking at all. We pore over books, take in an art show. We quiz university researchers on the science of vinegar. We let ideas percolate over the course of a daylong hike. Our team runs on trust, of one another and of our own intuition. Creativity means being intensely aware of your feelings and trusting your gut. It requires discipline and mental freedom. As we develop our dishes, these are the questions that guide us: Does it have Noma levels of taste and surprise? Does eating it ground you in time?

The new seasonal approach has pushed us to plan more. We draw up yearly plans for our farmers, for our garden, for the fermentation lab, for the wines and spirits, for foraging—and even for how to replenish our reservoir of creative ideas. It's forced me to develop new layers of discipline, even while carving out pockets for spontaneity and creative chaos.

Our physical spaces support this. We told Bjarke Ingels, our architect, that we wanted a place of work that felt like we were out of doors. I also wanted a space where, metaphorically, there was no ceiling, no heavy concrete to block our thoughts. Where we could think big, as far as the moon, if we wanted. In addition, our new setup is flexible, with separate buildings like you would find in a village. If we choose, we can close off an individual space. We could shrink Noma down to a ten-seat restaurant. This place has given us a home in which to think again, dream again, dare again.

We still sometimes head out into the world to hone our beginner's mind. In early 2020, our creative team returned to Japan. We wanted to immerse ourselves in Zen Buddhism, in part because of its deep ties to vegan cuisine. But sitting zazen in a temple, we forgot everything, including ourselves. We were like jelly afterward, ready to be molded into anything.

It may sound like a paradox, but at Noma we plan for spontaneity and commit to openness; it takes discipline to be curious. But the move also proved that some of the biggest decisions require you to take the plunge first and do your due diligence later. To make your home, sometimes you have to free-fall into it.

Twenty years have almost passed, and our guiding point has always been "time and place." What that has meant to us over the last twenty years has varied dramatically in our path to figuring out who we are. At the start of Noma, "time and place" was defined by the local ingredients that we sourced. The surrounding nature that tied us to our place in Scandinavia. We were where are ingredients were from: the north. Today "time and place" to us simply means to be Noma. To be in a situation where we're no longer defined by where we are; we are just defined by who we are—by being Noma.

Opposite: A portal through antlers.
Left: When greenery takes over.

Above: Pumpkin varietals.
Right: The fermentation lab at work.

Vegetable

May through August

Tomato Marinated with Sumac

Elderflower oil is drizzled into a serving bowl. Peeled and seeded tomatoes are arranged in the bowl, along with cucumber, nasturtium, anise hyssop, sage, and fireweed blossoms. Mussel and tomato broth is poured around everything, and sumac granita is spooned on as the final step. The dish is served on ice and oak leaves.

TOMATOES
Tomatoes, a mix of varieties and sizes

SUMAC-ADE
Filtered water
Whole sumac

SUMAC GRANITA
Simple syrup
Sumac-Ade

ICE-CLARIFIED MUSSEL JUICE
Mussels
White wine
Gelatin

MUSSEL AND TOMATO BROTH
Ice-Clarified Tomato Water*
Lacto Koji Water* (made with
  Rice Koji*)
Ice-Clarified Mussel Juice
Unripe sea buckthorn berries
Frozen Japanese quince
Salt

TO FINISH
Tomatoes
Mussel and Tomato Broth
Elderflower Oil*
Cucumber flowers
Nasturtium flowers
Anise hyssop flowers
Sage flowers
Fireweed flowers
Sumac Granita
Salt

Potato Magma

New potatoes are roasted in butter and passed through a sieve. A potato stock is made by boiling more new potatoes, straining off the cooking liquid, and infusing it with fresh elderflower.

    The roasted and passed potatoes are mixed with butter and potato stock to yield a smooth, magma-like potato broth, which is carefully poured into the bottom of a terra-cotta flower pot seasoned with elderflower oil. The pot is topped with an herb plant and fitted with a length of Japanese knotweed to serve as a straw for drinking the magma broth.

ROASTED NEW POTATOES
New potatoes
Butter

POTATO STOCK
New potatoes
Filtered water
Fresh elderflower blossoms with
  stems

MAGMA BROTH
New Potato Purée
Butter
Potato Stock

TO FINISH
Potted plant (parsley or lemon thyme)
Japanese knotweed
Elderflower Oil*
Magma Broth

White Asparagus and Pickles

A stalk of white asparagus is cooked in rose oil, then marinated in white wine vinegar and rose petal salt. The asparagus is dressed with saffron kelp salt and rose oil. Sprigs of pickled fresh elderflower, flowering marjoram, and lemon thyme are arranged on the plate as well, along with a candied pine cone marinated in pine vinegar and topped with roasted kelp salt and a halved nixtamalized larch cone dressed with spruce wood oil. The dish is finished with a spoonful of the asparagus marinade.

ROSE PETAL SALT
Wild beach rose petals
Flake sea salt
Ants

VINEGARED PINE CONES
Jarred candied pine cones
Pine Vinegar*

NIXTAMALIZED LARCH CONES
Larch cones
Grapeseed oil
Filtered water
Calcium hydroxide

SAFFRON KELP SALT
Filtered water
Kelp
Saffron

PICKLING LIQUID
White wine vinegar
Filtered water

COOKED WHITE ASPARAGUS
White asparagus
Rose Oil*

MARINATED WHITE ASPARAGUS
Cooked White Asparagus
Pickling Liquid
Rose Petal Salt

PICKLED HERBS
Flowering marjoram sprig
Flowering lemon thyme sprig
Elderflower blossoms and tender
  stems
Pickling Liquid

TO FINISH
Marinated White Asparagus
Saffron Kelp Salt
Rose Oil*
Pickled Herbs
Vinegared Pine Cone
Roasted Kelp Salt*
Nixtamalized Larch Cone
Spruce Wood Oil*

Zucchini Flower

Jerusalem artichokes are brined in citric koji and water, then marinated and aged in a paste made from sea buckthorn, bee pollen, pepper tamari, butternut squash vinegar, and salt to make a kimchi.

Zucchini flowers are cooked with koji oil and then dried until very crisp. More zucchini flowers are briefly brined in salt and calcium hydroxide to nixtamalize them.

Lightly cooked eggs are blended with lacto-fermented koji water, brined gooseberries, and lemon juice and emulsified with brown butter.

The nixtamalized zucchini flower is coated in tempura batter, fried, seasoned with Danish curry powder, and topped with salted mustard seeds and wedges of the Jerusalem artichoke kimchi. The brown butter emulsion is dotted on top. The face of the fried zucchini flower is scattered with fresh flowers, and spiced butter and horseradish juice are drizzled over the flowers. A zucchini flower crisp is placed on top.

SEA BUCKTHORN KIMCHI PASTE
Freeze-dried sea buckthorn berries
Bee pollen
Red Pepper Tamari*
Butternut Squash Vinegar*
Salt

JERUSALEM ARTICHOKE KIMCHI
Citric Koji*
Filtered water
Jerusalem artichokes
Sea Buckthorn Kimchi Paste

ZUCCHINI FLOWER CRISP
Zucchini flower
Koji Oil*

NIXTAMALIZED ZUCCHINI FLOWER
Zucchini flower
1% salt brine
Calcium hydroxide

DANISH CURRY POWDER
Toasted yellow mustard seeds
Toasted coriander seeds
Toasted fennel seeds
Saffron
Sumac powder
Dried Horseradish*
Dried Ginger*
Vinegar powder

TEMPURA BATTER
Tipo "00" flour
Cornstarch
Potato starch
Baking powder
Danish Curry Powder
Salt
Ethanol (96% ABV)
White wine vinegar
Sparkling water

BROWN BUTTER EMULSION
Eggs
Lacto Koji Water* (made with Øland Wheat Koji*)
Lemon juice
Brown Butter*
Salted Green Gooseberry Capers* (drained)

BLACK TRUMPET MUSHROOM TEA
Hot filtered water
Dried black trumpet mushrooms
Dried chanterelles
Dried ceps
Kelp

SALTED MUSTARD SEEDS
Yellow mustard seeds
Black Trumpet Mushroom Tea
Filtered water
Salt

JUN SPICE MIX
Dried ceps
Dried chanterelles
Black peppercorns
Juniper berries
Dried angelica buds
Freeze-dried lingonberry
Coriander seed
Arctic thyme leaves
Roasted Kelp*

SPICED BUTTER
Butter
Jun Spice Mix
Seeded morita chile
Seeded ancho chile
Roasted Kelp Salt*
Maitake Garum*
Chicken Wing Garum*

TO FINISH
Nixtamalized Zucchini Flower
Rice flour
Tempura Batter
Grapeseed oil
Danish Curry Powder
Salted Mustard Seeds
Jerusalem Artichoke Kimchi
Brown Butter Emulsion
Fresh flowers (kale flowers, rapeseed flowers, cabbage flowers, etc.)
Spiced Butter
Horseradish juice
Zucchini Flower Crisp

Hipberry Marinated with Marigold and Pollen

A rose hip is skinned, seeded, brushed with marigold oil, and dried until chewy. Japanese quince paste is gently folded with bee pollen and spooned into the rose hip, which is then garnished with green coriander seed halves.

Japanese quince paste is piped onto a trimmed nasturtium leaf and a thin slice of salted Japanese quince is laid on top. The quince slice is brushed with marigold oil, and marigold petals are arranged around the edge in a flower pattern. The center of the nasturtium leaf is piped with more Japanese quince paste and covered with bee pollen. The nasturtium "marigold" is positioned on the stuffed rose hip, hiding the rose hip beneath. A drizzle of marigold oil encircles the stuffed hipberry to finish the dish.

SEMI-DRIED ROSE HIP
Large rose hip
Burning Embers Marigold Oil*

JAPANESE QUINCE PASTE
Japanese quince
Butter
Dried Carrot Flowers*

TO FINISH
Japanese Quince Paste
Bee pollen
Semi-Dried Rose Hip
Green coriander seed halves
Small nasturtium leaf
Brined Japanese Quince*
Marigold (*Calendula officinalis*)
   flowers
Burning Embers Marigold Oil*

Seaweed Pie

Sugar kelp is simmered in sugar syrup, then in lacto-fermented koji water. The kelp is cut into rounds and dried in a tart mold to create a crisp shell.

Irish moss is cooked until tender in cucumber kelp broth. Sea lettuce and kelp grass are both cooked in yeast broth.

The sugar kelp tart shell is piped with lovage fudge and dusted with plankton powder. The Irish moss, sea lettuce, and kelp grass are spritzed with pine vinegar and arranged on top. The whole tart is finished with a spritz of ocean spray.

SUGAR SYRUP
Muscovado sugar
Filtered water

SUGAR KELP TART SHELL
Sugar Syrup
Fresh sugar kelp
Lacto Koji Water* (made with Øland
  Wheat Koji*)

LOVAGE HERB PASTE
Lovage leaves
Parsley leaves
Lovage Oil*
Yeast Broth Reduction*
Roasted Kelp Salt*

LOVAGE FUDGE
Lovage Herb Paste
Butter

COOKED IRISH MOSS
Irish moss
Cucumber-Kelp Broth*

MARINATED SEA LETTUCE
Fresh sea lettuce
Yeast Broth*

MARINATED KELP GRASS
Fresh kelp grass
Yeast Broth*

OCEAN SPRAY
Lemon thyme sprigs
Dried kelp
Dried Icelandic söl
Fresh Irish moss
Ethanol (60% ABV)

TO FINISH
Sugar Kelp Tart Shell
Marinated Sea Lettuce
Marinated Kelp Grass
Cooked Irish Moss
Pine Vinegar*
Lovage Fudge
Plankton powder
Ocean Spray

Courgette Dumpling

Honey-grilled baby zucchini are diced and folded with salted mustard seeds and strawberry-rhubarb tamari.

Female zucchini blossoms are trimmed and the stigmas removed and reserved. The blossoms are briefly cooked in a poaching liquid of lovage, lemon verbena, dried koji, lemon thyme, salt, and water and then cooled in a cold version of the same mixture.

The blossoms are filled with layers of lingonberry paste, seasoned parsley purée, roasted kelp salt, the dressed diced zucchini, chewy bee larvae, honey, horseradish juice, crispy bee larvae, bee pollen, and balsamic vinegar. The blossoms are twisted closed, trimmed again, brushed with elderflower oil, seasoned with salt, and spritzed with Japanese quince brine spray.

The stuffed blossom "dumpling" and its stigma are seasoned with cloudberry marinade and served on fresh leaves.

GRILLED BABY ZUCCHINI
Small zucchini
Noma honey

BLACK TRUMPET MUSHROOM TEA
Filtered water
Dried black trumpet mushrooms
Dried chanterelles
Dried ceps
Kelp

SALTED MUSTARD SEEDS
Yellow mustard seeds
Black Trumpet Mushroom Tea
Salt

ZUCCHINI COOKING LIQUID
Lovage leaves
Lemon verbena sprigs
Lemon thyme sprigs
Filtered water
Dried Koji*
Salt

BLANCHED ZUCCHINI FLOWERS
Female zucchini flowers
Zucchini Cooking Liquid

CLOUDBERRY MARINADE
Frozen cloudberry purée
Noma honey

MUSTARD SPICE MIX
Toasted yellow mustard seeds
Toasted fennel seeds
Toasted coriander seeds
Toasted seeded pasilla chile
Freeze-dried gooseberries
Black peppercorns
Juniper berries

SUNFLOWER SEED PASTE
Sunflower seeds
Brown Butter*
Ginger Powder*
Mustard Spice Mix
Celery Juice Reduction*
Peaso Water Reduction*
Roasted Kelp Salt*
Nordic Shoyu*

MUSHROOM SPICE MIX
Arctic thyme leaves
Yellow mustard seeds
Coriander seeds
Fennel seeds
Dried ceps
Dried morels

FRIED PARSLEY
Parsley leaves
Grapeseed oil

FRIED LOVAGE
Lovage leaves
Grapeseed oil

LINGONBERRY PASTE
Freeze-dried rhubarb
Freeze-dried lingonberries
Freeze-dried gooseberries
Cold-Infused Dashi*
Mushroom Spice Mix
Koji Oil*
Fried Parsley
Fried Lovage
Sunflower Seed Paste

SEASONED PARSLEY PURÉE
Parsley leaves
Beef Garum*

CHEWY BEE LARVAE AND CRISPY BEE LARVAE
Frozen bee larvae
Clarified butter
Salt

JAPANESE QUINCE BRINE SPRAY
Brine from Brined Japanese Quince*
White wine vinegar

TO FINISH
Finely diced Grilled Baby Zucchini
Salted Mustard Seeds
Strawberry-Rhubarb Tamari*
Blanched Zucchini Flower
Raw zucchini bud
Cloudberry Marinade
Lingonberry Paste
Seasoned Parsley Purée
Chewy Bee Larvae
Crispy Bee Larvae
Roasted Kelp Salt*
Horseradish juice
Noma honey
Italian balsamic vinegar
Bee pollen
Japanese Quince Brine Spray
Elderflower Oil*
Salt

Crudités

On the plate, a selection of raw or simply cooked seasonal vegetables, herbs, and flowers are arranged and served with Nordic pesto. Here the arrangement includes artichoke hearts cooked with a bit of Douglas fir oil and artichoke leaves cooked the same way and then compressed with parsley oil, as well as candied pine cones compressed with pine vinegar.

ARTICHOKE HEARTS AND LEAVES
Artichokes
Douglas Fir Oil*
Lemons
Salt

VINEGARED PINE CONE
Jarred candied pine cones
Pine Vinegar*

NORDIC PESTO
Unripe sea buckthorn berries
Salted Black Currant Capers*
Salted Green Gooseberry Capers*
Maitake Garum*
Black Currant Leaf Oil*
Parsley Oil*
Elderflower Peaso*
Parsley leaves
Coriander leaves
Lovage leaves
Basil leaves
Green coriander seeds
Salt

TO FINISH
Halved Artichoke Hearts
Artichoke Leaves compressed in
   Parsley Oil*
Raw oyster leaves
French breakfast radish (stem on)
Small white turnip slice
Mexican oregano leaf
Candied Pine Cone
Salted noble fir scale
Cucumber with flower
Zucchini with flower
Radish bud
2% salt brine spray
Nordic Pesto

A Cold Soup of Berries

Cherry tomatoes are peeled, seeded, and hollowed, then filled with semi-dried tomatoes. Raspberries are filled with a strawberry paste made from fresh strawberries deeply caramelized in koji oil and seasoned with roseroot spice blend. Fresh blueberries are filled with lemon thyme flowers.

The tomatoes, raspberries, and blueberries are grouped in a serving bowl and berry soup is poured around them. The soup is then seasoned with black currant wood and morita chile oils. The dish is garnished with grilled lemon thyme.

COOKED YELLOW BEETS
Yellow beets

BERRY SOUP BASE
Japanese quince
Halved red gooseberries
Lingonberries
Topped and seeded rose hips
  (skin on)
Lacto Mirabelle Plums*
Barley Koji*
Black Currant Wood Oil*
Morita Chile Oil*
Anise hyssop leaves
Oregano leaves
Lemon thyme leaves
Yarrow
Ramson leaves
Cooked Yellow Beets

TOMATO-SAFFRON WATER
Ice-Clarified Tomato Water*
Saffron

BERRY SOUP
Berry Soup Base
Tomato-Saffron Water
Smoked Koji Oil*

ROSEROOT SPICE BLEND
Dried roseroot
Dried carrot seeds
Toasted fenugreek
Toasted coriander seeds
Fennel seeds
Arctic thyme leaves

STRAWBERRY PASTE
Koji Oil*
Red strawberries
Roseroot Spice Blend

HOLLOWED CHERRY TOMATOES
Cherry tomatoes

GRAIN-GRILLED LEMON THYME
Lemon thyme
Konini Oil*

TO FINISH
Hollowed Cherry Tomatoes
Semi-Dried Tomatoes*
Raspberries
Strawberry Paste
Blueberries
Lemon thyme flowers
Berry Soup
Grain-Grilled Lemon Thyme
Black Currant Wood Oil*
Morita Chile Oil*

Cucumber Dolma

Cucumbers are cooked with koji oil and then dried until chewy but still juicy. The dried cucumbers are simmered in dashi with herbs and Douglas fir and then butterflied. The flesh is scraped off the skins and used to make a cucumber flesh paste. The cucumber skins are cut into rectangles, spread with parsley paste, and seasoned with elderflower oil, then piped with a rhubarb paste, the cucumber flesh paste, and a smoked parsley purée. Green coriander seed and pickled elderflower are arranged on top of the pastes and the skins are rolled up into dolma shapes. Flowering lemon thyme is tucked into each end, and the dolmas are brushed with more elderflower oil.

DRIED CUCUMBERS
Cucumbers
Koji Oil*

CUCUMBER SKINS
Dried Cucumbers
Cold-Infused Dashi*
Lemon thyme sprigs
Douglas fir sprigs
Parsley

CUCUMBER FLESH PASTE
Cucumber flesh (reserved from the
  Cucumber Skins)
Peaso* (blended and passed)
Sunflower seed oil

PARSLEY PASTE
Parsley leaves
Parsley Oil*
Yeast Broth Reduction*

PARSLEY PURÉE
Parsley leaves

SMOKED PARSLEY PURÉE
Parsley Purée
Peaso*
Parsley Oil*
Nordic Shoyu*
Toasted Hay*

DANISH CURRY POWDER
Toasted yellow mustard seeds
Toasted coriander seeds
Toasted fennel seeds
Saffron
Sumac powder
Horseradish Powder*
Ginger Powder*
Vinegar powder

SUNFLOWER SEED PASTE
Sunflower seeds
Butter
Ginger Powder*
Danish Curry Powder
Celery Juice Reduction*
Dried Tomato Powder*
Kelp Salt*
Nordic Shoyu*
Salt

CHILE NO CHILE POWDER
Horseradish Powder*
Yellow mustard seeds
Dried Ginger Skins*
Black peppercorns
Toasted coriander seeds

FRIED PARSLEY
Parsley leaves
Grapeseed oil

FRIED LOVAGE
Lovage leaves
Grapeseed oil

RHUBARB PASTE BASE
Freeze-dried rhubarb
Cucumber-Kelp Broth*
Salt
Chile No Chile Powder
Fried Parsley
Fried Lovage
Sunflower Seed Paste
Koji Oil*

RHUBARB PASTE
Rhubarb Paste Base
Peaso Water Reduction*
Roasted Kelp Salt*
Danish Curry Powder
Lacto Koji Water* (made with Øland
  Wheat Koji*)
Cucumber Juice Reduction*
Nordic Shoyu*
Coriander seeds
Sunflower Seed Paste

TO FINISH
Cucumber Skin
Parsley Paste
Elderflower Oil*
Rhubarb Paste
Cucumber Flesh Paste
Smoked Parsley Purée
Green coriander seeds
Pickled Elderflower* bunches
Flowering lemon thyme tips

Ice-Cold Beet Juice and Ladybug

The ladybug parts are created using black and red fruit leathers shaped in molds and dried until crisp. Strawberry paste is piped onto a half raspberry and topped with a semi-dried mulberry, a drop of chile de árbol oil, Japanese quince paste, and salt. The ladybug shell is brushed with rose oil and then fitted onto the stuffed raspberry.

Cylindra beet juice is blended with a purée of roasted beets, more beet juice, and dried black currants, along with clarified green apple juice, white peony tea, rose hip paste, strawberry-rhubarb tamari, freeze-dried black currants, dried beet powder, and plum kernels. The sweet-tart balance of the mixture is adjusted with Noma honey, lemon juice, and salt.

An icy mug gets a few drops of geranium oil before it's filled with the seasoned beet juice and garnished with a loose bouquet of bronze fennel, geranium leaves, and other wild flowers, herbs, and leaves. The bouquet is spritzed with geranium water and a ladybug gets placed among the flowers.

LADYBUG

BLACK GARLIC AND BERRY
LEATHER BASE
Japanese black garlic
Black currants
Seeded rose hips
Red gooseberries
Lingonberries
Muscovado sugar
Freeze-dried blueberries
Freeze-dried black currants
Charcoal powder

ROSE HIP PURÉE
Seeded rose hips

BERRY LEATHER BASE
Seeded rose hips
Red gooseberries
Black currants
Muscovado sugar
Freeze-dried raspberries
Freeze-dried beet powder

ROSE HIP AND BERRY LEATHER
BASE
Rose Hip Purée
Berry Leather Base

LADYBUG LEATHER
Black Garlic and Berry Leather Base
Rose Hip and Berry Leather Base

STRAWBERRY PASTE
Koji Oil*
Ripe red strawberries

JAPANESE QUINCE PASTE
Japanese quince
Butter
Dried Carrot Flowers*

TO FINISH THE LADYBUG
Ladybug Leather
Strawberry Paste
Fresh raspberry
Semi-Dried Mulberry* (small whole
   berry or half of a larger one)
Árbol Chile Oil*
Japanese Quince Paste
Salt
Rose Oil*

BEET JUICE

BEET JUICE
Cylindra beets

ROASTED BEETS
Cylindra beets
Grapeseed oil
Salt

BEET PURÉE
Roasted beets
Beet Juice
Freeze-dried black currants

CLARIFIED GREEN APPLE JUICE
Green apples

ROSE HIP PASTE
Rose hips

SEASONED BEET JUICE
Beet Purée
Beet Juice
Clarified Green Apple Juice
Cold-Infused White Peony Tea*
Rose Hip Paste
Strawberry-Rhubarb Tamari*
Freeze-dried black currants
Dried beet powder
Plum kernels
Noma honey
Lemon juice
Salt
Xantana

GERANIUM WATER SPRAY
Geranium leaves
Filtered water

TO FINISH THE BEET JUICE
Geranium Oil*
Seasoned Beet Juice
Bronze fennel
Geranium leaves
Other wild leaves and plants
Geranium Water Spray

VEGETABLE

Fava Beans and Berries

Lacto-fermented koji water, smoked tomato water, butter, and rose oil are blended to make rose sauce.

Fava beans are grilled in their pods, then the inner beans are peeled, split into tender green discs, and marinated in parsley oil.

Cherry tomatoes, brushed with koji oil and moistened with honey, are dried until dense but tender and chewy.

The favas and slices of cherry, gooseberry, strawberry, and dried tomato are arranged on a serving plate in overlapping concentric rings. Golden raspberry halves, wild cherries, and wild strawberries are scattered on top and parsley purée is dotted around. Soft herbs and flowers are strewn over the favas and fruits, along with coriander seeds, black currant shoots, and a few tiny mounds of pollen and morita oil.

The dish is sprinkled with ants and finished with rose sauce and drops of parsley oil.

ROSE SAUCE
Lacto Koji Water* (made with Øland
   Wheat Koji*)
Smoked Tomato Water*
Butter
Xantana
Salt
Rose Oil*

GRILLED FAVA BEANS
Fava beans
Parsley Oil*

PARSLEY PURÉE
Parsley leaves

POLLEN AND MORITA OIL PASTE
Morita Chile Oil*
Pollen

TO FINISH
Rose Sauce
Grilled Fava Beans
Parsley Oil*
Semi-Dried Tomato* halves
Pollen and Morita Oil Paste
Cherry slices
Gooseberry slices (green or red)
Strawberry slices
Golden raspberry halves
Small wild cherries
Wild strawberries
Parsley Purée
Oregano leaves
Marjoram leaves
Lemon thyme leaves
Grilled Lemon Thyme*
Lemon verbena leaves
Coriander flowers
Fennel flower halves
Fresh coriander seeds
Black currant shoot halves
Ants

Nordic Olives

Lemon verbena is frozen with liquid nitrogen, pulverized to a powder, and then mixed with finely chopped nasturtium stems, parsley leaves, parsley oil, and salt to form a paste.

Red gooseberries are partially hollowed out, stuffed with a white currant, a coriander seed, and a black currant bud, then filled with the nasturtium stem paste, skewered, and frozen.

Two stuffed gooseberries are transferred to black currant wood toothpicks and garnished with a halved salted sloeberry and a lavender bud. The "olives" are served on a small pool of spruce wood oil.

NASTURTIUM STEM PASTE
Lemon verbena leaves
Nasturtium stems
Parsley leaves
Parsley Oil*
Salt

TO FINISH
Ripe red gooseberries
Small white currants
Fresh coriander seeds
Black currant buds
Nasturtium Stem Paste
Black currant wood toothpicks
Pitted Salted Sloeberry* halves
Lavender bud
Spruce Wood Oil*

VEGETABLE

Onion Gel

New onions are hollowed out to create a vessel with a lid. Mature onions are slowly cooked with dashi and mushroom broth and then reduced. This bouillon base is seasoned and gelatin is stirred into the liquid.

The onion gel liquid is poured into the onion vessels. Once set, the surface of the gel is topped with toasted beechnuts, spruce wood oil, and a dollop of whipped cream.

ONION VESSELS
New onions

MUSHROOM BROTH
Cold-Infused Dashi*
Fresh maitake mushrooms
Dried chanterelles
Fresh lemon thyme
Ice-Clarified Tomato Water*

ONION BOUILLON BASE
Onions
Cold-Infused Dashi*
Mushroom Broth

ONION GEL
Onion Bouillon Base
Oregano Vinegar*
Salt
Gelatin

TO FINISH
Onion Gel
Onion Vessels and tops
Toasted beechnuts
Spruce Wood Oil*
Whipped cream
Salt

Vegetable Flatbread

Flatbread dough is rolled thin and grilled over charcoal until puffed, brown, and crispy.

Sliced radishes and an assortment of fresh herbs and flowers are dressed with rhubarb and sunflower seed paste, chicken wing garum, horseradish juice, pine vinegar, and a spoonful of warm berry spice smoked butter.

The grilled flatbread is brushed with brown butter and topped with the radish and herb mix, which is finished with morita chile paste and more berry spice smoked butter.

MALT FLATBREAD
Tipo "00" flour
Koji Flour*
Malt flour
Dried Rose Oil*
Butter
Salt
Kaelder Øl lager

DANISH CURRY POWDER
Toasted yellow mustard seeds
Toasted coriander seeds
Toasted fennel seeds
Saffron
Sumac powder
Horseradish Powder*
Ginger Powder*
Vinegar powder

SUNFLOWER SEED PASTE
Sunflower seeds
Butter
Ginger Powder*
Danish Curry Powder
Celery Juice Reduction*
Dried Tomato Powder*
Kelp Salt*
Nordic Shoyu*
Salt

CHILE NO CHILE POWDER
Horseradish Powder*
Yellow mustard seeds
Dried Ginger Skins*
Black peppercorns
Toasted coriander seeds

RHUBARB AND SUNFLOWER SEED PASTE
Freeze-dried rhubarb
Cucumber-Kelp Broth*
Salt
Chile No Chile Powder
Lemon verbena leaves
Scraps of dried Pickled Rose Petals*
Fried Parsley
Fried Lovage
Sunflower Seed Paste
Koji Oil*

BERRY SPICE
Toasted coriander seeds
Toasted fennel seeds
Toasted angelica
Dried Horseradish*
Dried Ginger*
Arctic thyme
Dried Strawberries*
Smoked Butter*

MORITA CHILE PASTE
Seeded morita chile
Grasshoppers
Spring garlic
Olive oil
Grapeseed oil
Grasshopper Garum*
Potato Stock Reduction*
Salt
Roasted Kelp Oil*

TO FINISH
Baby radishes
Lemon thyme tops with flowers
Tender ground elder shoots
Mustard flowers
Rocket flowers
Ground elder blossoms
Chervil flowers
Yarrow
Spanish chervil
Oregano tops
Wood sorrel bunches
Green coriander seed halves
Rhubarb and Sunflower Seed Paste
Chicken Wing Garum*
Horseradish juice
Pine Vinegar*
Berry Spice Smoked Butter
Malt Flatbread
Brown Butter*
Morita Chile Paste

Mushroom Skewer

Morels and other wild mushrooms are cooked in cep oil to preserve them. Fresh oyster mushrooms are pressure cooked with hay, spruce wood, lemon thyme, and yeast broth.

Chopped cooked mixed grains are folded with a mixture of muddled roasted kelp salt, green coriander seeds, celery and fennel reductions, and a lacto-fermented plum and tomato reduction emulsified with butter.

The three types of mushroom are lightly grilled. The grilled morels are piped with dressed mixed grains and the opening is filled with fried sourdough, then all the mushrooms are skewered onto a Douglas fir twig and grilled a second time with glaze over charcoal. Mushroom spice is sprinkled over the skewer and bee pollen and morita paste is brushed onto the morels. Two Mexican oregano leaves and some flaky salt finish the dish.

PRESERVED MORELS
Morel mushrooms
Cep Oil*

OYSTER MUSHROOMS
Oyster mushrooms
Hay
Spruce wood
Lemon thyme sprigs
Yeast Broth*

MIXED GRAINS
Spelt
Barley
Emmer
Konini wheat
Yellow mustard seeds

LACTO PLUM AND TOMATO
REDUCTION
Lacto Plum Juice*
Ice-Clarified Tomato Water*
Kelp
Dried Ginger*

DRESSED MIXED GRAINS
Roasted Kelp Salt*
Green coriander seeds
Celery Juice Reduction*
Fennel Juice Reduction*
Lacto Plum and Tomato Reduction
Xantana
Butter
Mixed Grains

FRIED SOURDOUGH
Sourdough bread
Butter

BEE POLLEN AND MORITA PASTE
Ants
Finely chopped pine shoots
Morita chile
Bee pollen

MUSHROOM SPICE
Dried ceps
Dried chanterelles
Dried black trumpet mushrooms
Toasted black peppercorns
Toasted coriander seeds
Toasted juniper berries
Dried angelica seeds
Freeze-dried lingonberries
Arctic thyme
Roasted Kelp Salt*

MUSHROOM GLAZE
Mushroom-Kelp Broth*
Yeast Broth*
Brown Butter*

TO FINISH
Preserved Morels
Preserved Mixed Mushrooms*
Oyster Mushrooms
Dressed Mixed Grains
Fried Sourdough
Douglas fir skewer
Mushroom Glaze
Mushroom Spice
Bee Pollen and Morita Paste
Mexican oregano leaves

Grilled Onion with Just-Pressed Walnut Oil

Onions with their green tops intact are deeply charred in white-hot coals and then cooked over direct heat until tender. The heart (inner layers) of the onion is scooped out and sliced, and the slices dressed with red pepper tamari, chives, and smoked salt. The onion heart is reassembled and slipped back into the outer layers of the onion. The interior is seasoned with just-pressed walnut oil and the onion is closed up and served.

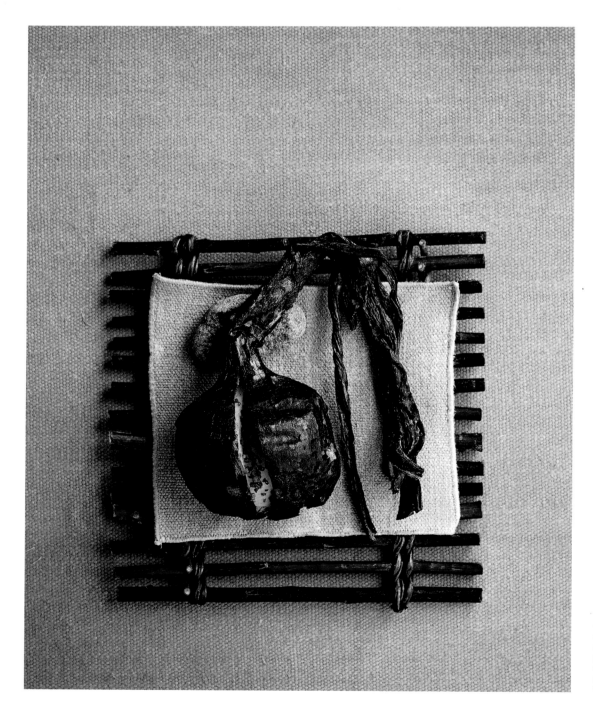

SMOKED SALT
Salt

GRILLED ONION HEARTS AND
VESSELS
Onions

TO FINISH
Grilled Onion Heart
Grilled Onion Vessel
Smoked Salt
Chopped chives
Red Pepper Tamari*
Walnut Oil*

Young Garlic Confit

Whole garlic heads are trimmed, blanched, and then simmered until tender in milk and lacto-fermented koji water seasoned with juniper berries.

The garlic cloves are served in a bowl of just-pressed walnut oil seasoned with salt and mixed with chopped fresh chives and lemon thyme leaves that have been grilled with smoked butter until slightly charred and crisp. Toasted beechnuts are nestled between the garlic cloves.

GARLIC CONFIT
Young garlic
Milk
Lacto Koji Water* (made with
  Rice Koji*)
Juniper berries

TOASTED BEECHNUTS
Beechnuts

TO FINISH
Garlic Confit
Chopped chives
Toasted Beechnuts
Walnut Oil*
Salt
Grilled Lemon Thyme*

VEGETABLE

Preserved Ramson and Soft-Boiled Egg

Ramson leaves are lightly grilled and then preserved in a mixture of kohlrabi shoyu, sugar, dried mushrooms, cloves, and vinegar.

Quail eggs are soft-boiled, pickled, and then cold-smoked over toasted hay.

A preserved grilled ramson leaf is trimmed and piped with some corn miso paste. A smoked pickled quail egg is placed on the leaf so it stands upright in the miso. More corn miso is dotted onto the egg, along with a confit gooseberry and a few drops of the ramson preserving liquid. The ramson leaf is wrapped around the egg to create a sealed packet, which is spritzed with more ramson preserving liquid.

RAMSON PRESERVATION LIQUID
Kohlrabi Shoyu*
Sugar
Dried Bluefoot Mushrooms*
Cloves
White wine vinegar

PRESERVED GRILLED RAMSONS
Ramsons
Ramson Preservation Liquid

RAMSON WRAPPER
Preserved Grilled Ramson leaves

QUAIL EGG PICKLING LIQUID
Apple balsamic vinegar
Cold-Infused Dashi*
Lemon thyme sprigs

SMOKED PICKLED QUAIL EGG
Quail Eggs
Quail Egg Pickling Liquid
Toasted Hay*

CONFIT GOOSEBERRIES
Freeze-dried gooseberries
Koji Oil*
Maitake Garum*
Freeze-dried rhubarb
Cold-Infused Dashi*
Lemon verbena leaves
Lemon thyme sprig

CORN MISO PASTE
Fresh Corn Miso*
Lacto Koji Water* (made with Øland
   Wheat Koji*)
Peaso Water Reduction*
Chicken Wing Garum*

TO FINISH
Ramson Wrapper
Corn Miso Paste
Smoked Pickled Quail Egg
Confit Gooseberry
Ramson Preservation Liquid

Rose Hip Sausage with Quail Egg

Quail eggs are soft-boiled and lightly smoked over hay.

Reeves plums are simmered in spiced dashi until tender, then peeled. The plum flesh is cooked down with rose hips, spices, and dried rose oil and the mixture is finely chopped to make a paste. Green coriander seeds and fennel flowers are chopped and folded into the rose hip and plum paste. The mixture is rolled into a sausage shape, dried, and brushed with plum juice reduction and chicken wing garum.

This rose hip and plum chorizo is sliced, laid over a warmed smoked soft-boiled quail egg, and seasoned with morita chile oil.

SMOKED SOFT-BOILED QUAIL
EGG
Quail eggs
Toasted Hay*

COOKED REEVES PLUMS
Cold-Infused Dashi*
Yellow mustard seeds
Coriander seeds
Fennel seeds
Dried Horseradish*
Dried Ginger Skins*
Juniper berries
Reeves plums

ROSE HIP AND PLUM PASTE
Toasted coriander seeds
Toasted fennel seeds
Toasted yellow mustard seeds
Dried Ginger Skins*
Dried Horseradish*
Saffron
Dried Rose Oil*
Cooked Reeves Plums
Seeded rose hips

ROSE HIP AND PLUM CHORIZO
Green coriander seeds
Fennel flowers
Rose Hip and Plum Paste
Chicken Wing Garum*
Plum Reduction*

TO FINISH
Smoked Soft-Boiled Quail Egg
Rose Hip and Plum Chorizo
Morita Chile Oil*

VEGETABLE

Flatbread with Buttered Vegetables

A malt dough is rolled thin, cut into rounds, and grilled until slightly puffed and browned to create a flatbread.

The flatbread is brushed with brown butter and piped with a bit of black currant wood fudge, morita chile paste, cep duxelles, and black currant shoots.

Cooked beets, raw turnips, and baby zucchini are sliced thin, barely cooked in a lacto-fermented koji water–butter emulsion, and arranged over the surface of the grilled flatbread. Onion cress flowers are also blanched in lacto-fermented koji water–butter emulsion and scattered over the flatbread, along with some grilled nettle leaves. The flatbread is finished with small drops of spiced butter and cut fresh chives.

BEETS
Candy cane beets
Yellow beets

CEP DUXELLES
Ceps reserved from making
  Cep Oil*

MORITA CHILE PASTE
Seeded morita chile
Thinly sliced spring garlic
Olive oil
Grapeseed oil
Potato Stock Reduction*
Salt
Roasted Kelp Oil*

BLACK CURRANT WOOD FUDGE
Cucumber Juice Reduction*
Peaso Water Reduction*
Black Currant Wood Oil*
Butter

MALT FLATBREAD
Tipo "00" flour
Koji Flour*
Malt flour
Rose Oil*
Butter
Salt
Kaelder Øl lager

LACTO KOJI WATER–BUTTER
EMULSION
Lacto Koji Water* (made with Øland
  Wheat Koji*)
Butter
Xantana

SPICED BUTTER SPICE BLEND
Toasted coriander seed
Toasted fennel seed
Toasted brown mustard seed
Arctic thyme leaves
Dried Horseradish*

SPICED BUTTER
Smoked Butter*
Roasted Kelp Salt*
Spiced Butter Spice Blend
Peaso Water Reduction*

GRILLED NETTLES
Stinging nettles
Smoked Butter*

TO FINISH
Beets
Hakurei turnips
Baby zucchini
Malt Flatbread
Brown Butter*
Black Currant Wood Fudge
Morita Chile Paste
Black currant shoot halves
Lacto Koji Water–Butter Emulsion
Grilled Nettles
Onion cress flowers
Chives
Spiced Butter

Grilled Preserved Morels

Maitake mushrooms are dry-aged, coated in koji oil, and cold-smoked. The smoked mushrooms are then baked with lemon thyme ant broth and Douglas fir ant broth and the resulting maitake broth is reduced over a charcoal fire.

Toasted beechnuts are pounded with kelp salt and dried lacto-fermented ceps and folded into brown butter emulsion to create a paste.

Morels preserved in koji oil are grilled until crisp, filled with the brown butter–beechnut paste, and dusted with mushroom-seaweed powder. The filled morels are placed in a ramekin, and maitake broth and cep oil are poured on top.

PRESERVED MORELS
Morel mushrooms
Cep Oil*

DOUGLAS FIR ANT BROTH
Filtered water
Small Douglas fir branches
Ants

LEMON THYME ANT BROTH
Filtered water
Lemon thyme sprigs
Ants

MAITAKE BROTH
Maitake mushrooms
Koji Oil*
Lemon Thyme Ant Broth
Peaso Water*
Peaso Water Reduction*
Douglas Fir Ant Broth

BROWN BUTTER EMULSION
Egg
Brown Butter*
Lemon juice

TOASTED BEECHNUTS
Beechnuts

DRIED LACTO CEPS
Lacto Ceps*

BROWN BUTTER–BEECHNUT
PASTE
Brown Butter Emulsion
Toasted Beechnuts
Roasted Kelp Salt*
Chopped Dried Lacto Ceps

MUSHROOM-SEAWEED POWDER
Dried ceps
Dried black trumpet mushrooms
Dried Icelandic söl
Roasted Kelp Powder*
Salt

TO FINISH
Preserved Morels
Brown Butter-Beechnut Paste
Mushroom-Seaweed Powder
Maitake Broth
Cep Oil*

A Stew of Summer Fruits and Vegetables with Koji and Elderflower

Fava pods are grilled over charcoal; the beans are shelled and peeled, their halves separated, and marinated in parsley oil. Zucchini rounds are grilled and brushed with smoked butter. A red raspberry and wine berries are piped with seasoned parsley purée.

A large spoonful of grilled favas is mounded in a bowl and seasoned with grilled lemon thyme, and the filled raspberry and wine berries are positioned next to the favas. From there, the other fruits and vegetables are arranged clockwise in a pleasingly loose fashion: the cooked turnip, blackberries, celtuce rounds, wild strawberries, radishes, grilled zucchini rounds, sweet onion petal half, baby cucumber, yellow raspberry, and sliced strawberries. The currants and halved gooseberry are tucked among the other ingredients, and the dried tomato pieces, ants, halved black currant shoots, and fresh coriander seeds are scattered throughout the dish, which is then finished with elderflower sauce and a few drops of parsley oil.

ELDERFLOWER SAUCE
Lacto Koji Water* (made with Øland
    Wheat Koji*)
Smoked Tomato Water* (smoked
    twice with hay)
Butter
Elderflower Oil*
Salt
Xantana

PARSLEY PURÉE
Parsley leaves

SEASONED PARSLEY PURÉE
Parsley Purée
Smoked Seaweed Shoyu*
Parsley Oil*
Peaso Water Reduction*
Fava Rice Shoyu*
Salt

CELTUCE ROUNDS
Celtuce stem

GRILLED ZUCCHINI ROUNDS
Small zucchini
Clarified Smoked Butter*

GRILLED FAVA BEANS
Fava beans
Parsley Oil*

GRILLED LEMON THYME
Lemon thyme
Koji Oil*

TO FINISH
Grilled Fava Beans
Grilled Lemon Thyme
Grilled Zucchini Rounds
Smoked Butter*
Semi-Dried Tomatoes*, cut into 2 or
    3 pieces each
Red raspberry
Yellow raspberry
Wine berries
Seasoned Parsley Purée
Ripe strawberry slices
Hakurei turnip
Sweet onion petal
Koji Oil*
Baby red radishes
Celtuce Rounds
Blackberries
Halved red gooseberry
Baby cucumber
Small string of currants
Wild strawberries
Ants
Black currant shoot halves
Fresh coriander seeds
Elderflower Sauce, in squeeze bottles
Parsley Oil*

VEGETABLE

Beet Wrap

Blackberries, black currants, and aronia juice are cooked together and dried to create a fruit leather.

Whole beets are cooked, then smoked with lemon thyme over charcoal until lightly charred. The smoked beets are then blended with lacto-fermented plums and gooseberries and cooked down to create a plum and beet paste.

Fennel broth is cooked with beeswax, strained, and lightly set into a gel.

The skins of more cooked beets are carefully pared off in one piece, simmered with aronia juice, black currants, arctic thyme, and juniper, and then dried and cut into strips.

Rectangles of the fruit leather are brushed with elderflower oil and fashioned into pockets, then filled with the aronia-scented beet skins, beeswax and fennel gel, Japanese quince paste, and black koji grains. The pocket edges are piped with plum and beet paste to seal, and the pocket is topped with a fennel flower crown, angelica seeds, bee pollen, and black currant shoots.

BLACKBERRY, BLACK CURRANT, AND ARONIA LEATHER
Blackberries
Black currants
Aronia berry juice
Muscovado sugar
Freeze-dried black currants
Salt

COOKED SMOKED BEETS
Cylindra beets
Grapeseed oil
Salt

PLUM AND BEET PASTE
Cooked Smoked Beets
Lacto Plums*
Freeze-dried gooseberries
Roasted Kelp Salt*
Gooseberry Reduction*

FENNEL BROTH
Fennel juice
Sliced fennel bulb
Koji Oil* (made with Rice Koji*)
Lacto Cep Water*
Douglas fir needles
Kelp
Dried chanterelles
Freeze-dried gooseberries
Lacto Koji Water* (made with Rice Koji*)

BEESWAX FENNEL BROTH
Fennel Broth
Beeswax

BEESWAX AND FENNEL GEL
Beeswax Fennel Broth
Agar
Kuzu starch

JAPANESE QUINCE PASTE
Japanese quince
Butter
Dried Carrot Flowers*

ARONIA-SCENTED BEETROOT SKINS
Cylindra beets
Aronia berry juice
Freeze-dried black currants
Arctic thyme leaves
Juniper berries
Kelp

TO FINISH
Blackberry, Black Currant, and Aronia Leather
Aronia-Scented Beetroot Skins
Beeswax and Fennel Gel
Pine shoot
Japanese Quince Paste
Elderflower Oil*
Black Koji Grains*
Plum and Beet Paste
Fennel flower crown
Fresh angelica seeds
Bee pollen
Fresh black currant shoots
Salt

Sweet Cooked Peas

Fresh peas are shelled and sorted by size and the husks are juiced. The pea husk juice is strained and seasoned with a bit of lacto-fermented koji water, pine vinegar, and a few drops of spruce wood oil.

Peas are charred with a flame and mixed with smaller raw peas. The pea husk juice is poured around the peas and the dish is seasoned with roasted kelp oil, roasted kelp salt, a halved black currant caper, black currant shoots, and green coriander seeds. A small spoonful of whipped cream is dolloped in the center of the peas.

PEAS
Peas in the pod

PEA HUSK JUICE
Pea husks
Lacto Koji Water* (made with Øland
  Wheat Koji*)
Pine Vinegar*
Spruce Wood Oil*

TO FINISH
Peas
Pea Husk Juice
Cream, whipped to soft peaks
Roasted Kelp Oil*
Roasted Kelp Salt*
Black currant shoot halves
Green coriander seed halves
Salted Black Currant Caper* halves

Barbecued Artichoke and Whisky Sauce

Danish whisky is seasoned with roasted kelp salt and emulsified with butter, using cold-infused dashi to adjust the consistency, to make a whisky butter glaze. Eggs are gently cooked; their yolks are removed and cured in beef garum. The cured yolks are whisked until smooth and seasoned with whisky vinegar, Danish whisky, more beef garum, and salt to make a sauce.

Artichoke leaves are separated from the hearts and blanched until tender. The hearts are quartered and pared, leaving just the fleshy core and stem with a few inner leaves attached. The quarters are steamed, brushed with whisky butter glaze, and then gently grilled over charcoal until lightly browned, tender, and juicy. They are finished with a spritz of whisky vinegar and seasoned with salt and cracked toasted black pepper.

On the plate, warmed artichoke leaves and a grilled artichoke heart quarter are served with a small ramekin of the whisky–egg yolk sauce on the side.

ARTICHOKE LEAVES AND
QUARTERS
Medium artichokes
Salt
10% salt brine

WHISKY BUTTER GLAZE
Danish whisky
Roasted Kelp Salt*
Unsalted Butter
Cold-Infused Dashi*

WHISKY–EGG YOLK SAUCE
Eggs
Beef Garum*
Whisky Vinegar*
Smoked Butter*
Danish whisky

TO FINISH
Artichoke Quarter
Artichoke Leaves
Whisky Butter Glaze
Whisky Vinegar*, in a spray bottle
Whisky–Egg Yolk Sauce
Cracked toasted black peppercorns
Salt

Cauliflower Waffle

A buckwheat batter is piped onto a waffle iron to create nicely browned waffles.

Thin slices of cauliflower florets are arranged on parchment in concentric rings to create a circle. The cauliflower is then seasoned with salted green gooseberry brine and Douglas fir oil.

The waffle is drizzled with Douglas fir oil and then spread with a thin layer of vegetable fudge and dotted with parsley and lovage paste and ancho chile paste. Two ants are placed on each dot of herb paste and a half sea buckthorn berry on each chile paste dot.

The waffle is flipped onto the cauliflower florets and gently pressed to join the two, then all is flipped again so the cauliflower is visible on top. Fennel and coriander blossoms are arranged on top of the cauliflower.

BUCKWHEAT WAFFLE
Buckwheat flour
Tipo "00" flour
Baking powder
Salt
Roasted Kelp Powder*
Cream
Buttermilk
Egg
Melted Brown Butter*

VEGETABLE FUDGE
Cucumber Juice Reduction*
Peaso Water Reduction*
Butter
Grapeseed oil

ANCHO CHILE PASTE
Finely chopped shallot
Grapeseed oil
Seeded ancho chile
Salt
Red Pepper Tamari*
Peaso Water Reduction*
Roasted Kelp Oil*

PARSLEY AND LOVAGE PASTE
Parsley leaves
Lovage leaves
Parsley Oil*
Yeast Broth Reduction*
Peaso Water Reduction*

CAULIFLOWER FLORETS
Cauliflower

TO FINISH
Buckwheat Waffle
Cauliflower Florets
Liquid from Salted Green
  Gooseberry Capers*
Douglas Fir Oil*
Vegetable Fudge
Parsley and Lovage Paste
Ancho Chile Paste
Ants
Seeded ripe sea buckthorn
  berry halves
Fennel flower
Coriander flowers

VEGETABLE

Jellied Peas

Fresh peas are removed from their husks. The husks are juiced and the solids reserved separately; the juice is racked off, infused with kelp, and then clarified by boiling.

The peas are sorted by size; the medium and small peas are blanched in the pea husk juice, and then the medium peas have their outer skins removed.

Grilled mushroom garum is cold-smoked, then combined with roasted kelp salt, oregano vinegar, Japanese quince brine, lemon thyme, mushroom tea, and gelatin. The mushroom tea is spooned into the serving bowl and set to form the base layer.

Lemon thyme is frozen with liquid nitrogen, pulverized, and then mixed with yeast and peaso reductions and lemon thyme and parsley oils to form a lemon thyme glaze.

Eggs are gently cooked in an immersion circulator; the yolks are removed and cured in beef garum, corn miso, and cep tamari. The cured eggs are passed through a fine sieve and emulsified with the solids reserved from making the pea husk juice, whisky vinegar, parsley oil, and salt to form a paste.

The blanched medium peas are gently mixed with the cured egg yolk paste, and then the small peas are added. The layer of mushroom tea gel is seasoned with lemon thyme glaze and the peas are gently spooned onto the gel. The peas are then seasoned with drops of black currant leaf oil, geranium oil, Japanese quince brine, clarified pea husk juice, and salt, adorned with a few geranium flowers, and finished with a small quenelle of soft whipped cream.

PEAS AND PEA HUSK JUICE
Peas in the pod
Kelp

MUSHROOM TEA
Dried ceps
Dried chanterelles
Dried shiitakes
Dried morels
Freeze-dried blueberries
Freeze-dried lingonberries
Kelp
Bay leaves
Filtered water
Ice-Clarified Tomato Water*

SMOKED MUSHROOM GARUM
Grilled Mushroom Garum*

MUSHROOM TEA GEL
Roasted Kelp Salt*
Smoked Mushroom Garum*
Oregano Vinegar*
Brine from Brined Japanese Quince*
Lemon thyme
Mushroom Tea
Gelatin

LEMON THYME GLAZE
Lemon thyme leaves
Yeast Broth Reduction*
Peaso Water Reduction*
Lemon Thyme Oil*
Parsley Oil*

CURED EGG YOLKS
Eggs
Beef Garum*
Fresh Corn Miso*
Cep Tamari*

CURED EGG YOLK AND PEA PASTE
Cured Egg Yolks
Solids reserved from making Pea
  Husk Juice
Whisky Vinegar*
Parsley Oil*
Salt

TO FINISH
Medium peas
Cured Egg Yolk and Pea Paste
Small peas
Mushroom Tea Gel
Lemon Thyme Glaze
Black Currant Leaf Oil*
Geranium Oil*
Brine from Brined Japanese Quince*
Clarified Pea Husk Juice
Salt
Geranium flowers
Soft whipped cream

Moldy Asparagus

Asparagus spears are cooked with black currant wood oil, then slightly dried, dusted with rice flour, inoculated with *Aspergillus oryzae* spores, and fermented for two days until the koji mold covers the asparagus.

The back sides of the fermented asparagus spears are brushed with an ant paste made by grinding black currant shoots, pine salt, ants, and roasted kelp salt and emulsifying the paste with black currant wood oil.

At the base of the asparagus spears, various fresh herbs and flowers are arranged, along with black currant shoots dressed with black currant wood oil and horseradish juice and some purslane clusters that have been sautéed in kelp oil and seasoned with horseradish juice. A small pool of split pumpkin seed oil sauce is poured around the asparagus.

BLANCHED ASPARAGUS
Green asparagus
Black Currant Wood Oil*

MOLDED ASPARAGUS
Koji tane (*Aspergillus oryzae* spores)
Rice flour
Blanched Asparagus

KOJI AND YEAST BROTH
EMULSION
Yeast Broth*
Lacto Koji Water* (made with Øland
　Wheat Koji*)
Butter
Xantana

SPLIT PUMPKIN SEED OIL SAUCE
Koji and Yeast Broth Emulsion
Pumpkin Seed Oil*
Parsley Oil*

ANT PASTE
Black currant shoots
Pine Salt*
Ants
Roasted Kelp Salt*
Black Currant Wood Oil*

TO FINISH
Molded Asparagus
Ant Paste
Young black currant shoots with
　leaves attached
Black Currant Wood Oil*
Horseradish juice
Sea purslane clusters
Roasted Kelp Oil*
Ground elder
Spanish chervil
Fennel tops
Pine shoots
Oxalis flowers
Split Pumpkin Seed Oil Sauce

Moldy Egg Tart

A beef garum–cured egg yolk is dusted with rice flour, inoculated with *Aspergillus oryzae* spores, and fermented for two days until the koji mold covers the yolk, then trimmed and gently flattened.

A seaweed dough is rolled thin and baked into tart shells, which are then lined with wedge-shaped pieces of nasturtium leaf. The leaves are dotted with horseradish oil and spread with koji truffle fudge. Preserved truffle slices are placed on the koji truffle fudge. The truffle slices are then covered with a layer of truffle purée. The moldy egg yolk is placed on the truffle purée and more purée is piped around it. The ring of purée is sprinkled with finely chopped preserved truffle and topped with individual grains of koji.

MOLDY EGG
Eggs
Beef Garum*
Smoked Seaweed Shoyu*
Rice flour
Koji tane (*Aspergillus oryzae* spores)

SEAWEED PASTE
Dried Sea Lettuce*
Roasted Kelp Salt*
Rice flour
Cold-Infused Dashi*

SEAWEED TART
Tipo "00" flour
Roasted Kelp Powder*
Seaweed Paste
Söl Oil*
Butter

TRUFFLE PURÉE
Truffles
Roasted Yeast Oil*
Cep Oil*
Mushroom-Kelp Broth*
Lacto Cep Water*
Celery Juice Reduction*

INDIVIDUAL KOJI GRAINS
Koji* (any type)

KOJI TRUFFLE FUDGE
Cucumber Juice Reduction*
Peaso Water Reduction*
Koji Oil*
Butter
Chopped Preserved Truffle*

NASTURTIUM LEAVES
Nasturtium leaves

PRESERVED TRUFFLE SLICES
Preserved Truffle*

TO FINISH
Seaweed Tart
Nasturtium Leaves
Horseradish Oil*
Koji Truffle Fudge
Preserved Truffle Slices
Cep Oil*
Truffle Purée
Moldy Egg
Finely chopped Preserved Truffle*
    scraps
Individual Koji Grains

Savory Mold Crepe

Cooked barley is puréed, rolled out into a thin sheet, inoculated with koji spores, and fermented for two days. The mold sheet is then cut into round crepes.

Cheese and milk are blended, set with gelatin, and folded with whipped cream to make a mousse-like sponge. The cheese mousse is put under vacuum, aerated, and frozen, then sliced into strips and punched into half-moon shapes.

The inside of the mold crepe is spread with mushroom fudge, and preserved truffle slices are arranged around the perimeter of the crepe so they overhang it like a skirt. The center of the crepe is piped with a parsley and lemon thyme paste and roasted kelp salt is applied. A half-moon slice of the cheese sponge is laid over half the crepe, which is then folded over like a sandwich to close, taking care not to touch the delicate mold on the outside of the crepe.

MOLD CREPE
Pearl barley
Koji tane (*Aspergillus oryzae* spores)

MUSHROOM-KELP BROTH
REDUCTION
Mushroom-Kelp Broth*

MUSHROOM FUDGE
Mushroom-Kelp Broth Reduction
Cep Oil*
Butter

LEMON THYME PASTE
Lemon thyme leaves
Yeast Broth Reduction*
Peaso Water Reduction*
Koji Oil* (made with Awamori Koji*)
Roasted Kelp Salt*

PARSLEY AND LEMON THYME
PASTE
Parsley leaves
Lemon Thyme Paste

CHEESE SPONGE
Gammel Knas cheese
Milk
Gelatin
Whipped cream

PRESERVED TRUFFLE SLICES
Preserved Truffles*
Cep Oil*

TO FINISH
Mold Crepe
Mushroom Fudge
Preserved Truffle Slices
Parsley and Lemon Thyme Paste
Roasted Kelp Salt*
Cheese Sponge
Cracked toasted black peppercorns

VEGETABLE

Potatoes Cooked in Soil

Maitake and oyster mushroom "soils" are made by puréeing the mushrooms separately with oil, slowly cooking the purées until caramelized, straining off all the oil, and drying the resulting pulp. The maitake soil and oyster mushroom soil are mixed together and seasoned with roasted kelp salt.

Roasted potatoes are passed through a sieve, then beaten with potato stock, truffle juice, and butter to yield a smooth purée.

A ramekin is placed into a terra-cotta herb pot and both are heated. Small new potatoes are boiled in a potato stock infused with fresh elderflower. One of the boiled new potatoes is positioned in the center of the ramekin; the others are removed from the potato stock and warmed in elderflower emulsion, then added to the ramekin. All the new potatoes are dotted with elderflower fudge, sprinkled with elderflower blossoms, and seasoned with elderflower oil. The potato purée is spread over everything. The mushroom soil is distributed over the top and a nasturtium vine is inserted into the center new potato.

POTATO STOCK
New potatoes
Filtered water
Fresh elderflower

BOILED NEW POTATOES
New potatoes
Potato Stock
Salt

ELDERFLOWER PEASO EMULSION
Butter
Elderflower Peaso* (passed)
Potato Stock
Xantana

ELDERFLOWER FUDGE
Cucumber Juice Reduction*
Peaso Water Reduction*
Elderflower Oil*
Butter

OYSTER MUSHROOM SOIL
Oyster mushrooms
Grapeseed oil

MAITAKE SOIL
Maitake mushrooms
Grapeseed oil

MUSHROOM SOIL
Oyster Mushroom Soil
Maitake Soil
Roasted Kelp Salt*
Salt

PASSED POTATO
Potatoes
Butter
Salt

POTATO PURÉE
Passed Potato
Butter
Potato Stock
Truffle juice

TO FINISH
Boiled New Potatoes
Elderflower Peaso Emulsion
Potato Purée
Mushroom Soil
Elderflower Oil*
Fresh elderflower (picked into
   individual flowers)
Elderflower Fudge
Nasturtium stem with flower

Butterfly Flatbread

Flatbread dough is shaped into a butterfly and baked until golden brown. The body and antennae of the butterfly are brushed with rose fudge and sprinkled with bee pollen. Coriander seeds, ants, black currant shoots, and confit gooseberry quarters are arranged on the wings, a bit of parsley paste is dabbed on, and sage and nasturtium flower petals are dipped into rose fudge and placed on the wings. The butterfly is finished with small drops of rose oil and spritzes of rose-pollen aquavit spray.

BUTTERFLY FLATBREAD
Tipo "00" flour
Koji Flour*
Rose Oil*
Butter
Salt
Amber beer

ROSE FUDGE
Cucumber Juice Reduction*
Peaso Water Reduction*
Rose Oil*
Butter

PARSLEY-KOJI OIL
Koji Oil*
Parsley

PARSLEY PASTE
Parsley leaves
Yeast Broth Reduction*
Parsley-Koji Oil

CONFIT GOOSEBERRIES
Freeze-dried gooseberries
Koji Oil*
Maitake Garum*
Freeze-dried rhubarb
Cold-Infused Dashi*
Lemon verbena leaves
Lemon thyme sprig

ROSE-POLLEN AQUAVIT SPRAY
Quince aquavit
Beach rose petals
Bee pollen

TO FINISH
Butterfly Flatbread
Rose Fudge
Bee pollen
Green coriander seeds
Ants
Black currant shoot halves
Confit Gooseberry quarters
Parsley Paste
Nasturtium flowers
Purple sage flowers
Pink sage flowers
Rose Oil*
Rose-Pollen Aquavit Spray

Boiled Artichoke

Trimmed artichoke leaves and hearts are cooked separately in truffle juice seasoned with a few pieces of roasted kelp salt.

ARTICHOKE HEARTS AND LEAVES
Small artichokes
Truffle juice
Salt

TO FINISH
Steamed artichoke leaves
Steamed artichoke hearts
Roasted Kelp Salt*

Warm Summer Salad with Vegetarian Demi-Glace

A rose millefeuille is made by layering elderflower syrup–brushed rose petals with lemon verbena fudge, red currant and rose hip paste, and black currant capers. The top petal is finished with salt and rose oil.

A truffle millefeuille is made by layering sliced truffles, spinach leaves that have been brushed with clarified smoked butter and grilled, and fresh mushroom crudités that were marinated with cep oil and lacto cep water, using truffle purée to bind the layers together.

A peeled and seeded rose hip is marinated in rose hip seed oil and filled with peeled pumpkin seeds that were marinated in rose oil.

Very thinly sliced rhubarb stalks are marinated in pepper tamari, then grilled while being brushed with smoked butter, spruce wood oil, and pepper tamari. The grilled rhubarb slices are rolled into loose curls, topped with angelica buds, and seasoned with spruce wood oil and salt.

A bloodred ribbed seaweed leaf is brushed with reduced dashi and dried until crisp. Trimmed artichokes are cooked with corn miso water, lacto koji water, and hazelnut oil, then cold smoked. Before serving, the artichokes are deep-fried and brushed with a whisky butter glaze, then spritzed with horseradish juice and seasoned with salt.

Nixtamalized potatoes are baked and then mashed into a dough, which is shaped into rounds. Nixtamalized larch cones are cooked in grapeseed oil, then halved before serving. Noble fir and Norwegian spruce cones are brined for one month, after which the scales are peeled off. All cones and scales are marinated in söl vinaigrette for serving.

A red radish and broccoli floret are simmered in butter emulsion; a Swiss chard leaf, green oxalis stem, and hop shoot are bathed in the same cooking liquid. The chard leaf is wrapped around just-wilted Spanish chervil leaves, chickweed leaves, and chamomile buds.

Before serving, the potato rounds are deep-fried, then brushed with roasted kelp butter and topped with marjoram and grilled lemon thyme.

The chard wrap is placed on a serving plate with the hop shoot and oxalis stem on its right and left. The rose and truffle millefeuilles, smoked artichoke, seaweed leaf, rhubarb curl, potato round, hop shoots, marinated pine scales, spruce shoots, and radish are arranged around it, along with purslane flowers and a coriander flower crown. The dish is served with a truffle sauce, which is spooned on tableside.

ROSE MILLEFEUILLE

LEMON VERBENA FUDGE
Lemon Verbena Oil*
Yeast Broth Reduction*
Peaso Water Reduction*
Lemon verbena leaves
Butter

RED CURRANT AND ROSE HIP PASTE
Dried meadowsweet
Angelica buds
Geranium Oil*
Red currants
Rose hips

ROSE MILLEFEUILLE
Fresh rose petals
Redcurrant and Rose Hip Paste
Lemon Verbena Fudge
Salted Black Currant Capers*
Elderflower Syrup*
Rose Oil*
Salt

TRUFFLE MILLEFEUILLE

TRUFFLE PURÉE
Truffles
Roasted Yeast Oil*
Cep Oil*
Mushroom-Kelp Broth*
Lacto Cep Water*
Celery Juice Reduction*

GRILLED SPINACH LEAVES
Baby spinach
Clarified Smoked Butter*

TRUFFLE MILLEFEUILLE
Fresh Australian winter truffles
Truffle Purée
Grilled Spinach Leaves
Fresh mushroom crudités
Lacto Cep Water*
Cep Oil*

STUFFED ROSE HIP

PEELED PUMPKIN SEEDS
Fresh Hokkaido pumpkin seeds
Rose Oil*

ROSE HIP SEED OIL
Rose hip seeds
Grapeseed oil

STUFFED ROSE HIP
Rose hip
Rose Hip Seed Oil
Peeled Pumpkin Seeds
Rose Oil*

SMOKED RHUBARB

GRILLING BUTTER
Smoked Butter*
Spruce Wood Oil*
Red Pepper Tamari*

SMOKED RHUBARB
Rhubarb stalks
Red Pepper Tamari*
Spruce Wood Oil*
Grilling Butter
Fresh angelica buds

BLOODRED RIBBED SEAWEED LEAF

Bloodred ribbed seaweed
Cold-Infused Dashi*

SMOKED ARTICHOKE

CORN MISO WATER
Filtered water
Fresh Corn Miso*

WHISKY BUTTER GLAZE
Danish whisky
Roasted Kelp Salt*
Butter
Cold-Infused Dashi*

ARTICHOKE COOKING LIQUID
Corn Miso Water
Lacto Koji Water* (made with Rice Koji*)
Hazelnut Oil*

SMOKED ARTICHOKE
Purple artichokes
Lemons
Artichoke Cooking Liquid
Grapeseed oil
Whisky Butter Glaze
Horseradish juice

POTATO ROUNDS

ROASTED KELP BUTTER
Roasted Kelp Salt*
Butter

POTATO ROUNDS
Potatoes
Calcium hydroxide
Roasted Kelp Butter
Marjoram
Grilled Lemon Thyme*

MARINATED PINES

SÖL VINAIGRETTE
Pickling liquid from Pickled Rose Petals*
Söl
Douglas Fir Oil*

NIXTAMALIZED LARCH CONES
Large larch cones
Grapeseed oil
Filtered water
Calcium hydroxide

SALTED NOBLE FIR CONES
Noble fir cones
Filtered water
Salt

SALTED NORWEGIAN SPRUCE CONES
Norwegian spruce (Picea abies) cones
Filtered water
Salt

MARINATED PINE CONES
Nixtamalized Larch Cone halves
Noble Fir Cone scales
Salted Norwegian Spruce Cone scales
Söl Vinaigrette

SPRUCE SHOOTS
Fresh spruce shoots
Spruce Wood Oil*

STEAMED GREENS AND SAUCE

TRUFFLE SAUCE
Reduced Mushroom-Kelp Broth* (reduced to 43 °Bx)
Truffle juice
Brown Butter*
Black truffle
White Wine Reduction*

BUTTER EMULSION
Lacto Koji Water* (made with Rice Koji*)
Butter
Rose Oil*

STEAMED GREENS
Hops shoots
Green oxalis stem
Round red radish
Broccoli Floret half
Swiss chard leaf
Spanish chervil leaves
Chickweed leaves
Chamomile buds
Salt

TO FINISH
Rose Millefeuille
Truffle Millefeuille
Smoked Artichoke half
Stuffed Rose Hip
Bloodred Ribbed Seaweed
Smoked Rhubarb curl
Halved Potato Round
Marinated Pine scales
Spruce Shoots
Purslane flowers
Coriander flower crown
Truffle Sauce

Milk Skin and Truffle

Full-fat milk is reduced in a wide skillet until all that's left is a skin, which is slowly cooked until lightly caramelized. The caramelized milk skin is punched into rounds, and two rounds are sandwiched around parsley, lemon thyme, and a disc of soft cheese with a bit of its rind.

The milk skin pocket is fried and truffle purée is piped on top. Sliced preserved truffles are shingled over the whole surface and the dish is finished with salt and cep oil.

CARAMELIZED MILK SKINS
3.5% milk

LEMON THYME PASTE
Lemon thyme leaves
Yeast Broth Reduction*
Peaso Water Reduction*
Koji Oil* (made with Awamori Koji*)
Roasted Kelp Salt*

CHOPPED PARSLEY
Parsley leaves
Lemon Thyme Paste

TRUFFLE PURÉE
Truffles
Roasted Yeast Oil*
Cep Oil*
Mushroom-Kelp Broth*
Lacto Cep Water*
Celery Juice Reduction*

MILK SKIN POCKET
Flour slurry
Caramelized Milk Skin discs
Chopped Parsley
Lemon thyme leaves
Benedict Hvid Kloster cheese
Chopped Benedict Hvid Kloster
  cheese rind

TO FINISH
Preserved Truffles*
Milk Skin Pocket
Grapeseed oil
Truffle Purée
Cep Oil*

Carrot Terrine

Carrots are slowly cooked in rhubarb root oil with roasted kelp and dried carrot flowers until caramelized and tender. The cooked carrots are bundled and wrapped tightly to form a roulade, then sliced crosswise to create a mosaic-like puck. The slice of carrot terrine is wrapped with a long piece of kelp that's been braised in aronia juice, dried mushrooms, and other aromatics.

    Black currant wood fudge and grilled lemon thyme paste are piped into a serving bowl and the wrapped carrot terrine is placed on top. The carrots are dressed with rose oil, Danish curry powder, and salt to finish.

CARROT ROULADE
Orange and purple carrots with tops
Rhubarb Root Oil*
Roasted Kelp*
Dried Carrot Flowers*

ARONIA KELP
Kelp (thick center-cut pieces only)
Aronia berry juice
Filtered water
Muscovado sugar
Dried ceps
Dried morels
Freeze-dried lingonberries
Roasted juniper wood
Quince tea
Rose Oil*

DANISH CURRY POWDER
Toasted yellow mustard seeds
Toasted coriander seeds
Toasted fennel seeds
Saffron
Sumac powder
Horseradish Powder*
Ginger Powder*
Vinegar powder

GRILLED LEMON THYME
Lemon Thyme Oil*
Lemon thyme sprigs

GRILLED LEMON THYME PASTE
Grilled Lemon Thyme leaves
Yeast Broth Reduction*
Lemon Thyme Oil*

BLACK CURRANT WOOD FUDGE
Cucumber Juice Reduction*
Peaso Water Reduction*
Butter
Black Currant Wood Oil*

TO FINISH
Carrot Roulade
Strip of Aronia Kelp
Black Currant Wood Fudge
Grilled Lemon Thyme Paste
Rose Oil*
Danish Curry Powder

Pumpkin Seed Tofu and Walnut Mole

Pumpkin seed tofu begins by blending pumpkin seeds with water, then straining the liquid and thickening it with carrageenan. The liquid is poured into a serving vessel and steamed until set.

Walnut butter is made by blending blanched walnuts with water, straining the resulting walnut milk, and then slowly reducing it on the stove for two days until caramelized and butter-like.

Grasshoppers are cooked in butter with berry spice until crisp and then ground into a paste, which is cooked until dark and roasted. The grasshopper butter and walnut butter are whisked with cucumber and peaso water reductions and some roasted kelp oil to make a walnut and grasshopper mole.

The pumpkin seed tofu is dressed with pumpkin seed oil, roasted kelp salt, thyme, and oregano leaves and flowers. The mole is served alongside, surrounded by grilled rose petals.

PUMPKIN SEED TOFU
Pumpkin seeds
Filtered water
Carrageenan

WALNUT BUTTER
Walnuts
Filtered water

BERRY SPICE
Toasted coriander seeds
Toasted fennel seeds
Toasted dried angelica buds
Dried Horseradish*
Dried Ginger*
Arctic thyme leaves
Dried Strawberries*

GRASSHOPPER BUTTER
Butter
Grasshoppers
Berry Spice

WALNUT AND GRASSHOPPER MOLE
Cucumber Juice Reduction*
Roasted Kelp Oil*
Walnut Butter
Grasshopper Butter
Peaso Water Reduction*
Salt

TO FINISH
Pumpkin Seed Tofu vessel
Rose petals
Pumpkin Seed Oil*
Roasted Kelp Salt*
Thyme flowers
Oregano flowers
Oregano leaves
Walnut and Grasshopper Mole

VEGETABLE

Wax Broth

Cloudberry juice is sweetened with honey, emulsified with beeswax, strained, and chilled.

The wax-infused cloudberry juice is served in a wax bowl with mini bouquets of mixed flowers and a pile of bee pollen in one corner.

CLOUDBERRY JUICE
Cloudberry pulp
Filtered water

WAX-INFUSED CLOUDBERRY JUICE
Cloudberry Juice
Chopped beeswax
Noma honey

FLOWERS
Oxalis
Wood sorrel
Cucumber
Lavender
Cowslip
Spanish chervil
Marigold
Pea
Nettle
Oregano

TO FINISH
Wax bowl
Bee pollen
Wax-Infused Cloudberry Juice

Marigold and Whisky Sauce

Marigold blossoms are coated in tempura batter, deep-fried, and dusted with Danish curry powder.

Raw and lightly cooked egg yolks cured in beef garum are whisked with smoked butter, smoked butter whey, and Danish whisky. The fried marigolds are served with the whisky–egg yolk sauce.

TEMPURA BATTER
Rice flour
Cornstarch
Baking soda
Baking powder
White wine vinegar
Grapeseed oil
Cold filtered water
Ethanol (96% ABV)

WHISKY–EGG YOLK SAUCE
Eggs
Beef Garum*
Danish whisky
Smoked Butter*
Smoked Butter Whey*

MARIGOLD FLOWERS
Marigold (*Calendula officinalis*)
   flowers
1% salt brine
Calcium hydroxide

DANISH CURRY POWDER
Toasted yellow mustard seeds
Toasted coriander seeds
Toasted fennel seeds
Saffron
Sumac powder
Horseradish Powder*
Ginger Powder*
Vinegar powder

TO FINISH
Marigold Flowers
Rice flour
Tempura Batter
Grapeseed oil
Danish Curry Powder
Grapeseed oil
Whisky–Egg Yolk Sauce

Strawberry Ceviche

A ceviche sauce is made by infusing a mixture of white currant juice, tomato water, lacto-fermented koji water, and whisky simple syrup with muddled white currants, sea buckthorn, spices, and pine shoots, and then straining the mixture.

Fruit and vegetable slices—including Hakurei turnips marinated in lacto-koji water and horseradish juice, grilled fava beans dressed in parsley oil and pumpkin seed oil, and semi-dried cherry tomatoes and lacto-fermented plums—are arranged in an overlapping pattern in a serving bowl. Fresh herbs and herb flowers are strewn across the top, and the dish is finished with the ceviche sauce, elderflower oil, and árbol chile oil.

SEMI-DRIED CHERRY TOMATOES
Ripe yet firm cherry tomatoes
Koji Oil*
Noma honey

SEMI-DRIED LACTO PLUMS
Lacto Plums*
Elderflower Oil*

WHISKY SIMPLE SYRUP
Filtered water
Sugar
Danish whisky
Seeded morita chile

CEVICHE SAUCE
White currants
Unripe sea buckthorn berries
Dried Ginger Skins*
Angelica seeds
Green coriander seeds
Pine shoots
White Currant Juice*
Ice-Clarified Tomato Water*
Whisky Simple Syrup
Lacto Koji Water* (made with Øland
   Wheat Koji*)
Elderflower Oil*

MARINATED TURNIPS
Hakurei turnips
Lacto Koji Water* (made with Øland
   Wheat Koji*)
Horseradish juice

FAVA BEANS
Fava beans
Parsley Oil*
Pumpkin Seed Oil*

GREEN STRAWBERRIES
Green Danish strawberries

RED STRAWBERRIES
Red Danish strawberries

TO FINISH
Seeded ripe sea buckthorn berries
Angelica seed halves
Green coriander seed halves
Black currant shoot halves
Semi-Dried Cherry Tomato halves
Semi-Dried Lacto Plums
Marinated Turnips, cut into
   half-moons
Fava Bean halves
Sliced Red Strawberry
Sliced Green Strawberry
Sliced fresh red radish
Lemon verbena leaves
Oregano leaves
Lemon thyme flowers
Marigold leaves
Ceviche Sauce
Elderflower Oil*
Árbol Chile Oil*

Celeriac Shawarma

Thin slices of celeriac are cooked in truffle juice and brown butter, then sandwiched with alternating fine layers of linseed fudge, truffle purée, and celeriac purée and sliced to reveal the strata.

The slices are slowly grilled over coals laid with Douglas fir, and brushed generously with shawarma cooking glaze until lightly smoked and caramelized.

Greens are barely wilted by bathing with a butter emulsion. Large leaves embrace smaller greens and herbs to form a wrap.

White currants are moistened with elderflower oil and seasoned with salt. Apple wedges are glazed with dashi, truffle, and brown butter, then lightly grilled.

At the table, the celeriac shawarma is dressed with a sauce of mushroom-kelp broth, truffle, a touch of vinegar and white wine, along with brown butter.

CELERIAC
Celeriac
Truffle juice
Brown Butter*

CELERIAC PURÉE
Celeriac
Truffle juice
Brown Butter*

LINSEED OIL
Linseeds

LINSEED FUDGE
Roasted Kelp Salt*
Celery Juice Reduction*
Linseed Oil
Cep Oil*
Brown Butter*

TRUFFLE PURÉE
Truffles
Roasted Yeast Oil*
Cep Oil*
Mushroom-Kelp Broth*
Lacto Cep Water*
Celery Juice Reduction*

SHAWARMA COOKING GLAZE
Cold-Infused Dashi*
Truffle juice
Brown Butter*

GRILLED CELERIAC SHAWARMA
Douglas fir branches
Celeriac
Linseed Fudge
Truffle Purée
Celeriac Purée
Shawarma Cooking Glaze

CARAMELIZED APPLES
Apples (cut into seedless eighths)
Shawarma Cooking Glaze

TRUFFLE SAUCE
Reduced Mushroom-Kelp Broth*
Truffle juice
Brown Butter*
Chopped black truffle
White wine vinegar
White Wine Reduction*

BUTTER EMULSION
Lacto Koji Water* (made with Øland
    Wheat Koji*)
Yeast Broth*
Butter

STEAMED GREENS WRAP
Spinach
Tatsoi
Ground elder
Goose tongue (*Plantago maritima*)
Goosefoot
Lovage leaves
Chamomile buds
Butter Emulsion

TO FINISH
Elderflower Oil*
Chopped white currants
Steamed Greens Wrap
Grilled Celeriac Shawarma
Caramelized Apples
Truffle Sauce
Warmed half slice of bread
Butter

Celeriac Pasta

Celeriac is thinly sliced into large sheets, which are cooked, then brushed with koji-dashi reduction and oven-dried. The sheets are then brushed with egg yolk sauce, air-dried, and cut into squares.

The celeriac squares are blanched in butter emulsion to soften, lined with oyster leaves, seasoned with roasted kelp salt spice mix, and rolled into garganelli shapes. The "pasta" rolls are served with whipped cream and more roasted kelp salt spice mix.

CELERIAC STRIPS
Celeriac

KOJI-DASHI REDUCTION
Cold-Infused Dashi*
Barley Koji*

EGG YOLK SAUCE
Eggs
Smoked Seaweed Shoyu*
Smoked Butter*
Smoked Butter Whey*

CELERIAC SQUARES
Celeriac Strips
Egg Yolk Sauce
Koji-Dashi Reduction

ROASTED KELP SALT SPICE MIX
Toasted black peppercorns
Toasted coriander seed
Arctic thyme
Roasted Kelp Salt*

BUTTER EMULSION
Filtered water
Butter
Xantana

TO FINISH
Celeriac Squares
Butter Emulsion
Oyster leaves
Whipped cream
Roasted Kelp Salt Spice Mix

Asparagus and Magnolia

White asparagus spears are trimmed and peeled, then cooked in asparagus juice (made from the trimmings) seasoned with lemon thyme and verbena until they yield a juicy bite. The spears are then cooled in a similar broth.

The spears are pierced through the cut end with an apple blossom skewer, then seasoned with salt and balsamic vinegar. Fresh strawberry slices are shingled on top, leaving the asparagus tip unseasoned and uncovered.

The strawberry slices are seasoned with a few small drops of elderflower oil, then topped with a thin piping of strawberry paste, made from fresh strawberries caramelized in koji oil and then puréed. A brined magnolia leaf is spritzed with ginger juice, then gently pressed onto the paste. To finish, three or four brined magnolia pistils are placed on the tip of the white asparagus.

WHITE ASPARAGUS AND
ASPARAGUS JUICE
White asparagus

STRAWBERRY PASTE
Koji Oil*
Ripe red strawberries

SALTED MAGNOLIA BLOSSOMS
Magnolia blossoms
8% salt brine

ASPARAGUS COOKING BROTH
White asparagus juice
Filtered water
Salt
Lemon thyme sprigs
Lemon verbena sprigs

ASPARAGUS COOLING BROTH
White asparagus juice
Lemon thyme sprigs
Lemon verbena sprigs
Green oxalis sprigs

GINGER JUICE
Fresh ginger

TO FINISH
White asparagus spear
Asparagus Cooking and Cooling
   Broths
Apple blossom skewers
   (or other flowering branches,
   like elderflower)
Salt
Italian balsamic vinegar
Thinly sliced ripe red strawberry
Elderflower Oil*
Strawberry Paste
Large Salted Magnolia Blossom leaf
Ginger Juice spray
Magnolia pistils

Smoked White Asparagus

White asparagus is cooked in mushroom broth and white asparagus juice, spritzed with Danish whisky, and then hot-smoked over hay.

Lightly cooked egg yolks are cured in beef garum, then whisked with smoked butter whey and kimchi tamari to make smoked egg yolk sauce.

The smoked asparagus is coated in tempura batter and fried, then seasoned with smoked salt.

A nasturtium leaf is affixed to a serving plate with a dot of smoked egg yolk sauce, then piped with quince paste and horseradish yeast paste. Two lines of smoked egg yolk sauce are piped onto the fried asparagus, which is set on the pastes on the nasturtium leaf and garnished with samphire and fennel, wood sorrel, oxalis, red oxalis, and lemon thyme flowers.

MUSHROOM BROTH
Cold-Infused Dashi*
Maitake mushrooms
Dried chanterelles
Lemon thyme
Ice-Clarified Tomato Water*

WHITE ASPARAGUS COOKING LIQUID
White asparagus juice
Mushroom Broth

SMOKED WHITE ASPARAGUS
Thick white asparagus stalks
White Asparagus Cooking Liquid
Danish whisky

CURED EGG YOLKS
Eggs
Beef Garum*

SMOKED EGG YOLK SAUCE
Cured Egg Yolks
Smoked Butter Whey*
Kimchi Tamari*
Salt

JAPANESE QUINCE PASTE
Japanese quince
Butter
Dried Carrot Flowers*

HORSERADISH YEAST PASTE
Grated fresh horseradish
Unripe sea buckthorn berries
Yeast Broth Reduction*
Black Currant Wood Oil*
Black currant shoots
Roasted Kelp Salt*

SMOKED SALT
Salt
Clarified Smoked Butter*

ARCTIC THYME SPICE MIX
Arctic thyme sprigs
Toasted coriander seeds
Toasted juniper berries

TEMPURA BATTER
Tipo "00" flour
Cornstarch
Potato starch
Baking powder
Arctic Thyme Spice Mix
Salt
Ethanol (96% ABV)
White wine vinegar
Sparkling water
Rye whiskey

TO FINISH
Rice flour
Grapeseed oil
Smoked Salt
Smoked Egg Yolk Sauce
Nasturtium leaf
Japanese Quince Paste
Horseradish Yeast Paste
Samphire
Fennel flower
Wood sorrel flower petals
Oxalis flowers
Red oxalis leaves
Lemon thyme flowers

Leeks in Vinaigrette

Whole leeks are slowly grilled and smoked over coals and pine branches until tender, then split. The tender cores are removed and brushed with a Nomite–smoked butter glaze. The cores are then halved and drizzled with ancho koji fudge and parsley and egg yolk sauce, topped with grilled lemon thyme and horseradish juice, and surrounded by grilled ground elder leaves.

NOMITE-SMOKED BUTTER GLAZE
Nomite*
Smoked Butter*

ANCHO CHILE-KOJI OIL
Ancho chile
Koji Oil*

ANCHO KOJI FUDGE
Cucumber Juice Reduction*
Peaso Water Reduction*
Ancho Chile-Koji Oil
Butter

PARSLEY PURÉE
Parsley leaves

SMOKED PARSLEY PURÉE
Parsley Purée
Peaso* (passed)
Parsley Oil*
Nordic Shoyu*
Toasted Hay*

EGG YOLK SAUCE
Eggs
Beef Garum*
Smoked Butter*
Smoked Butter Whey*

PARSLEY AND EGG YOLK SAUCE
Egg Yolk Sauce
Smoked Parsley Purée
Smoked Seaweed Shoyu*

GRILLED GROUND ELDER
Ground elder
Clarified Smoked Butter*

TO FINISH
Leeks
Pine branches
Nomite-Smoked Butter Glaze
Ancho Koji Fudge
Parsley and Egg Yolk Sauce
Grilled Lemon Thyme*
Grilled Ground Elder leaves
Horseradish juice

Barbecued Baby Corn

Tender young ears of corn are cooked in their husks with koji oil. The husks are split lengthwise and the corn is removed, keeping the husks intact; the husks are reserved.

The corn is then wrapped in a nasturtium leaf with herbs, butter, and red pepper tamari and steamed over a grill. The nasturtium leaf is removed and the steamed corn is cut into five pieces.

Fresh black currant and blueberry halves are marinated with herbs, spices, and berries in kombucha, lacto-fermented koji water, and black currant oil. The marinated berries are spooned into a reserved corn husk, along with a walnut fudge, and the corn pieces are arranged in the husk.

The corn is finally seasoned with more walnut fudge, tamari, and grilled lemon thyme paste, and finished with lemon thyme flowers.

BABY CORN
Baby corn
Koji Oil*

NASTURTIUM-WRAPPED STEAMED CORN
Baby Corn cob
Nasturtium leaves
Lemon thyme sprigs
Geranium leaves
Lemon verbena leaves
Marigold leaves
Butter
Red Pepper Tamari*

MARINATED BERRIES
Fennel seeds
Coriander seeds
Lavender
Black peppercorns
Arctic thyme
Oxalis stems
Lemon thyme leaves
Unripe sea buckthorn berries
Blackberries
Green gooseberries
Lemon Verbena Kombucha*
Lacto Koji Water* (made with Øland Wheat Koji*)
Black Currant Wood Oil*
Black currant halves
Blueberry halves

WALNUT FUDGE
Cucumber Juice Reduction*
Peaso Water Reduction*
Butter
Walnut Oil*

QUINCE REDUCTION
Quince

GRILLED LEMON THYME
Maitake Oil*
Lemon thyme sprigs

GRILLED LEMON THYME PASTE
Grilled Lemon Thyme
Maitake Oil*
Quince Reduction
Yeast Broth Reduction*

TO FINISH
Grilled Baby Corn
Baby Corn husk
Marinated Berries
Red Pepper Tamari*
Walnut Fudge
Grilled Lemon Thyme Paste
Lemon thyme flowers

VEGETABLE

Stuffed Padrón Pepper

Padrón peppers are charred over hot charcoal and peeled. Some are seeded and reserved for a filling, and the rest are kept intact (including their stems) and seeded through an incision on one side.

Red bell peppers are also charred and peeled and then cut into quarters and dried. The semi-dried bell peppers and the seeded charred padrón peppers are chopped to make a filling.

Fava beans are peeled and blanched and then seasoned with a parsley–spruce wood oil marinade. The favas are mixed with the chopped pepper filling, bell pepper marinade, and parsley, and stuffed into the whole peeled padrón peppers, along with semi-dried cherry tomato halves, confit gooseberry halves, semi-dried lacto-fermented plum pieces, fresh coriander seeds, and lemon thyme. The incision in the stuffed padrón pepper is sealed with a lemon verbena leaf and the front side of the pepper is brushed with smoked parsley purée.

CHARRED PADRÓN PEPPERS
Padrón peppers

SEMI-DRIED BELL PEPPERS
Red bell peppers

CHOPPED PEPPER FILLING
Charred Padrón Peppers
Semi-Dried Bell Peppers

BELL PEPPER MARINADE
Red Pepper Tamari*
White Currant Juice*
Bell pepper liquid
  (reserved from making the
  Semi-Dried Bell Peppers)
Ancho Chile Oil*

PARSLEY–SPRUCE WOOD OIL
MARINADE
Parsley Oil*
Spruce Wood Oil*

FAVA BEANS
Fava beans
Lacto Koji Water* (made with Øland
  Wheat Koji*)
Parsley–Spruce Wood Oil Marinade
Salt

CONFIT GOOSEBERRIES
Freeze-dried gooseberries
Koji Oil*
Maitake Garum*
Freeze-dried rhubarb
Cold-Infused Dashi*
Lemon verbena leaves
Lemon thyme sprig

SEMI-DRIED LACTO PLUMS
Lacto Plum* halves

PARSLEY PURÉE
Parsley leaves

SMOKED PARSLEY PURÉE
Strained Parsley Purée
Strained Peaso*
Parsley Oil*
Nordic Shoyu*
Parsley–Spruce Wood Oil Marinade
Toasted Hay*

TO FINISH
Charred Padrón Pepper
Semi-Dried Tomatoes*
Fava Bean halves
Bell Pepper Marinade
Confit Gooseberry half
Semi-Dried Lacto Plums
Fresh coriander seeds
Lemon thyme leaves
Parsley leaf
Lemon verbena leaf
Chopped Pepper Filling
Smoked Parsley Purée

VEGETABLE

Radish and Nasturtium Butterfly

A dough is made from flour, kelp in several forms, and butter, then rolled thin, cut into a butterfly shape, and baked into a tart shell.

Fresh coriander leaves are flash frozen, ground, and then mixed with yeast broth reduction to make a paste. Radishes are cooked in an infused liquid, then sliced thin and cut into half-moons.

The butterfly pastry is piped with vegetable fudge and coriander paste. The bottom wing sections are covered with radish slices folded in half and shingled onto the pastry in a ruffled pattern. The upper wing sections are layered with overlapping nasturtium and sage blossom petals. The butterfly's body and antennae are showered with grated horseradish and the whole dish is seasoned with salt and drops of horseradish juice and horseradish oil.

RAW KELP POWDER
Kelp

KELP THICKENER
Raw Kelp Powder
Cold filtered water

BUTTERFLY TART SHELL
Tipo "00" flour
Roasted Kelp Powder*
Butter
Kelp Thickener
Roasted Kelp Oil*

VEGETABLE FUDGE
Cucumber Juice Reduction*
Peaso Water Reduction*
Butter
Grapeseed oil

CORIANDER PASTE
Yeast Broth Reduction*
Fresh coriander leaves

RADISH COOKING LIQUID
Filtered water
Lemon verbena sprigs
Lemon thyme sprigs
Dried Cucumber*
Dried woodruff
Kelp
Freeze-dried gooseberries
Douglas fir needles

RADISHES
Round red radishes
Radish Cooking Liquid

TO FINISH
Butterfly Tart
Half-moon slices of Radish
Veg Fudge
Coriander Paste
Nasturtium flowers of different colors
Sage flowers of different colors
Grated fresh horseradish
Horseradish juice
Horseradish Oil*
Salt

Mold Pancake and
Plum Kernel Dessert

Cooked barley is puréed, rolled out into a thin sheet, inoculated with koji spores, and fermented for two days. The mold sheet is then cut into round pancakes.

    Ice cream is flavored with peeled plum kernels and set into half-moon shapes. A half-moon of plum kernel ice cream is set inside the mold crepe and drizzled with aged balsamic vinegar. The mold crepe is then folded around the ice cream.

MOLD CREPE
Pearl barley
Koji tane (*Aspergillus oryzae* spores)

PLUM KERNEL ICE CREAM
Milk
Cream
Peeled plum kernels
Dextrose
Sugar
Milk powder
Trimoline
Salt
Procrema

TO FINISH
Plum Kernel Ice Cream
Mold Crepe
10-year-old DOP Balsamico
  di Modena

Garden Flower, Chocolate, and Berries

Dark chocolate (70% cacao) is blended with cocoa butter, tempered, and brushed onto Mexican oregano leaves. A darker chocolate (72% cacao) is blended with cocoa butter, tempered, and poured into discs. A tiny fennel blossom is pressed into one disc of melted chocolate and coriander seed tops into another, and the chocolate is allowed to set. The chocolate discs and chocolate-coated oregano leaves are lightly salted and served with a bowl of wild summer berries.

MEXICAN OREGANO AND
CHOCOLATE
70% chocolate
Cocoa butter
Mexican oregano leaves

GREEN FENNEL SEED AND
CHOCOLATE
72% chocolate
Cocoa butter
Green fennel bud tops from the
    garden

GREEN CORIANDER SEED AND
CHOCOLATE
72% chocolate
Cocoa butter
Green coriander seed tops from
    the garden

TO FINISH
Mexican Oregano and Chocolate
Green Fennel Seed and Chocolate
Green Coriander Seed and
    Chocolate
Salt
Raspberries
Wild blackberries
Wine berries

Sea Buckthorn Cake

A bee larvae sponge cake is made with flour, almond flour, sugar, egg whites, and butter infused with bee larvae. The cake is brushed with bee pollen glaze and grilled until caramelized on both sides, then brushed with sea buckthorn syrup.

Italian meringue, whipped cream, and sea buckthorn base are folded together and set with gelatin to make sea buckthorn mousse.

Two rounds of cake are layered and coated with chopped elderflower pulp and sea buckthorn mousse to form a dome-shaped cake, which is then glazed with sea buckthorn glaze. The top is sprinkled with bee pollen and marigold petals are placed around the cake.

QUINCE REDUCTION
Quince

BEE POLLEN GLAZE
Bee pollen
Quince Reduction
Elderflower Oil*

SEA BUCKTHORN JUICE
Ripe sea buckthorn berries

SEA BUCKTHORN SYRUP
Sea Buckthorn Juice
Elderflower Syrup*
Plum schnapps

BEE LARVAE BUTTER
Bee larvae
Butter

BEE LARVAE SPONGE
Sugar
Egg whites
Bee Larvae Butter
Tipo "00" flour
Almond flour
Salt
Bee Pollen Glaze
Sea Buckthorn Syrup

SEA BUCKTHORN BASE
Sea Buckthorn Juice
Freeze-dried sea buckthorn berries
Noma honey

ITALIAN MERINGUE
Egg whites
Sugar
Filtered water

SEA BUCKTHORN MOUSSE
Sea Buckthorn Base
Cream
Italian Meringue
Gelatin

SEA BUCKTHORN GLAZE
Sea Buckthorn Juice
Sugar
Glucose syrup
Gelatin
Elderflower Oil*

SEA BUCKTHORN CAKE
Chopped elderflower pulp (reserved
    from making Elderflower Syrup*)
Sea Buckthorn Mousse
Bee Larvae Sponge
Sea Buckthorn Glaze

TO FINISH
Sea Buckthorn Cake
Bee pollen
Marigold flowers

VEGETABLE

Crispy Bee Larvae and
Caramelized Chocolate

Bee larvae are gently cooked in foaming butter until crispy.

Filtered water and beeswax are emulsified, strained, and cooked with sugar to form a syrup.

Caramelized chocolate is tempered, spread into a thin layer, and topped with the crispy bee larvae and an assortment of flowers. Once cooled and set, the chocolate is cracked into a large shard, which is served with sweet licorice syrup, the beeswax syrup, and rose oil.

CRISPY BEE LARVAE
Bee larvae
Butter

BEESWAX SYRUP
Filtered water
Beeswax
Sugar

CARAMELIZED CHOCOLATE
Blond milk chocolate
Cocoa butter

FLOWERS
White oxalis
Red oxalis
Pink oxalis
Yellow oxalis
Marigold
Thyme
Lavender
Fennel

CHOCOLATE SHARD
Tempered Caramelized Chocolate
Crispy Bee Larvae
Flowers

TO FINISH
Chocolate Shard, dressed
Sweet licorice syrup
Beeswax Syrup
Rose Oil*

Woodruff Ice Cream with Pine

A quenelle of woodruff ice cream, scented with plum kernels, is scooped into a frozen bowl. A well is formed in the center of the ice cream and green strawberry paste is spooned into the well, followed by ant paste.

Cooked blueberries and candied pine cone halves dotted with plum kernel paste and topped with Scots pine cones are arranged around the ice cream, with pine shoots tucked in between. Birch water kombucha gel is piped over the ant paste and the dish is finished with a pinch of salt and drops of black currant wood oil.

WOODRUFF ICE CREAM
Milk
Fresh woodruff
Plum kernels
Cream
Sugar
Dextrose
Trimoline
Salt
Procrema

STEAMED GREEN STRAWBERRIES
Green strawberries
Black Currant Wood Oil*

GREEN STRAWBERRY PASTE
Steamed Green Strawberries
Unripe sea buckthorn berries
Black currant shoots
Elderflower Syrup*
Black Currant Wood Oil*
Salt

PLUM KERNEL PASTE
Peeled plum kernels
Salt
Douglas Fir Oil*

ANT PASTE
Ants
Green coriander seeds
Muscovado sugar
Black Currant Wood Oil*

SCOTS PINE
Mini Scots pine cones
Douglas Fir Oil*

BLUEBERRIES
Blueberries
Black Currant Wood Oil*

BIRCH WATER KOMBUCHA GEL
Birch Water Kombucha*
Gelatin

TO FINISH
Woodruff Ice Cream
Blueberries
Jarred candied pine cone halves
Scots Pine
Plum Kernel Paste
Green Strawberry Paste
Ant Paste
Pine shoots
Birch Water Kombucha Gel
Black Currant Wood Oil*

A Pile of Pies

Five different pie shells are made: The cream pie shell is simply heavy cream into which a frozen pie shell mold is dipped; the frozen cream shell is released and popped back into the blast freezer.

The berry powder cream pie shell is a cream pie shell that's completely coated with berry powder.

The rhubarb emulsion pie shell is made by infusing sweetened clarified rhubarb juice with green coriander, quince tea, dried roseroot, and sweet licorice syrup, setting the mixture with gelatin, and emulsifying with rose oil. The mixture is frozen onto a pie mold.

The raspberry pie shell is made simply of frozen honey-sweetened raspberry purée.

The rhubarb crisp pie shell is made from clarified rhubarb juice, a purée of cooked apple skins and flesh, and sugar. The mixture is spread thin and dried, then circles are stamped out, warmed, and gently shaped around pie molds.

To assemble the dish, a cold rock is placed in the serving dish and topped with a tall stack of the pie shells, each arranged slightly off-center and shingled over the edge of the one below, with mulberry cream and rhubarb gel between them to hold the shells together.

CLARIFIED RHUBARB JUICE
Rhubarb

RHUBARB EMULSION PIE SHELL
Clarified Rhubarb Juice
Green coriander seeds
Quince tea
Dried roseroot
Sweet licorice syrup
Birch syrup
Sugar
Gelatin
Rose Oil*

RASPBERRY PIE SHELL
Raspberries
Honey

CREAM PIE SHELL
Cream

APPLE PURÉE
Danish apples

RHUBARB CRISP PIE SHELL
Clarified Rhubarb Juice
Apple Purée
Gellan gum
Glucose powder
Sugar

BERRY POWDER
Freeze-dried black currants
Freeze-dried blueberries
Freeze-dried rhubarb
Dried rose petals
Dried Ginger*

BERRY POWDER CREAM PIE SHELL
Berry Powder
Cream Pie Shell

MULBERRY PURÉE
Frozen Semi-Dried Mulberries*

MULBERRY CREAM
Gently whipped cream
Mulberry Purée

TO FINISH
Rhubarb Crisp Pie Shell
Berry Powder Cream Pie Shell
Cream Pie Shell
Rhubarb Emulsion Pie Shell
Raspberry Pie Shell
Mulberry Cream
Raspberry halves

Rose Terra Cotta

Elderflower sponge cake batter is baked in a sheet. The cake is then cut into rounds, brushed with elderflower oil, and lightly grilled. Elderflower paste is spread on both sides of the grilled cake rounds.

Malt soil is made from a mix of flours, malt powder, sugar, bilberry powder, and butter; the mixture is baked, cooled, and pounded to a crumble along with the brunost.

Lavender-infused cream is folded with crème fraîche, whipped cream, Italian meringue, and red gooseberry and rose emulsion to make a gooseberry and rose mousse.

The mousse and the grilled elderflower sponge rounds are layered in a flowerpot-shaped silicone mold. The assembled pot-shaped cake is glazed with terra-cotta glaze and the surface is coated with malt soil. Oxalis, oregano, and lemon verbena are then "planted" in the cake.

ELDERFLOWER PASTE
Elderflower Syrup*
Elderflower pulp (reserved from
    making Elderflower Syrup*)
Lemon verbena
Elderflower Oil*

ELDERFLOWER SPONGE
Sugar
Eggs
Egg yolk
Lemon juice
Elderflower Oil*
Tipo "00" flour
Baking powder

RED GOOSEBERRY PURÉE
Red gooseberries

RED GOOSEBERRY AND ROSE EMULSION
Red Gooseberry Purée
Rose Oil*
Gelatin

MALT SOIL
Hazelnut flour
Malt flour
Tipo "00" flour
Sugar
Bilberry powder
Melted butter
Brunost (brown cheese)

LAVENDER CREAM
Cream
Lavender

ITALIAN MERINGUE
Sugar
Egg whites

GOOSEBERRY AND ROSE MOUSSE
Gelatin
Lavender Cream
Crème fraîche
Italian Meringue
Cream, whipped to stiff peaks
Red Gooseberry and Rose Emulsion

MILK CRUMB
Milk powder
Tipo "00" flour
Sugar
Melted butter
Cornstarch
Salt

TERRA-COTTA GLAZE
Milk Crumb
Rose Oil*
Butter
Aronia Berry Reduction*

TO FINISH
Gooseberry and Rose Mousse
Elderflower Sponge discs
Terra-Cotta Glaze
Rose terra-cotta cake
Malt Soil
Oxalis branches
Oregano branches
Lemon verbena stalks

Berries and Cream

White currant juice is sweetened with honey and steeped with flowers. The juice is strained and reduced until lightly set like jelly. The jelly is spread into a thin layer, further dried, and cut into squares.

Plums are simmered in seasoned dashi until soft, then peeled and pitted. The plum flesh is cooked with rose hips, rose oil, and spices to make a compote.

The rose hip and plum compote is piped into the white currant jelly squares, which are folded to make a packet. The packets are arranged in the serving bowl with fresh flowers, and everything is surrounded by fresh cream.

WHITE CURRANT JELLY
White Currant Juice*
Danish honey
Geranium leaves
Citrus marigold (*Tagetes tenuifolia*)
Lemon verbena leaves
Lavender flower clusters

COOKED PLUM FLESH
Cold-Infused Dashi*
Yellow mustard seeds
Coriander seeds
Fennel seeds
Dried Horseradish*
Dried Ginger Skins*
Juniper berries
Tophit plums

ROSE HIP AND PLUM COMPOTE
Cooked Plum Flesh
Seeded rose hips
Dried Rose Oil*
Toasted coriander seeds
Toasted fennel seeds
Toasted yellow mustard seeds
Dried Ginger Skins*
Dried Horseradish*
Saffron

TO FINISH
White Currant Jelly squares
Rose Hip and Plum Compote
Wood sorrel
Oxalis leaves
Oxalis flowers
Marigold petals
Geranium petals
Cream
Geranium Oil*

Sweet Woodruff and Plum Dessert

Laetitia plum juice is reduced until thick, then spread into circles to create plum leather discs. The discs are molded around dome-shaped cups of woodruff ice cream made from woodruff-infused milk, cream, and honey to form flowerlike dumplings.

The dumplings are topped with a dusting of woodruff powder, small drops of Gammel Dansk syrup, Italian balsamic vinegar, a tender pine shoot, and a small amount of ant paste. To finish, cream is spooned around the dumplings in the serving bowl and black currant wood oil is drizzled onto the cream.

PLUM LEATHER
Laetitia plums
Noma honey

WOODRUFF MILK
Milk
Fresh woodruff

WOODRUFF ICE CREAM
Woodruff Milk
Cream
Dextrose
Honey
Milk powder
Trimoline
Salt
Procrema

PLUM AND WOODRUFF
DUMPLINGS
Plum Leather discs
Quail egg trays
Woodruff Ice Cream

ANT PASTE
Ants
Green coriander seeds
Muscovado sugar
Black Currant Wood Oil*

GAMMEL DANSK SYRUP
Gammel Dansk
Glucose syrup

TO FINISH
Plum and Woodruff Dumplings
Ground dried woodruff
Ant Paste
Pine shoots
Italian balsamic vinegar
Gammel Dansk Syrup
Black Currant Wood Oil*
Cream (38% milkfat)

Cardamom-Scented Candle

Toasted cardamom and saffron-infused cream are cooked with sugar, glucose, and salt, finished with melted butter and vinegar, and thickened with agar and more cream to make a caramel. The cardamom-saffron caramel is poured into chilled silicone molds to form candles. The candles are kept frozen.

To shape the candlewicks, lightly dried and skinned walnuts are cut into thin matchstick shapes.

A serving plate is glossed with cardamom-infused oil. The candle is set on the plate and spritzed with cardamom perfume made from cardamom-infused water. A walnut wick is affixed to the candle and lit.

CARDAMOM-SAFFRON CANDLE
Cardamom pods
Saffron
Cream
Glucose syrup
Sugar
Salt
Butter
White wine vinegar
Agar

CARDAMOM OIL
Grapeseed oil
Cardamom pods

WALNUT WICK
Walnuts

CARDAMOM PERFUME
Filtered water
Cardamom pods

TO FINISH
Cardamom Oil
Cardamom-Saffron Candle
Walnut Wick
Cardamom Perfume

Between gardens and wilderness   Piet Oudolf

Noma is about transformation. At the start: local ingredients, foraged in the wild. On the plate: works of art, exquisitely arranged and imbued with complex flavors. The perennial garden I designed for Noma is also about change. But to a diner, the hundreds of meticulous steps that go into making each of René's dishes remain hidden. In my work, you see the transformation unfold, from beginning to end. My garden is a process.

It's also an experience: Visitors to Noma walk the length of a perennial meadow dotted with bulbs in spring and flowers in summer. A mix of grasses evokes wild landscapes and undulates in the slightest breeze. The garden moves with the seasons, too. Plants grow to a high point in summer and then decay, revealing their skeletal stems and seed heads. Insects and birds come and go.

One of my best-known public projects is the High Line in New York City, built on a two-kilometer stretch of abandoned elevated train tracks. The brief there was to create a narrative, as visitors walk through successive zones evoking woodland, meadow, nature preserve, and grasslands. The garden at Noma is smaller, but it is also a walk designed as discovery. It's part of the ritual the restaurant offers its guests. With each step, visitors shed the constraints and conventions of the city and open their senses to new experiences. And when it comes to connecting to the human yearning for an untamed, natural state, grasses are the perfect guide.

René's mission has been to rediscover and elevate ingredients most of us didn't know were edible. Much of my work has been with plants that until not long ago

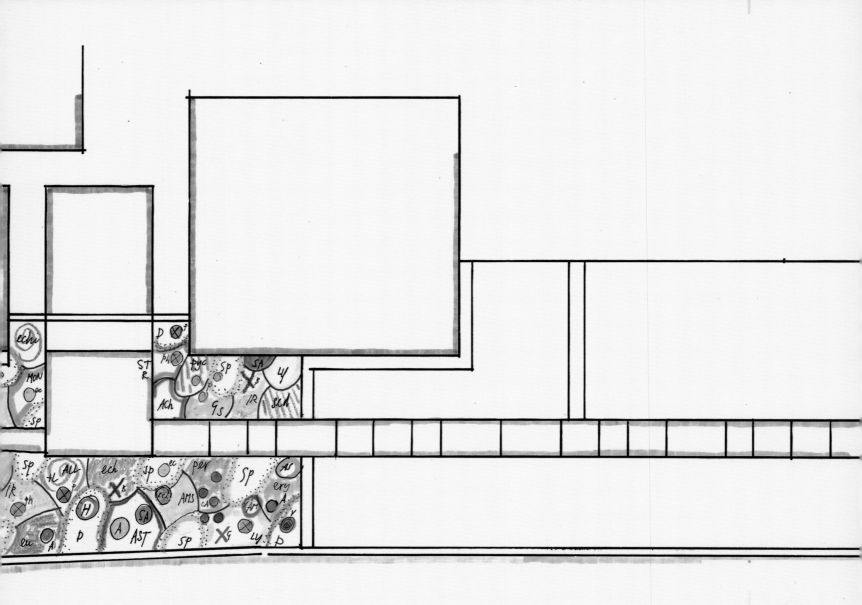

PLANT GROUPS

Ach	ACHILLEA TERRA COTTA + SCABIOSA		eup	EUPATORIUM HYSSOPIFOLIUM	sed	SEDUM MATRONA
ALL L+	ALLIUM SUMMERBEAUTY + LIMONIUM		G s	GERANIUM SANG. ELSBETH	SP	SPOROBOLUS HETEROLEPIS
ALL +CA	ALLIUM SUMMERBEAUTY + CALAMINTHA		IMP	IMPERATA CYLINDRICA	ST B	STACHYS BIG EARS
AMS	AMSONIA HUBRICHTII		IR	IRIS PERRY'S BLUE	ST R	STACHYS MON. ROSEA
AST	ASTER TWILIGHT		LY	LYTHRUM VIRG. SWIRL		
P	DESCHAMPSIA GOLDTAU		MON N	MONARDA NEON		
ech	ECHINACEA H. DANCER + SAPO		MON B	MONARDA BRADBURIANA		
echi	ECHINOPS BANN. VEITCH BLUE		per	PERSICARIA AMPL. ALBA		
era	ERAGROSTIS SPECTABILIS		pyc	PYCNANTHEMUM MUTICUM		
ery	ERYNGIUM BIG BLUE		scu	SCUTELLARIA INCANA		

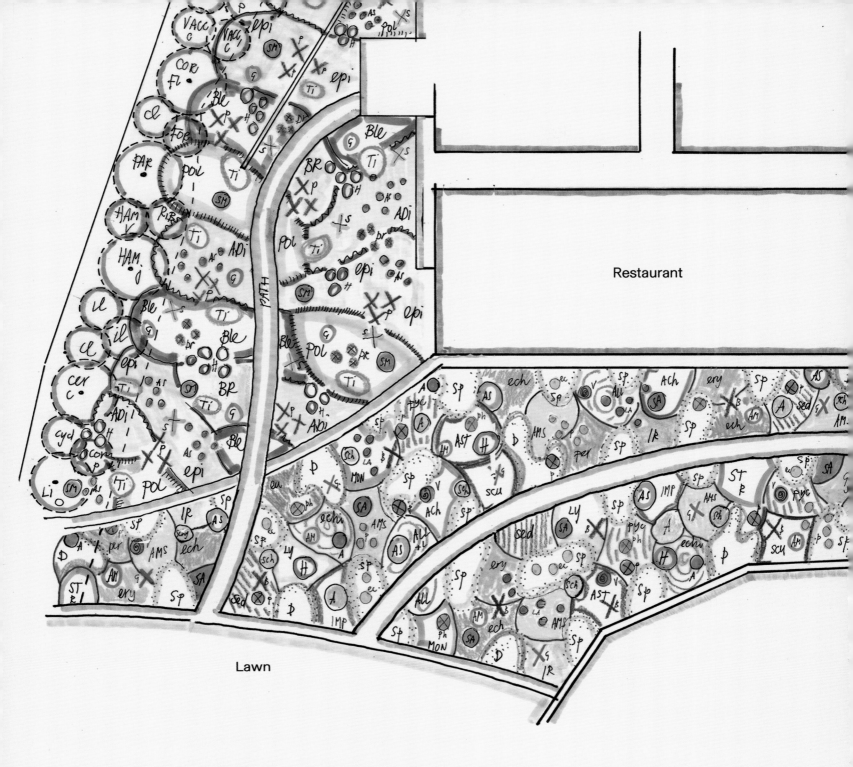

Restaurant

Lawn

PLANT GROUPS

ADi	ADIANTHUM PEDATUM
Ble	BLECHNUM SPICANT
POL	POLYPODIUM VULGARE
BR	BRUNNERA MACROPHYLLA
epi	EPIMEDIUM WHITE QUEEN

INDIVIDUAL PLANTS

As	ASPLENIUM SCOLOPENDRIUM
BR	DRYOPTERIS ERYTHROSORA
g	GERANIUM BUXTON'S VAR.
H	HAKONECHLOA MACRA
P	POLYSTICHUM HERRENHAUSEN
SM	SMILACINA RACEMOSA
Ti	TIARELLA SPRING SYMPHONY

were considered unworthy of gardens. My love of grasses might be a product of my childhood in the Netherlands, growing up on the edge of the dunes. There was only a fence separating my parents' house from a nature preserve.

Grasses became a way for me to create more spontaneity than I saw in the stiff, decorative gardens of the past with their clipped boxwood hedges. In combination with other plants, grasses can act like filters, breaking stronger colors and softening the overall palette. Grasses have more staying power and start flowering late. They bring sensual movement to a landscape.

More important, they remind you of the wild and where we come from.

They evoke the prairie and other untouched landscapes. It's a romantic idea. As our longing for those untouched spaces grows stronger because of our built-up environments and the loss of diversity, gardens have become more naturalistic.

I work in four dimensions. Even in the design stage, I have to have timing in mind. With every plant I choose, I have to know what it will do this summer, and the summer after, and maybe five years from now. And I have to consider its character. It's a bit like casting. When I start on a new project, I create a palette of plants that I think I can use. Then I start intuitively putting them on paper, considering their qualities as individuals and as team players. A plant might be beautiful on its own but not get along well with others. You can't have all prima donnas. But you can make the same plant a prima donna in one garden and a chorus member in another.

The menu at Noma is determined by the seasons: in the summer, food comes from the garden; in the autumn, from the forest; in the winter, from the sea. My perennial gardens make the seasons tangible by honoring the life cycle of plants. In traditional horticulture, if a plant was no longer in flower, you'd cut it back or pull it out of the earth and replace it with another. The aim was to maximize color and bloom for as long as the climate allowed. There was a constant in-and-out of plants, which required a lot of labor.

Planting for all seasons reconnects us with the natural process of transformation. Allowing a plant to grow and flower, to die and decay in full view, can remind us of our own mortality, like skulls in the still lifes of the old Dutch painters. But it also invites us to discover the beauty of structure, the sculptural intricacy of a seed head, the way a plant's skeleton appears etched against the sky. A tree without leaves is still beautiful. Besides, plant skeletons can animate a garden in winter, providing shelter for insects and seed for birds. A good skeleton can be as beautiful as a flower, and more personal.

My gardens are probably an expression of my inner self. I try to create a vision that moves people as it moves me. What's important to me is the depth of a visitor's experience. A good garden activates multiple layers of emotions, sensations, and thoughts.

I want people to feel more than they see.

A color palette is to a painter as plants are to Oudolf.

Clockwise from left: Sun streaming through the Noma greenhouse; a heron at the edge of the garden; the perennial master: Piet Oudolf.

Forest

September through December

Stag Beetle

Blackened Conference pears are blended and reduced to make a purée. More black pears are juiced and the juice is reduced to enhance sweetness.

The reduced black pear purée and juice are blended with blackberries and Japanese black garlic to create beetle leather, which is shaped into rounds and beetle parts using a stencil.

A beetle leather round is filled with herbs, fresh and semi-dried fruits, and red currant and rose hip paste, then sealed like a dumpling. The beetle's body parts are applied to the dumpling using more red currant and rose hip paste, and the finished beetle is brushed with spruce wood oil and presented in a glass specimen box with pins.

REDUCED BLACK PEAR PURÉE
Black Pears*

REDUCED BLACK PEAR JUICE
Black Pears*

BEETLE LEATHER
Reduced Black Pear Purée
Reduced Black Pear Juice
Blackberries
Japanese black garlic
Activated charcoal powder

SEMI-DRIED LACTO PLUMS
Lacto Plums*

SEMI-DRIED STRAWBERRIES
Danish strawberries
Koji Oil*

RED CURRANT AND ROSE HIP
PASTE
Dried meadowsweet
Angelica seeds or buds
Geranium Oil*
Red currants
Seeded rose hips

TO FINISH
Beetle Leather disc
Wood sorrel leaves
Marigold leaves
Lemon verbena leaves
Green coriander seeds
Lavender buds
Red Currant and Rose Hip Paste
Diced Semi-Dried Lacto Plums
Blueberries
Diced Semi-Dried Strawberries
Beetle Leather body segments
Spruce Wood Oil*

Oregano Leaf and Reindeer Brain

Reindeer brain is brined, cold-smoked over hay, and poached in dashi. The brain is sliced, glazed with a mushroom spice smoked butter, and cut into smaller bits.

The brain is gently mixed with an assortment of herbs and herb flowers, horseradish juice, more mushroom spice smoked butter, and a few drops of morita chile oil.

The center of a Mexican oregano leaf is brushed with a layer of brain salad paste and the brains are mounded on the leaf.

BRAIN SPICE MIX
Toasted fennel seeds
Toasted yellow mustard seeds
Toasted coriander seeds
Toasted black peppercorns
Toasted seeded pasilla chile
Freeze-dried gooseberries
Juniper berries

MUSHROOM SPICE MIX
Toasted yellow mustard seeds
Toasted coriander seeds
Toasted fennel seeds
Arctic thyme leaves
Dried ceps
Dried morels

SUNFLOWER SEED PASTE
Sunflower seeds
Brown Butter*
Ginger Powder*
Brain Spice Mix
Celery Juice Reduction*
Peaso Water Reduction*
Roasted Kelp Salt*
Kohlrabi Shoyu*

BRAIN SALAD PASTE
Freeze-dried rhubarb
Freeze-dried lingonberries
Cold-Infused Dashi*
Mushroom Spice Mix
Koji Oil*
Fried Parsley
Fried Oregano
Sunflower Seed Paste

BRAIN BRINE
Filtered water
Salt
Arctic thyme leaves
Dried Ginger Skins*
Toasted yellow mustard seeds
Toasted brown mustard seeds
Toasted fennel seeds
Toasted star anise
Toasted coriander seeds

MUSHROOM SPICE SMOKED
BUTTER
Smoked Butter*
Mushroom Spice Mix

BRAINS
Reindeer or fallow deer head
Brain Brine
Cold-Infused Dashi*
Mushroom Spice Smoked Butter

HERBS
Chamomile leaves
Ground elder leaves
Spanish chervil leaves
Lemon thyme leaves
Fennel flowers
Coriander flowers
Wasabi flowers
Coriander seeds
Yarrow leaves
Wood sorrel leaves
Marjoram leaves
Lemon verbena leaves
Soft oregano leaves
Soft lovage leaves
Chickweed
Watercress

TO FINISH
Mexican oregano leaf
Brain Salad Paste
Brains
Herbs
Japanese Quince brunoise
Horseradish juice
Mushroom Spice Smoked Butter
Morita Chile Oil*

Reindeer Brain Pie

Reindeer brains are lightly brined, cold-smoked, and then poached in dashi and sliced. The slices are glazed with mushroom spice smoked butter and seasoned with egg white garum and horseradish juice.

Full-fat milk is reduced in a wide skillet until all that's left is a skin, which is slowly cooked until lightly caramelized. The caramelized milk skin is punched into a round and spread with black currant wood fudge, and a nasturtium leaf is pressed onto the fudge. The leaf is spread with parsley paste and dotted with cep paste and chanterelle umami paste. The glazed reindeer brain goes onto the pastes and the milk skin is folded up and sealed to create a reindeer pie.

The pie is fried and tucked into another nasturtium leaf that's been piped with a bit of truffle purée.

BLACK CURRANT WOOD FUDGE
Cucumber Juice Reduction*
Peaso Water Reduction*
Butter
Black Currant Wood Oil*

PARSLEY PASTE
Parsley leaves
Yeast Broth Reduction*
Parsley Oil*

PAN-ROASTED CEP OIL
Ceps
Grapeseed oil

CEP PASTE
Pan-Roasted Cep Oil solids
Cucumber Juice Reduction*
Peaso Water Reduction*

CHANTERELLE UMAMI PASTE
Finely chopped Pickled Chanterelles*
Peaso Water Reduction*
Roasted Kelp Salt*
Sweet Koji Water Reduction*

CARAMELIZED MILK SKIN
3.5% milk

TRUFFLE PURÉE
Truffles
Roasted Yeast Oil*
Cep Oil*
Mushroom-Kelp Broth*
Lacto Cep Water*
Celery Juice Reduction*

BRAIN BRINE
Filtered water
Salt
Arctic thyme leaves
Dried Ginger Skins*
Toasted yellow mustard seeds
Toasted brown mustard seeds
Toasted fennel seeds
Toasted star anise
Toasted coriander seeds

MUSHROOM SPICE MIX
Dried Horseradish*
Toasted yellow mustard seeds
Toasted black peppercorns
Toasted coriander seeds
Dried Ginger*
Dried ceps
Juniper berries

MUSHROOM SPICE SMOKED BUTTER
Smoked Butter*
Mushroom Spice Mix

REINDEER BRAINS
Reindeer or fallow deer head
Brain Brine
Cold-Infused Dashi*
Mushroom Spice Smoked Butter
Egg White Garum*
Horseradish juice

REINDEER PIE
Caramelized Milk Skin
Cep Paste
Black Currant Wood Fudge
Parsley Paste
Chanterelle Umami Paste
Fried Parsley
Nasturtium leaf
Flour slurry

TO FINISH
Reindeer Pie
Grapeseed oil
Nasturtium leaf
Truffle Purée

Reindeer Brain Jelly

Reindeer skulls are trimmed, cleaned, and bleached.

Chestnuts are cold-smoked and then simmered in cream and puréed.

Reindeer brains are brined with spices, puréed, and blended with eggs, milk, cream, and smoked chestnut cream to form a custard base. The custard base is steamed in a reindeer skull and chilled.

Pheasants are roasted with butter and then simmered with lemon thyme and roasted duck garum. The broth is seasoned with oregano vinegar and beef garum, then set with gelatin, and a brunoise of braised mushroom kelp is folded in. The pheasant gel is set on top of the reindeer brain custard and the dish is finished with freshly pressed hazelnut oil.

REINDEER SKULLS
Reindeer heads

BRAISED KELP
Kelp reserved from Mushroom-Kelp
    Broth*

SMOKED CHESTNUT CREAM
Chestnuts
Cream
Roasted Kelp Salt*

BRAIN BRINE
Toasted black peppercorns
Toasted green cardamom pods
Toasted juniper berries
Toasted fennel seeds
Kelp
Dried Ginger*
Filtered water
Salt

BRINED BRAINS
Reindeer or fallow deer
Brain Brine

BRAIN CUSTARD BASE
Brined Brains
Eggs
Milk
Cream
Smoked Chestnut Cream
Salt

PHEASANT BROTH
Pheasants
Butter
Lemon thyme sprigs
BBQ Duck Garum*
Salt

STEAMED BRAIN CUSTARD
Brain Custard Base
Reindeer Skulls

PHEASANT GEL
Pheasant Broth
Salt
Oregano Vinegar*
Gelatin
Beef Garum*

TO FINISH
Steamed Brain Custard
Braised Kelp
Pheasant Gel
Hazelnut Oil*
Salt

Forest Broth

Fresh and dried mushrooms, lemon thyme, dashi, and tomato water are cooked into a broth, which is served in a bowl filled with pine sprigs and reindeer moss and garnished with pine cones.

MUSHROOM AND MOSS BROTH
Cold-Infused Dashi*
Fresh maitake mushrooms
Dried chanterelles
Fresh lemon thyme sprigs
Ice-Clarified Tomato Water*

TO FINISH
Mushroom and Moss Broth
Reindeer moss
Douglas fir needles
Pine cones

Reindeer Tongue Skewer

Reindeer tongue is spritzed with Danish whisky and cut into medallions. The tongue is pan-roasted in smoked butter with lemon thyme, then cut into quarters and skewered, alternating with pine shoots. The tongue is finished with warmed roasted kelp butter and a brushing of ant–morita chile paste.

REINDEER TONGUE
Reindeer tongue
Danish whisky

ANT-MORITA CHILE PASTE
Ants
Pine Salt*
Morita Chile Oil*

ROASTED KELP BUTTER
Roasted Kelp Salt*
Butter

TO FINISH
Reindeer Tongue
Smoked Butter*
Lemon thyme sprigs
Ant-Morita Chile Paste
Roasted Kelp Butter
Pine shoots

Rose Hip Berry Dumpling

A rose hip is seeded from the bottom and then peeled, leaving the stem end intact. The seeded rose hip is brushed with rose oil and lightly dried. The top of the semi-dried rose hip is cut off and the cut edge is piped with Japanese quince paste and pinched to seal, creating a hollow dumpling.

The interior is filled with diced Japanese quince, a red currant, and a drop of black currant wood oil. The mirabelle gel is added, then the Japanese quince paste, and finally the rose hip–red currant paste; the stuffed rose hip dumpling is then sealed. The dumpling is finished with rose oil, morita chile oil, and cut coriander seeds.

ROSE HIP–RED CURRANT PASTE
Seeded rose hips
Red currants
Pitted Lacto Mirabelle Plums*
Black Currant Wood Oil*
Freeze-dried black currants
Söl
Arctic thyme leaves
Salt

SEMI-DRIED ROSE HIPS
Rose hips
Rose Oil*

MIRABELLE GEL
Ice-Clarified Mirabelle Plum Juice*
Noma honey
Kuzu
Agar
Salt

JAPANESE QUINCE PASTE
Japanese quince
Butter
Dried Carrot Flowers*

TO FINISH
Semi-Dried Rose Hip
Rose Hip–Red Currant Paste
Mirabelle Gel
Cubes of freshly frozen Japanese quince
Red currant
Green coriander seed halves
Japanese Quince Paste
Rose Oil*
Black Currant Wood Oil*
Morita Chile Oil*
Moss plate
Salt

Rose Hip and Japanese Quince

Brined Japanese quince are sliced into thin discs and the discs are quartered.

A peeled and seeded rose hip is filled with Japanese quince paste and sweet rose hip purée. The rose hip is brushed with rose oil and topped with three salted Japanese quince quarters and tiny piles of pollen mixed with rose oil.

SEEDED ROSE HIPS
Rose hips

SWEET ROSE HIP PURÉE
Seeded Rose Hips
Honey

POLLEN MIX
Pollen
Rose Oil*

JAPANESE QUINCE PASTE
Japanese quince
Butter
Dried Carrot Flowers*

TO FINISH
Brined Japanese Quince*
  (made using an 8% salt brine)
Seeded Rose Hip
Japanese Quince Paste
Sweet Rose Hip Purée
Rose Oil*
Pollen Mix

Pheasant Gel and Caviar

Roasted pheasants are simmered in water with lemon thyme and roasted duck garum to make a broth, which is then strained and lightly set with gelatin.

The pheasant gel is poured into lidded beeswax bowls and chilled to set. Small drops of spruce wood oil are dotted around the edge of the pheasant gel and the center is dressed with a spoonful of caviar and another spoonful of whipped cream.

PHEASANT BROTH
Pheasants
Lemon thyme sprigs
Roasted duck garum
Salt

PHEASANT GEL
Pheasant Broth
Salt
Oregano Vinegar*
Gelatin

TO FINISH
Pheasant Gel
Spruce Wood Oil*
White sturgeon caviar
Whipped cream
Beeswax bowl

Beet Sashimi

Golden beets are roasted, infused with rose oil, and then sliced into thin fans.

Freeze-dried black currants, dried ceps, söl, and Madagascar pepper are dehydrated and then ground into a fine powder, which is blended with black currant wood oil, marigold oil, and kanzuri oil to make a praline.

Three rings of thinly sliced fresh plum are arranged in a serving bowl. The centers of the rings are filled with berry praline and the edges of the rings are dotted with vegetable fudge, pollen paste, and ant paste. Semi-dried cloudberries and semi-dried lacto-fermented mirabelle plums are tucked alongside.

Three beet fans are placed on top of the plum clusters, beet sauce is spooned around, and the dish is finished with sprays of whisky vinegar and small drops of rose oil and morita chile oil.

GOLDEN BEET FANS
Golden beets
Roasted Kelp Oil*
Lemon thyme sprigs
Rose Oil*
Salt

BEET JUICE
Golden beets
Roasted beet cores

BEET SAUCE
Beet Juice
Ice-Clarified Tomato Water*
Lacto Koji Water* (made with Rice
 Koji*)
Salt

SEMI-DRIED CLOUDBERRIES
Frozen cloudberries
Birch syrup

ANT PASTE
Ants
Green coriander seeds
Juniper skins
Black Currant Wood Oil*

PLUM RINGS
Plum

BERRY PRALINE
Freeze-dried black currants
Dried ceps
Söl
Madagascar peppercorns
 (voatsiperifery)
Black Currant Wood Oil*
Marigold Oil*
Kanzuri Oil*

POLLEN PASTE
Bee pollen
Rose Oil*
Cold-Infused Dashi*

VEGETABLE FUDGE
Cucumber Juice Reduction*
Peaso Water Reduction*
Butter
Grapeseed oil

SEMI-DRIED LACTO MIRABELLE
PLUMS
Lacto Mirabelle Plums*
Koji Oil*

TO FINISH
Whisky Vinegar,* in a spray bottle
Rose Oil*
Morita Chile Oil*
Golden Beet Fans
Plum Rings
Pollen Paste
Ant Paste
Berry Praline
Semi-Dried Cloudberries
Semi-Dried Lacto Mirabelle
 Plum halves
Vegetable Fudge
Beet Sauce

Plum and Bee Larvae

Sunflower seeds are cooked in brown butter and then ground with spices, reductions, roasted kelp salt, and Nordic shoyu to make a smooth paste. This paste is combined with freeze-dried rhubarb, lingonberries, and gooseberries soaked in dashi and seasoned with mushroom spice mix, all cooked down and caramelized in koji oil. The caramelized lingonberry–sunflower seed mixture is ground with fried parsley and fried lovage to make a paste.

Plums are peeled and pitted but left whole, then dried until slightly chewy. Bee larvae are gently cooked in butter until the soft larvae firm up and then become crisp.

Lingonberry paste, Japanese quince paste, and seasoned parsley purée are piped into the cavity of the plum. Lemon thyme, coriander seeds, and morita chile also flavor the interior of the plum. The filled plum is then sliced.

A teaspoon of elderflower-pollen oil is poured into a serving bowl and seasoned with cherry vinegar. Two slices of the filled plum are placed in the bowl and then brushed with more elderflower-pollen oil, dotted with Japanese quince paste, and topped with crispy bee larvae. The bowl is served on a frame of beeswax.

DRIED PLUMS
Danish Tophit plums

MUSTARD SPICE MIX
Toasted fennel seeds
Toasted yellow mustard seeds
Toasted coriander seeds
Toasted black peppercorns
Seeded pasilla chile
Freeze-dried gooseberries
Juniper berries

SUNFLOWER SEED PASTE
Sunflower seeds
Brown Butter*
Ginger Powder*
Mustard Spice Mix
Celery Juice Reduction*
Peaso Water Reduction*
Roasted Kelp Salt*
Nordic Shoyu*

MUSHROOM SPICE MIX
Toasted fennel seeds
Toasted yellow mustard seeds
Toasted coriander seeds
Dried ceps
Arctic thyme leaves
Dried morels

FRIED PARSLEY
Parsley leaves
Grapeseed oil

FRIED LOVAGE
Lovage leaves
Grapeseed oil

LINGONBERRY PASTE
Freeze-dried rhubarb
Freeze-dried lingonberries
Freeze-dried gooseberries
Cold-Infused Dashi*
Mushroom Spice Mix
Koji Oil*
Fried Parsley
Fried Lovage
Sunflower Seed Paste

PARSLEY PURÉE
Parsley leaves

SEASONED PARSLEY PURÉE
Strained Parsley Purée
Smoked Seaweed Shoyu*
Parsley Oil*
Peaso Water Reduction*
Fava Rice Shoyu*
Salt

JAPANESE QUINCE PASTE
Japanese quince
Butter
Dried Carrot Flowers*

ELDERFLOWER-POLLEN OIL
Bee pollen
Elderflower Oil*

CRISPY BEE LARVAE
Bee larvae
Butter

TO FINISH
Lingonberry Paste
Dried Plum
Japanese Quince Paste
Seasoned Parsley Purée
Lemon thyme leaves
Green coriander seeds
Morita Chile Oil*
Elderflower-Pollen Oil
Cherry Vinegar*
Crispy Bee Larvae

Potato and Pumpkin Tart

A shallow tart shell is made from very thin slices of Danish potato shingled over each other in concentric circles to create a round. The round of potatoes is cooked, cooled, brushed with koji oil, and dried in the oven, then brushed again with koji oil and gently sandwiched between two tart molds to give the potato round a slight concave shape. The potato tart shell is baked until crisp and golden.

Crown Prince pumpkins are cut into slices, steamed, and then sculpted into batons from which thin slices are shaved off. Three slices are shingled together and brushed with pumpkin seed oil.

The pumpkin slices are curved around a nasturtium flower, brushed with hazelnut–grilled mushroom garum oil, seasoned with a drop of honey, salt, and crushed black pepper, and then placed on the potato tart shell.

POTATO TART SHELL
Danish potatoes
Koji Oil*

CROWN PRINCE PUMPKIN SHEETS
Crown Prince pumpkin
Pumpkin Seed Oil*
Salt

HAZELNUT–GRILLED MUSHROOM
GARUM OIL
Piedmont hazelnuts
Grilled Mushroom Garum*

TO FINISH
Nasturtium flower
Potato Tart Shell
Cracked toasted black peppercorns
Hazelnut–Grilled Mushroom
  Garum Oil
Noma honey
Crown Prince Pumpkin Sheets

Mushroom Sauté

A mix of wild mushrooms that have been preserved in cep oil is sautéed and dressed with a little truffle sauce made by reducing mushroom kelp broth and truffle juice, whisking in brown butter, and finishing with chopped truffles.

Some of these mushrooms are scattered in the base of a heated serving dish and fresh raw greens are added, followed by the rest of the mushrooms. More truffle sauce is added to the dish, and fresh cep slices brushed with cep oil and spritzed with dryad saddle garum are laid inside.

TRUFFLE SAUCE
Reduced Mushroom-Kelp Broth*
Truffle juice
Brown Butter*
Black truffle
White wine vinegar
White Wine Reduction*

GREENS
Oregano leaves
Watercress
Chickweed
Ground elder leaves
Yarrow leaves
Beach mustard
Spanish chervil leaves
Cabbage flowers
Rocket flowers
Fennel flowers
Coriander flowers
Nasturtium flowers
Halved green coriander seeds

TO FINISH
Truffle Sauce
Ceps
Cep Oil*
Dryad Saddle Garum*
Salt
Greens
Preserved Mixed Mushrooms*

Chestnut Dumpling

Chestnuts and water are blended and the liquid is strained. This chestnut milk is reduced for up to two days until thick, then further reduced until it begins to caramelize and thicken, at which point the mixture is beaten in a mortar and pestle to smooth and aerate the chestnut mochi. The chestnut mochi is rolled thin in a pasta machine with cep oil and punched into round wrappers.

Walnuts are blanched, puréed, and strained, and the walnut milk is then cooked down to a paste. The walnut paste is folded with whipped cream and set with gelatin, then aerated and frozen to create a walnut sponge. The sponge is sliced and cut into half-rounds.

Chickens and ducks are simmered to make a stock, which is strained and left to settle. The fat is skimmed off the surface of the stock and reserved. The stock is reduced to a light glaze.

The glaze is then mixed with some of the reserved fat, brought to a boil, and left to cool until a skin forms on top. The skin is delicately transferred from the saucepan to parchment and the parchment is placed in a skillet, where the skin is cooked until it begins to crisp. Pickled beech leaves are laid on the duck skins and dried until the fused leaves and duck skins are completely crisp. The fused beech leaves are then cut out.

Two mochi wrappers are filled with preserved truffle rings, parsley and lemon thyme paste, truffle purée, and a half round of frozen walnut sponge. The wrapper is folded to enclose the fillings, brushed with cep oil, dotted with truffle purée and a piece of peeled walnut, and topped with a crispy pickled beech leaf.

CHESTNUT MOCHI
Chestnuts
Filtered water

CHESTNUT MOCHI WRAPPER
Chestnut Mochi
Cep Oil*

WALNUT PASTE
Walnuts
Filtered water

WALNUT SPONGE
Walnut Paste
Gelatin
Cream

LEMON THYME PASTE
Lemon thyme leaves
Yeast Broth Reduction*
Peaso Water Reduction*
Koji Oil* (made with Awamori Koji*)
Roasted Kelp Salt*

PARSLEY AND LEMON THYME PASTE
Parsley leaves
Lemon Thyme Paste

DUCK SKINS
Whole chickens
Whole ducks
Chicken wings
Duck fat

CRISPY PICKLED BEECH LEAVES
Duck Skins
Pickled beech leaves
Filtered water

TRUFFLE PURÉE
Truffles
Roasted Yeast Oil*
Cep Oil*
Mushroom-Kelp Broth*
Lacto Cep Water*
Celery Juice Reduction*

PEELED WALNUTS
Fresh walnuts

PRESERVED TRUFFLE RINGS
Preserved Truffles*
Cep Oil*

TO FINISH
Chestnut Mochi Wrapper
Preserved Truffle Rings
Parsley and Lemon Thyme Paste
Truffle Purée
Cracked toasted black peppercorns
Walnut Sponge semicircles
Cep Oil*
Crispy Pickled Beech Leaves
Peeled Walnut

Forest Ceviche

Peeled walnuts, rounds of sliced apple, salted noble fir scales, semi-dried mulberries, candied pine cones, blackberries, black currant shoots, coriander seeds, arctic thyme, and lemon thyme are arranged in an alternating pattern in the serving bowl. The dish is finished with mirabelle marinade, spruce wood oil, and spritzes of mirabelle aquavit.

PEELED WALNUTS
Walnuts

MIRABELLE MARINADE
Ice-Clarified Mirabelle Plum Juice*
Unripe sea buckthorn berries
Juniper berries
Angelica seeds or buds
Green coriander seeds
Pine shoots
Douglas fir needles

TO FINISH
Peeled Walnut quarters
Salted Noble Fir Cone* scales
Jarred candied pine cone halves
Semi-Dried Mulberry* halves
Blackberry halves
Red Aroma apple rounds
Pine shoots
Black currant shoot halves
Green coriander seeds
Arctic thyme leaves
Lemon thyme leaves
Mirabelle Marinade
Spruce Wood Oil*
Mirabelle plum aquavit

New Season Apple

A juice is made from elderflower kombucha, jasmine tea, green gooseberry water, elderflower syrup, lemon juice, lemon thyme, and sea buckthorn. The juice is carbonated and mixed with a bit of black currant wood oil to create a sauce.

    A whole fresh apple, with stem and leaves attached, is hollowed out from the bottom, filled with fresh apple brunoise, salted Japanese quince, coriander seeds, black currant shoots, lemon thyme, ants, and anise hyssop flowers, and dressed inside with the apple sauce. The filled apple is served right-side up so the filling is hidden until the diner lifts the apple.

APPLE VESSEL
Apples, with stems and leaves
   attached

APPLE SAUCE BASE
Elderflower Kombucha*
Cold-Infused Jasmine Tea*
Green Gooseberry Water*
Elderflower Syrup*
Lemon juice
Lovage leaves
Lemon thyme leaves
Unripe sea buckthorn berries
Salt

FINISHED APPLE SAUCE
Apple Sauce Base
Black Currant Wood Oil*

DICED APPLE
Ahrista apples

TO FINISH
Apple Vessel
Diced Apple
Diced Brined Japanese Quince*
Coriander seeds
Black currant shoots
Lemon thyme leaves
Ants
Anise hyssop flowers
Finished Apple Sauce

Wild Boar and Nasturtium

Nasturtium leaves are compressed with parsley oil, then folded over dots of gooseberry-coriander paste and smoked egg yolk paste to form nasturtium ravioli.

Chestnuts are cooked in smoked butter until crisp and caramelized, glazed in roasted kelp salt, peaso reduction, and smoked seaweed shoyu, and then diced.

Fermented wild boar belly is fried to brown its surface and then sliced. Smoked egg yolk paste is piped onto the boar slices, which are then topped with the diced roasted chestnuts and folded to enclose the fillings.

Three fermented wild boar belly wraps are brushed with chestnut smoked butter and briefly grilled over charcoal. The belly wraps and one nasturtium ravioli are skewered with a black currant wood skewer. The belly wraps are brushed with cep tamari and seasoned with ancho chile paste, quince vinegar, salt, and black pepper. The skewer is served on a hay plate with a wedge of Japanese quince.

CURED EGG YOLKS
Eggs
Beef Garum*

SMOKED EGG YOLK PASTE
Cured Egg Yolks
Smoked Mushroom Garum*
Smoked Butter Whey*
Cep Tamari*
Salt

GOOSEBERRY-CORIANDER PASTE
Salted Green Gooseberry Capers*
Frozen green coriander seeds
Spruce Wood Oil*

ROASTED CHESTNUTS
Chestnuts
Smoked Butter*
Salt
Roasted Kelp Salt*
Peaso Water Reduction*
Smoked Seaweed Shoyu*

NASTURTIUM WRAPPERS
Nasturtium leaves
Parsley Oil*

NASTURTIUM RAVIOLI
Nasturtium Wrappers
Gooseberry-Coriander Paste
Smoked Egg Yolk Paste
Parsley Oil*

FERMENTED WILD BOAR BELLY
WRAPS
Fermented Wild Boar Belly*
Smoked Egg Yolk Paste
Diced Roasted Chestnuts

CHESTNUT SMOKED BUTTER
Leftover butter from Roasted
  Chestnuts
Smoked Butter*

ANCHO CHILE PASTE BASE
Grapeseed oil
Seeded morita chile
Seeded ancho chile
Roasted Kelp*

ANCHO CHILE PASTE
Ancho Chile Paste Base
Chicken Wing Garum*
Red Pepper Tamari*

TO FINISH
Ancho Chile Paste
Quince Vinegar*
Cep Tamari* (reduced to 66 °Bx)
Toasted cracked black peppercorns
Frozen Japanese quince
Black currant wood skewer
Chestnut Smoked Butter
Nasturtium Ravioli
Fermented Wild Boar Belly Wrap
  skewer
Hay plate

Quail Egg and Beech Leaf

Chickens and ducks are simmered to make a stock, which is strained and left to settle. The fat is skimmed off the surface of the stock and reserved. The stock is reduced to a light glaze.

The glaze is then mixed with some of the reserved fat, brought to a boil, and left to cool until a skin forms on top. The skin is delicately transferred from the saucepan to parchment and the parchment is placed in a skillet, where the skin is cooked until it begins to crisp. Pickled beech leaves are laid on the duck skins and dried until the fused leaves and duck skins are completely crisp. The fused beech leaves are then cut out.

Quail eggs are soft-boiled, pickled, and smoked. The eggs are then warmed, spritzed with some of their pickling liquid, and seasoned with smoked salt and cep and coriander spice mix. Smoked egg yolk sauce is piped onto the eggs and then topped with some roasted kelp salt, and a crispy pickled beech leaf is laid on top. The egg is arranged in a moss plate and finished with three drops of cep tamari.

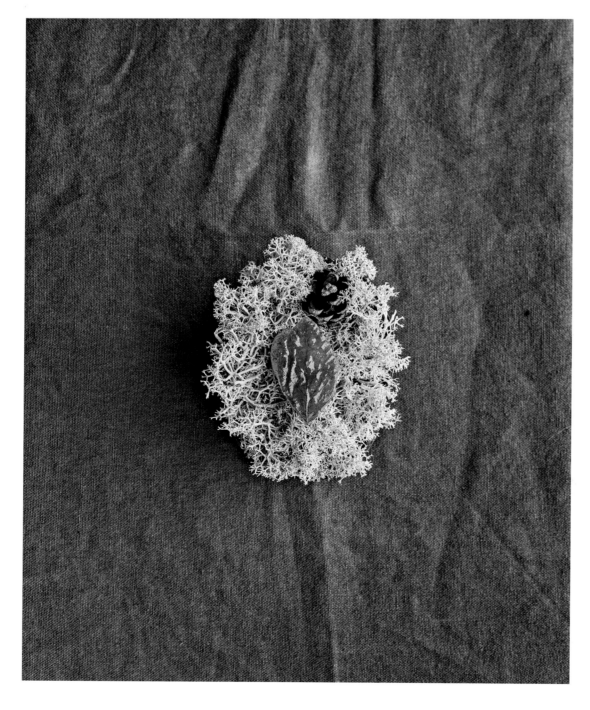

QUAIL EGG PICKLING LIQUID
Apple balsamic vinegar
Cold-Infused Dashi*
Lemon thyme sprigs

SMOKED PICKLED QUAIL EGG
Quail eggs
Quail Egg Pickling Liquid

SMOKED SALT
Salt

CURED EGG YOLKS
Eggs
Beef Garum*

SMOKED EGG YOLK SAUCE
Cured Egg Yolks
Smoked Butter*
Roasted Kelp Salt*
Salt

CEP AND CORIANDER SPICE MIX
Dried ceps
Dried chanterelles
Black peppercorns
Juniper berries
Angelica seeds or buds
Freeze-dried lingonberry
Coriander seeds
Arctic thyme leaves
Roasted Kelp*

DUCK SKINS
Whole chickens
Whole ducks
Chicken wings
Duck fat

CRISPY PICKLED BEECH LEAVES
Duck Skins
Pickled beech leaves
Filtered water

TO FINISH
Smoked Pickled Quail Egg
Crispy Pickled Beech Leaf
Quail Egg Pickling Liquid
Smoked Egg Yolk Sauce
Roasted Kelp Salt*
Cep and Coriander Spice Mix
Cep Tamari*
Smoked Salt

Hen of the Woods and Madagascar Pepper

Madagascar peppercorns are marinated in maitake oil, slowly smoked over birchwood, and then finely chopped.

Fresh wild mushroom slices are basted with mushroom cooking glaze as they're being grilled over charcoal. The grilled mushroom slices are brushed with dashi reduction, seasoned with rose oil, pine vinegar, salt, and cold-infused kelp salt and finished with finely chopped smoked Madagascar peppercorns.

SMOKED MADAGASCAR PEPPER
Maitake Oil*
Madagascar peppercorns
   (voatsiperifery)

SLICED MUSHROOMS
Cep, coral, hen of the woods, or
   hedgehog mushroom

MUSHROOM COOKING GLAZE
Butter
Lemon thyme
Truffle juice

TO FINISH
Sliced Mushrooms
Mushroom Cooking Glaze
Cold-Infused Kelp Salt*
Smoked Madagascar Pepper
Rose Oil*
Pine Vinegar*
Dashi Reduction*

Reindeer Penis Salad

Reindeer penis is brined in mushroom brine, cooked under pressure with more brine, dashi, and mushroom-kelp broth, and finally soaked in more dashi and brine.

Butter-roasted pheasants are cooked in oil with herbs, spices, chile, and birchwood to create pheasant and birchwood oil.

Thinly sliced reindeer penis is folded with cooked barley, spelt, and emmer, along with cooked mustard seeds, savory granola, and forest pesto. The mixture is mounded on a fig leaf–lined plate and surrounded by dots of smoked egg yolk paste, lingonberry paste, rice koji fudge, and Pablo chile paste. A loose showering of oregano leaves, a squeeze of Douglas fir vinaigrette, and a pinch of reindeer penis spice mix finish the dish.

MUSHROOM BRINE
Filtered water
Salt
Muscovado sugar
Bay leaves
Toasted juniper berries
Toasted coriander seeds
Toasted black peppercorns
Lemon thyme sprigs
Dried ceps
Dried Ginger Skins*
Arctic thyme leaves

BRINED REINDEER PENIS
Reindeer penis
Ice water
Mushroom Brine

PRESSURE-COOKED REINDEER
PENIS
Brined Reindeer Penis
Cold-Infused Dashi*
Mushroom-Kelp Broth*
Mushroom Brine
Cold-Infused Dashi*

COOKED MUSTARD SEEDS
Yellow mustard seeds
Bay leaves
Filtered water

COOKED GRAINS
Barley
Spelt
Emmer

REINDEER PENIS AND GRAIN MIX
Pressure-Cooked Reindeer Penis
Cooked Grains
Cooked Mustard Seeds

CURED EGG YOLKS
Eggs
Beef Garum*

SMOKED EGG YOLK PASTE
Cured Egg Yolks
Smoked Butter Whey*
Cep Tamari*
Beef Garum*
Salt

FOREST PESTO
Unripe sea buckthorn berries
Green coriander seeds
Lacto Cep Water*
Smoked Mushroom Garum*
Peaso Water Reduction*
Yeast Broth Reduction*
Cep Oil*
Lemon Thyme Vinegar*

DOUGLAS FIR VINAIGRETTE
Douglas Fir Oil*
Black Currant Leaf Oil*
Oregano Vinegar*

REINDEER PENIS SPICE MIX
Toasted juniper berries
Toasted black peppercorns
Toasted coriander seeds
Toasted cardamom pods
Dried Ginger*
Fennel seeds
Dried ceps
Roasted Yeast*
Salt

PHEASANT AND BIRCHWOOD OIL
Pheasants
Bay leaves
Juniper berries
Black peppercorns
Seeded pasilla chiles
Grapeseed oil
Birchwood

SAVORY GRANOLA
Pheasant and Birchwood Oil
Toasted coriander seeds
Toasted sunflower seeds
Toasted pumpkin seeds
Toasted black peppercorns

Lemon thyme sprig
Shallot
Seeded ancho chile

MUSTARD SPICE MIX
Toasted fennel seeds
Toasted yellow mustard seeds
Toasted coriander seeds
Toasted black peppercorns
Seeded pasilla chile
Freeze-dried gooseberries
Juniper berries

SUNFLOWER SEED PASTE
Sunflower seeds
Brown Butter*
Ginger Powder*
Mustard Spice Mix
Celery Juice Reduction*
Peaso Water Reduction*
Roasted Kelp Salt*
Nordic Shoyu*

MUSHROOM SPICE MIX
Toasted fennel seeds
Toasted yellow mustard seeds
Toasted coriander seeds
Dried ceps
Arctic thyme leaves
Dried morels

FRIED PARSLEY
Parsley leaves
Grapeseed oil

FRIED LOVAGE
Lovage leaves
Grapeseed oil

LINGONBERRY PASTE
Freeze-dried rhubarb
Freeze-dried lingonberries
Freeze-dried gooseberries
Cold-Infused Dashi*
Mushroom Spice Mix
Koji Oil*
Fried Parsley

Fried Lovage
Sunflower Seed Paste

PABLO CHILE PASTE
Finely chopped shallot
Grapeseed oil
Seeded ancho chile
Salt
Red Pepper Tamari*
Peaso Water Reduction*
Roasted Kelp Oil*

RICE KOJI FUDGE
Cucumber Juice Reduction*
Peaso Water Reduction*
Butter
Koji Oil* (made with Rice Koji*)

TO FINISH
Reindeer Penis and Grain Mix
Chopped Savory Granola
Forest Pesto
Salt
Smoked Egg Yolk Paste
Lingonberry Paste
Rice Koji Fudge
Pablo Chile Paste
Oregano leaves
Douglas Fir Vinaigrette
Reindeer Penis Spice Mix

Whole Mallard

Wild mallards are plucked, leaving the feathers on the head and wings, then aged for five days. The ducks are lightly cured with koji cure, then grilled over charcoal, with birch bark creating smoke.

As the duck is grilling, it's brushed with a glaze made by reducing duck stock, ryeso water, and mushroom-kelp broth. The remaining glaze is further reduced to make a finishing glaze.

The breasts are carved from the duck and sliced, and duck marinade is brushed in between the slices, which are reassembled, repositioned on the duck, and brushed with finishing glaze.

KOJI CURE
Koji* (any type)
Filtered water
Salt

LIGHT CHICKEN STOCK
Whole chickens

DUCK GLAZE
Light Chicken Stock
Duck carcasses

COOKING GLAZE
Ryeso Water*
Mushroom-Kelp Broth*
Duck Glaze

FINISHING GLAZE
Cooking Glaze

DUCK MARINADE
Lemon thyme leaves
Cep Oil*
Spruce Wood Oil*
Juniper skins
Arctic thyme leaves
Brine from Salted Unripe Plums*

BBQ DUCK
Wild mallards
Koji Cure
Birch bark
Cooking Glaze

TO FINISH
BBQ Duck
Duck Marinade
Finishing Glaze

Whole Teal

Wild teal are plucked, leaving the feathers on the head and wings, then aged for a few days. The teal are lightly cured with koji cure, then grilled over charcoal, with birch bark creating smoke.

As the teal is grilling, it's brushed with a glaze made by reducing duck stock, ryeso water, and mushroom-kelp broth. The remaining glaze is further reduced to make a finishing glaze.

The breasts are carved from the teal and sliced, then reassembled, repositioned on the teal, and brushed with finishing glaze.

KOJI CURE
Koji* (any type)
Filtered water
Salt

LIGHT CHICKEN STOCK
Whole chickens

DUCK GLAZE
Light Chicken Stock
Duck carcasses

COOKING GLAZE
Ryeso Water*
Mushroom-Kelp Broth*
Duck Glaze

FINISHING GLAZE
Cooking Glaze

BBQ TEAL
Wild teal
Koji Cure
Birch bark
Cooking Glaze

TO FINISH
BBQ Teal
Finishing Glaze

Duck Caramel

Wild duck meat and bones are simmered in dashi with dried ceps, lemon thyme, juniper wood, and an apple. The broth is strained, reduced, and then further reduced with some cep oil to a thick and fudgy consistency.

   The reduction is piped decoratively onto a Mexican oregano leaf and seasoned with crushed toasted black pepper and salt.

WILD DUCK REDUCTION
Wild duck scraps and bones
Cold-Infused Dashi*
Dried ceps
Lemon thyme sprigs
Juniper wood
Chopped apple
Cep Oil*

TO FINISH
Mexican oregano leaf
Crushed toasted black peppercorns
Tempered Wild Duck Reduction
Salt

Pumpkin Salad

Hokkaido pumpkin is peeled, cooked with marigold oil, cold-smoked, dried with marigold glaze until chewy, and then scooped into leaflike shapes.

Peeled and seeded rose hip quarters are stuffed with strawberry and pasilla paste, then topped with coriander seeds, noble fir cone scales, and peeled pumpkin seeds.

A broth is made from deer dashi, beef garum, plum reduction, and some strawberry-infused koji water.

The rose hip quarters are arranged in a serving bowl, alternating with leaves of dried Hokkaido pumpkin and brined Japanese quince rings. The dish is dressed with coriander flowers and finished with the broth and marigold oil.

QUINCE REDUCTION
Quince

MARIGOLD GLAZE
Burning Embers Marigold Oil*
Quince Reduction

DRIED HOKKAIDO PUMPKIN
Hokkaido pumpkin
Burning Embers Marigold Oil*
Marigold Glaze

STRAWBERRY AND PASILLA PASTE
Koji Oil*
Green cardamom pods
Dried Ginger*
Dried Strawberries*
Rose hips
Seeded pasilla chiles
Coriander seeds
Cold-Infused Dashi*
Chicken Wing Garum*
Lacto Koji Water* (made with
  Rice Koji*)

STUFFED ROSE HIP
Peeled and seeded rose hip
Green coriander seeds
Halved noble fir cone scales*
Hulled raw pumpkin seeds marinated
  in Rose Oil*
Strawberry and Pasilla Paste

JAPANESE QUINCE
Brined Japanese Quince* (made
  using an 8% salt brine)

LARDO SPICE MIX
Star anise
Juniper berries
Toasted black peppercorns
Toasted coriander seeds
Dried Ginger*

SMOKED DEER MEAT
Deer leg meat
Salt
Lardo Spice Mix

DEER DASHI
Cold-Infused Dashi*
Smoked Deer Meat
Lemon thyme sprigs
Juniper wood
Douglas fir needles
White wine vinegar

DEER AND PLUM BROTH
Plum Reduction*
Beef Garum*
Deer Dashi
Strawberry-infused Lacto Koji Water*
  (reserved from making Strawberry
  and Pasilla Paste)
Filtered water

TO FINISH
Coriander flowers
Japanese Quince
Dried Hokkaido Pumpkin
Stuffed Rose Hip quarters
Deer and Plum Broth
Burning Embers Marigold Oil*

Apple and Beetle

A beetle is created by shaping black fruit leather made from dark berries and berry juice, black garlic, sugar, and charcoal for color. The beetle body is a tiny fruit-leather envelope filled with a semi-dried mulberry, black currant bud, coriander seed, and angelica seed. The beetle's other parts are made from fruit leather shaped using a template, with oxalis leaves layered under the wings. The parts are affixed to the body with red currant and rose hip paste.

Balls of fresh apple are macerated in apple ceviche liquid. The top of an apple, complete with stem and leaves, is sliced off and reserved. The apple is hollowed out to form a vessel and half the macerated apple balls are placed inside. The apple balls are dotted with red currant and rose hip paste, then garnished with lemon thyme leaves and sprinkled with green coriander seeds, green angelica seeds, and black currant shoots. The remaining apple balls are placed on top and dressed with a sauce made from the apple macerating liquid blended with rose oil. More coriander seeds, angelica seeds, and black currant shoots are arranged on top and seasoned with elderflower oil. The beetle is perched on the edge of the apple vessel, the top of the apple is placed on top, and the vessel is served in a hay bowl.

APPLE CEVICHE LIQUID
Ice-Clarified Mirabelle Plum Juice*
Ice-Clarified Tomato Water*
Lacto Koji Water* (made with Øland
  Wheat Koji*)
Unripe sea buckthorn berries
Dried Ginger*
Dried juniper berries
Green coriander seeds
Pine shoots
Douglas fir needles

APPLE SAUCE
Apple Ceviche Liquid
Rose Oil*

RED CURRANT AND ROSE HIP
PASTE
Dried meadowsweet
Dried angelica
Geranium Oil*
Red currants
Seeded rose hips

BLACKBERRY AND BLACK GARLIC
LEATHER
Japanese black garlic
Blackberries
Black currants
Aronia berry juice
Muscovado sugar
Freeze-dried black currants
Activated black charcoal powder

BEETLE BODY
Semi-Dried Mulberries*
Black currant bud
Green coriander seed
Young green angelica seed

BEETLE TOP
Red Currant and Rose Hip Paste
Green oxalis leaves
Fruit leather beetle segments

APPLE BALLS
Apples
Apple Ceviche Liquid

APPLE VESSEL
Apples, with stems and leaves
  attached

TO FINISH
Halved green coriander seeds
Young green angelica seeds
Halved black currant shoots
Lemon thyme leaves
Elderflower Oil*
Apple Balls
Apple Vessel
Beetle Top and Beetle Body
Apple Sauce

Duck Leg Skewer

A duck leg bone is cleaned and sculpted into a skewer. Duck skin is simmered in seasoned liquid, dried, cut into squares, and fried until crisp.

Chicken stock and duck stock are reduced to a glaze and blended with BBQ duck garum and blueberry reduction. Duck meat is slid onto the bone skewer and grilled over hot charcoal while being basted with the duck glaze.

The grilled duck leg skewer is bathed in warm roasted kelp butter and seasoned with berry spice. Squares of crispy duck skin and tiny pine shoots are tucked between the pieces of grilled duck on the skewer.

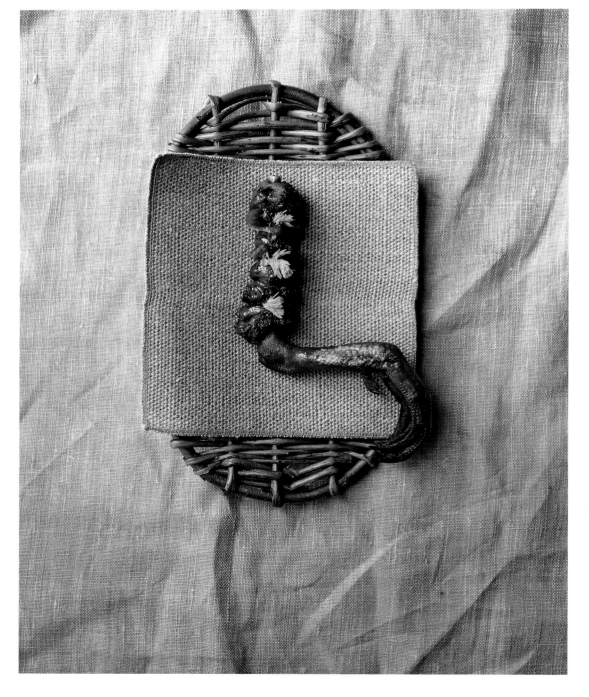

DUCK LEGS
Duck legs

CRISPY DUCK SKIN
Filtered water
White wine vinegar
Salt
Coriander seeds
Juniper berries
Arctic thyme leaves
Duck leg skin

DUCK LEG SKEWER
Duck leg meat
Sharpened duck leg bone

BLUEBERRY REDUCTION
Blueberries

LIGHT CHICKEN STOCK
Whole chickens

DUCK GLAZE BASE
Light Chicken Stock
Duck carcasses

DUCK GLAZE
Duck Glaze Base
BBQ Duck Garum*
Blueberry Reduction

ROASTED KELP BUTTER
Roasted Kelp Salt*
Butter

BERRY SPICE
Dried Horseradish*
Dried Ginger*
Arctic thyme leaves
Toasted coriander seeds
Toasted angelica seeds
Toasted fennel seeds
Dried Strawberries*

ANT PASTE
Ants
Berry Spice
Black Currant Wood Oil*

TO FINISH
Duck Leg Skewer
Duck Glaze
Roasted Kelp Butter
Crispy Duck Skin
Pine shoots
Berry Spice
Salt

Truffle Feather

Truffles are blended with mushroom-kelp broth, lacto-fermented cep water, and celery reduction and then emulsified with yeast oil and cep oil to create a thick, creamy truffle purée.

A flatbread dough is made from several flours, butter, beer, and dried rose oil. The dough is rolled thin and cut out with a feather-shaped stencil. A thin piece of dough is applied to make the quill, and the feather flatbread is baked.

Cooked barley is puréed, rolled to a thin sheet, inoculated with koji spores, and fermented for two days. The koji sheet is cut to a shape just smaller than the feather flatbread.

The quill of the feather flatbread is brushed with cep oil and black trumpet mushroom powder is dusted over it. The vanes of the feather are created by affixing thin strips of preserved truffle to the flatbread with some truffle purée.

Soft cheese is melted onto the back of the mold shape and truffle purée is piped around the edge. The feather flatbread is placed on the mold shape, sandwiching the purée. Warmed truffle sauce is drizzled over the truffle vanes and the dish is served on a hay plate.

TRUFFLE PURÉE
Truffles
Roasted Yeast Oil*
Cep Oil*
Mushroom-Kelp Broth*
Lacto Cep Water*
Celery Juice Reduction*

TRUFFLE SAUCE
Reduced Mushroom-Kelp Broth*
Truffle juice
Brown Butter*
Black truffle
White wine vinegar
White Wine Reduction*

PRESERVED TRUFFLE FEATHERS
Preserved Truffles*

FEATHER FLATBREAD
Tipo "00" flour
Koji Flour*
Malt flour
Dried Rose Oil*
Butter
Salt
Kaelder Øl lager
Rolling flour

BLACK TRUMPET MUSHROOM
POWDER
Dried black trumpet mushrooms

MOLD CREPE
Pearl barley
Koji tane (*Aspergillus oryzae* spores)

TROLDHEDE ASK CHEESE
Troldhede Ask cheese

TO FINISH
Feather Flatbread
Cep Oil*
Black Trumpet Mushroom Powder
Truffle Purée
Preserved Truffle Feathers
Mold Crepe
Troldhede Ask Cheese
Truffle Sauce

Pheasant Salad

Lightly cooked egg yolks are cured in beef garum, oyster garum, and lacto-fermented cep water, then whisked until smooth with sunflower seed and beef garum oil and yeast broth reduction; chicken wing garum toasted sunflower seeds are chopped and folded into the paste.

A ring of the cured egg yolk paste is piped into a serving bowl. More garum toasted sunflower seeds are arranged in concentric circles over the paste. Marigold petals are arranged around the outside of the "flower," and some rose petals and salted fresh hazelnuts in hazelnut oil are tucked around the perimeter.

Mixed greens are dressed in Jun-spiced butter and gently grilled, then seasoned with horseradish juice and chicken wing garum. Fresh greens are dressed with juniper rose vinaigrette. The grilled greens and fresh greens are arranged around the sunflower and the dish is finished with ancho chile oil. A jug of warmed pheasant koji yeast sauce is served at the table.

CHICKEN WING GARUM TOASTED
SUNFLOWER SEEDS
Sunflower seeds
Chicken Wing Garum*

CURED EGG YOLKS
Eggs
Beef Garum*
Oyster Garum*
Lacto Cep Water*

CURED EGG YOLK PASTE
Cured Egg Yolks
Sunflower Seed and Beef Garum Oil*
Yeast Broth Reduction*
Finely chopped Chicken Wing
　Garum Toasted Sunflower Seeds

PHEASANT OIL
Pheasants
Spruce branches
Bay leaves
Juniper berries
Seeded pasilla chile
Coriander seeds
Halved garlic head
Juniper wood
Lemon thyme
Star anise
Grapeseed oil

PHEASANT KOJI YEAST SAUCE
Lacto Koji Water* (made with Øland
　Wheat Koji*)
Yeast Broth*
Butter
Pheasant Oil
Xantana

JUN SPICE MIX
Dried ceps
Dried chanterelles
Black peppercorns
Juniper berries
Angelica seeds
Freeze-dried lingonberry
Coriander seeds
Arctic thyme leaves
Roasted Kelp*

JUN-SPICED BUTTER
Butter
Jun Spice Mix
Kelp
Halved seeded ancho chile

SALTED FRESH HAZELNUTS
Fresh hazelnuts
8% salt brine

SOAKED JUNIPER BERRY SKINS
Juniper berries
Lacto Koji Water* (made with Øland
　Wheat Koji*)

JUNIPER ROSE VINAIGRETTE
Dryad Saddle Garum*
Green coriander seeds
Finely chopped Soaked Juniper
　Berry Skins
Rose Oil*
Lemon juice

FRESH GREENS
Yarrow leaves
Chickweed
Oxalis stem and leaves
Coriander flowers
Oregano leaves
Watercress
Sage leaves
Ground elder
Beach mustard leaves and flower
Spanish chervil leaves

GRILLED GREENS
Jerusalem artichoke leaves
Gold cress
Beach cress
Moneywort
Winter cress
Baby radishes
Spanish chervil
Goose tongue (*Plantago maritima*)
Goosefoot
Wild rocket
Dandelion
Hemp
Beach horseradish
Sage leaves

TO FINISH
Cured Egg Yolk Paste
Chicken Wing Garum Toasted
　Sunflower Seeds
Marigold petals
Salted Fresh Hazelnuts
Hazelnut Oil*
Pickled Rose Petal* halves
Grilled Greens
Jun-Spiced Butter
Horseradish juice
Chicken Wing Garum*
Fresh Greens
Juniper Rose Vinaigrette
Ancho Chile Oil*
Pheasant Koji Yeast Sauce

Tomatoes and Rabbit

Rabbit pieces are roasted and then simmered in dashi with dried ceps, lemon thyme, juniper wood, and an apple. The broth is strained, reduced, and then further reduced with some cep oil to a thick and fudgy consistency.

Semi-dried tomatoes are filled with bee pollen paste and dressed with the rabbit reduction and half a black currant bud. Semi-dried strawberries are filled with coriander seeds, semi-dried lacto-fermented plums, and half a salted sloeberry, sealed with Japanese quince paste, and dusted with noble fir salt spice mix.

A serving bowl is dressed with some rabbit oil mixed with bee pollen paste, and seasoned with salt and chopped chives. The filled tomatoes and strawberries are arranged casually in the bowl and finished with a sprinkling of salt.

SEMI-DRIED STRAWBERRIES
Strawberries
Koji Oil*

SEMI-DRIED LACTO PLUMS
Lacto Plums*
Elderflower Oil*
Salt

RABBIT OIL
Rabbit
Juniper berries
Ancho chile
Icelandic söl
Freeze-dried gooseberries
Freeze-dried lingonberries
Coriander seeds
Dried Carrot Flowers*
Star anise
Garlic
Douglas fir twigs
Lemon thyme sprigs
Grapeseed oil

BEE POLLEN PASTE
Bee pollen
Morita Chile Oil*
Filtered water

JAPANESE QUINCE PASTE
Japanese quince
Butter
Dried Carrot Flowers*

RABBIT REDUCTION
Rabbit pieces
Cold-Infused Dashi*
Dried ceps
Lemon thyme sprigs
Juniper wood
Chopped apple
Cep Oil*

NOBLE FIR SALT SPICE MIX
Noble Fir Salt*
Dried Lacto Plum Skins*
Freeze-dried lingonberries
Freeze-dried rhubarb

TO FINISH
Semi-Dried Tomatoes*
Bee Pollen Paste
Rabbit Reduction
Black currant bud halves
Semi-Dried Strawberries
Coriander seeds
Japanese Quince Paste
Finely diced Semi-Dried Lacto Plums
Salted Sloeberry* halves
Noble Fir Salt Spice Mix
Chives
Salt

Reindeer Sweetbreads and Moss

Both raw and lightly cooked egg yolks are cured in beef garum, then whipped with smoked butter whey until smooth to make a sauce.

Reindeer sweetbreads are cooked in brown butter and dredged in rice flour and egg whites. The dredged sweetbreads are then coated in pieces of cleaned reindeer moss, deep-fried, and seasoned with Nordic punch, salt, and black pepper.

The egg yolk sauce, topped with ants, is served in a separate dish that's been brushed with kelp paste.

SWEETBREADS
Reindeer sweetbreads
Brown Butter*

REINDEER MOSS
Fresh reindeer moss

MOSS-BREADED SWEETBREADS
Sweetbreads
Egg whites
Rice flour
Reindeer Moss

NORDIC PUNCH
Roasted Yeast*
Ginger Powder*
Koji Flour*
Toasted green cardamom pods
Toasted juniper berries
Toasted coriander seeds

KELP PASTE
Roasted Kelp Salt*
Filtered water

EGG YOLK SAUCE
Eggs
Beef Garum*
Smoked Butter Whey*

TO FINISH
Moss-Breaded Sweetbreads
Grapeseed oil
Nordic Punch
Black peppercorns
Kelp Paste
Egg Yolk Sauce
Ants

Mallard Wing

The wings of a whole mallard are removed from the duck, with a portion of the thickest part of each breast still attached to the wing. The wings are plucked to just past the first joint, then wrapped in twine, leaving the breast meat exposed.

The breast meat is coated in sourdough tempura batter, deep-fried, and then seasoned with roasted kelp butter, arctic kelp salt, horseradish juice, and pine vinegar.

TEMPURA BATTER DRY MIX
Rice flour
Cornstarch
Potato starch
Baking soda
Baking powder

TEMPURA BATTER WET MIX
White wine vinegar
Grapeseed oil
Ethanol (96% ABV)

SOURDOUGH TEMPURA BATTER
Sourdough starter
Carbonated water
Tempura Batter Dry Mix
Tempura Batter Wet Mix
Arctic thyme leaves
Salt

ARCTIC KELP SALT
Arctic thyme leaves
Roasted Kelp Salt*
Freeze-dried rhubarb

ROASTED KELP BUTTER
Roasted Kelp Salt*
Butter

DUCK WINGS
Mallard ducks

TO FINISH
Duck Wings
Horseradish juice
Pine Vinegar*
Arctic Kelp Salt
Roasted Kelp Butter
Rice flour
Sourdough Tempura Batter
Grapeseed oil

Reindeer Heart Tartare

Raw reindeer heart is sliced into fine strips and arranged in a rectangular layer.

Both raw and lightly cooked egg yolks are cured in beef garum, then whipped with smoked butter whey until smooth to make a sauce.

The reindeer heart is transferred to a serving plate, seasoned with horseradish juice, beef garum, and koji oil, and sprinkled with tartare spice mix and rye bread crumbs toasted in butter. Strips of fresh horseradish are laid over the reindeer heart and the wood sorrel leaves are arranged to completely cover the tartare.

The egg yolk sauce, topped with ants, is served in a separate dish that's been brushed with kelp paste. The diner takes a pinch of wood sorrel and tartare and drags it through the egg yolk sauce and kelp paste.

REINDEER HEART
Reindeer heart

RYE CRUMBLE
Rye bread
Butter

TARTARE SPICE MIX
Caraway
Coriander seeds
Juniper berries

WOOD SORREL
Wood sorrel leaves

KELP PASTE
Roasted Kelp Salt*
Filtered water

EGG YOLK SAUCE
Eggs
Beef Garum*
Smoked Butter Whey*

TO FINISH
Reindeer Heart
Fresh horseradish
Beef Garum*
Koji Oil*
Horseradish juice
Wood Sorrel
Rye Crumble
Tartare Spice Mix
Kelp Paste
Egg Yolk Sauce
Ants

Duck Leg Stewed with Roses

Diced duck meat is sautéed in duck fat and flambéed with Danish whisky. The meat is folded with a mix of raw duck heart brunoise, cold-smoked maitake crumbles, fried sourdough bread crumbs, diced pickled chanterelles, and tiny cubes of dried lacto-fermented plum.

    The stew is spooned into a bowl and topped with pickled chanterelles, fresh lingonberries, and a scoop of fresh cheese. The dish is finished with a few drops of cep oil and lightly grilled beach rose petals.

LACTO PLUM GLAZE
Mushroom-Kelp Broth*
Beef Garum*

DRIED LACTO PLUMS
Lacto Plums*
Lacto Plum Glaze

LACTO PLUM AND TOMATO REDUCTION
Lacto Plum Juice*
Ice-Clarified Tomato Water*
Kelp
Dried Ginger*

FRESH CHEESE
Milk
Cream
Buttermilk
Rennet

DUCK LEG STEW BASE
Roasted Kelp Salt*
Green coriander seeds
Celery Juice Reduction*
Fennel Juice Reduction*
Blanched juniper skins
Lacto Plum and Tomato Reduction
Butter

COLD-SMOKED MAITAKE
Maitake mushrooms
Brown Butter*

FRIED SOURDOUGH
Sourdough bread (crusts removed)
Grapeseed oil

DUCK LEGS
Wild mallard thighs

DUCK HEARTS
Duck hearts

DUCK LEG STEW
Duck Hearts
Duck Legs
Dried Lacto Plums
Cold-Smoked Maitake
Duck Leg Stew Base
Duck fat
Fried Sourdough
Arctic thyme leaves
Pickled Chanterelles*
Danish whisky

TO FINISH
Duck Leg Stew
Pickled Chanterelles*
Fresh lingonberries
Fresh Cheese
Cep Oil*
Beach rose petals

Reindeer Feast

Sweetbreads are cooked with smoked koji oil, toasted hay, Douglas fir, and lemon thyme, then cold-smoked over Douglas fir. Reindeer marrow bones are marinated. A cluster of white currants is glazed with honey and seasoned with chicken wing garum, spruce wood oil, and a salted green gooseberry seed. A pickled pine cone is brushed with ant paste and skewered with a pine shoot.

Reindeer tongue is sautéed in smoked butter and lemon thyme, and seasoned with coriander and gooseberry paste and black pepper. The marinated bone marrow is seared in butter and skewered with a pine shoot.

When it's time to serve the dish, the sweetbreads are dredged in tempura batter and fried, brushed with sweetbread glaze, seasoned with sumac spice mix, and speared onto a pine shoot.

The reindeer tongue is drizzled with reindeer tongue spiced butter and speared with a pine shoot.

A fresh cep is seared and glazed with mushroom glaze, dressed with Douglas fir oil, and skewered on a pine shoot.

A serving bowl is lined with reindeer moss. The sweetbread, reindeer tongue, reindeer bone marrow, ceps, white currant cluster, and pickled pine cone are arranged on top. The mushroom broth is poured into the bowl and the dish is spritzed with Douglas fir distillate.

TEMPURA BATTER
Tipo "00" flour
Cornstarch
Potato starch
Baking powder
Arctic thyme leaves
Salt
Ethanol (96% ABV)
White wine vinegar
Sparkling water

SWEETBREAD GLAZE
Reindeer tongue
Cold-Infused Dashi*
Cep and Birch Bark Vinegar*
Yeast Broth Reduction*
Grapeseed oil

SWEETBREADS
Sweetbreads
White wine vinegar
Sparkling water
Douglas fir branches
Toasted Hay*
Lemon thyme sprigs
Smoked Koji Oil*

SUMAC SPICE MIX
Sumac powder
Toasted black peppercorns
Toasted juniper berries
Toasted coriander seeds
Green cardamom pods
Fennel seeds
Dried Ginger*
Salt

REINDEER TONGUE
Reindeer tongue

CORIANDER AND GOOSEBERRY PASTE
Green coriander seeds
Chopped Salted Green Gooseberry Capers*
Spruce Wood Oil*

REINDEER TONGUE SPICE
Toasted juniper berries
Toasted black peppercorns
Toasted coriander seeds
Toasted green cardamom pods
Dried Ginger*
Fennel seeds
Dried ceps
Roasted Yeast*
Salt

REINDEER TONGUE SPICE BUTTER
Butter
Beef Garum*
Cep and Birch Bark Vinegar*
Chicken Wing Garum*
Reindeer Tongue Spice
Chopped Salted Ramson Capers*

BONE MARROW MARINADE
Elderberry Balsamic Vinegar*
Beef Garum*
Lacto Cherry Juice*

BONE MARROW VINAIGRETTE
Toasted juniper berries
Elderberry Balsamic Vinegar*
Chicken Wing Garum*
Cep Oil*
Ground freeze-dried rhubarb

REINDEER BONE MARROW
1% salt brine
Reindeer marrow bones
Bone Marrow Marinade

MUSHROOM GLAZE
Lacto Cep Water*
Yeast Broth Reduction*
Beef Garum*

ANT PASTE
Black currant shoots
Douglas fir needles
Ants
Roasted Kelp Salt*
Black Currant Wood Oil*

PICKLED PINE CONE
1% salt brine
Cep and Birch Bark Vinegar*
Jarred candied pine cones
Ant Paste

NORDIC SEAWEED SPICE
Toasted coriander seeds
Yellow mustard seeds
Arctic thyme leaves
Dried ceps
Roasted Yeast*
Fennel seeds
Salt
Koji Flour*
Roasted Kelp Powder*

MUSHROOM TEA BASE
Filtered water
Chicken Wing Garum*
Beef Garum*
Mushroom-Kelp Broth*
Seeded pasilla chile
Dried ceps
Dried chanterelles
Dried black trumpet mushrooms
Dried morels
Dried slippery jack mushrooms
Freeze-dried lingonberries
Kelp
Nordic Seaweed Spice

MUSHROOM BROTH
Sliced ceps
Sliced maitake mushrooms
Reindeer moss
Toasted juniper wood
Pounded Douglas fir needles
Cut marrow bone
Fresh Koji*
Brined Onion Cress*
Dried woodruff
Salted Air Onion Capers*
Mushroom Tea Base
Maitake Garum*
Salt
Filtered water
Lingonberries
Blackberries

TO FINISH THE MUSHROOM BROTH
Maitake Garum*
Salt
Lingonberries
Pounded Douglas fir needles

DOUGLAS FIR DISTILLATE
Douglas fir needles
Ethanol (60% ABV)

TO FINISH THE SWEETBREADS
Sweetbreads
Tipo "00" flour
Grapeseed oil
Tempura Batter
Sweetbread Glaze
Sumac Spice Mix
Pine skewer

TO FINISH THE TONGUE
Reindeer Tongue
Lemon thyme sprigs
Smoked Butter*
Coriander and Gooseberry Paste
Cracked black peppercorns
Reindeer Tongue Spice Butter
Pine skewer

TO FINISH THE REINDEER BONE MARROW
Reindeer Bone Marrow
Butter
Pine skewer
Bone Marrow Vinaigrette

TO FINISH THE CEPS
Ceps
Mushroom Glaze
Douglas Fir Oil*
Pine shoot
Salt
Pine skewer

TO FINISH THE WHITE CURRANT CLUSTER
White currants
Noma honey
Salted Green Gooseberry Caper* seed
Spruce Wood Oil*
Chicken Wing Garum*
Salt

TO FINISH THE PINE CONE
Pickled Pine Cone
Ant Paste

TO FINISH THE DISH
Sweetbread
Reindeer Tongue
Reindeer Bone Marrow
Ceps
White Currant Cluster
Pine Cone
Mushroom Broth
Reindeer moss bowl
Douglas Fir Distillate

Quail Egg and Kelp

Quail eggs are soft-boiled, lightly pickled, and then smoked over toasted hay.

Quail is roasted and then simmered in dashi with apples that have been grilled with koji oil, herbs, and pepper. The broth is strained, reduced, and then further reduced with some koji oil to a thick and fudgy consistency.

Kelp "hats" are made from kelp left over from making dashi. The kelp is layered with sediment left from making kelp oil and then baked, separated into leaves, dried, rehydrated in truffle juice, trimmed into squares, and split to make a hatlike pocket.

The soft-boiled quail eggs are warmed in melted smoked butter, seasoned with salt and Jun spice mix, and dotted on the narrow end with smoked egg yolk paste, ant and black currant caper paste, and a piece of roasted kelp salt.

A kelp hat is filled with quail caramel and the dressed quail egg is tucked inside. The kelp hat is seasoned with kelp oil and served on a layer of kelp.

PICKLING LIQUID
Apple balsamic vinegar
Cold-Infused Dashi*
Lemon thyme sprigs

SMOKED PICKLED SOFT-BOILED
QUAIL EGG
Quail eggs

CURED EGG YOLKS
Eggs
Beef Garum*

SMOKED EGG YOLK PASTE
Cured Egg Yolks
Smoked Butter Whey*
Cep Tamari*
Beef Garum*
Salt

JUN SPICE MIX
Dried ceps
Dried chanterelles
Black peppercorns
Juniper berries
Angelica
Freeze-dried lingonberry
Coriander seeds
Arctic thyme
Roasted Kelp*

ANT AND BLACK CURRANT CAPER
PASTE
Ants
Salted Black Currant Capers*
Salted Black Currant Caper* liquid
Lemon Thyme Oil*
Yeast Broth Reduction*
Arctic thyme

QUAIL CARAMEL
Whole quail
Cold-Infused Dashi*
Grilled Lemon Thyme*
Toasted black peppercorns
Bay leaves
Apples
Koji Oil*

KELP HAT
Kelp reserved from making Cold-
   Infused Dashi*
Roasted Kelp Oil* and sediment
Truffle juice

TO FINISH
Smoked Pickled Soft-Boiled
   Quail Egg
Smoked Butter*
Smoked Egg Yolk Paste
Roasted Kelp Salt*
Jun Spice Mix
Ant and Black Currant Caper Paste
Quail Caramel
Kelp Hat
Kelp Oil*

Pumpkin and Koji Butter

Slices of Hokkaido pumpkin are cooked in pumpkin seed oil and trimmed into portions.

   Leaves from a conical cabbage are cooked in an aromatic liquid, cooled in a separate aromatic liquid, and then trimmed into rounds. The pumpkin portions are spread with pumpkin bushi paste and seasoned with salt and kelp-quince butter. The exterior of a cabbage round is brushed with parsley-pumpkin oil and the interior is brushed with pumpkin seed fudge, layered with a dressed pumpkin slice, and folded over to enclose the fillings. The pumpkin-cabbage dumpling is served with warmed and foamed koji-tomato sauce and finished with chopped fresh chives.

CABBAGE COOKING LIQUID
Filtered water
Salt
Parsley sprigs
Juniper berries
Lemon thyme sprigs
Bay leaves

CABBAGE COOLING LIQUID
Filtered water
Kelp
Arctic thyme leaves
Coriander seeds
Fresh Corn Miso*
Lemon thyme sprigs
Lemon verbena sprigs
Juniper berries

PUMPKIN BUSHI PASTE
Ground pumpkin bushi
Chopped Dried Strawberries*
Peaso Water Reduction*
Roasted Kelp Salt*
Koji Oil* (made with Øland Wheat
   Koji*)

KELP-QUINCE BUTTER
Roasted Kelp Salt*
Black Pepper Tamari*
Quince Vinegar*
Butter

KOJI-TOMATO SAUCE
Lacto Koji Water* (made with Øland
   Wheat Koji*)
Ice-Clarified Tomato Water*
Butter
Salt
Xantana

HOKKAIDO PUMPKIN
Hokkaido pumpkin
Pumpkin Seed Oil*
Salt

PARSLEY-PUMPKIN OIL
Parsley Oil*
Pumpkin Seed Oil*

PUMPKIN SEED FUDGE
Cucumber Juice Reduction*
Peaso Water Reduction*
Butter
Pumpkin Seed Oil*

TO FINISH
Spidskål conical cabbage
Cabbage Cooking Liquid
Cabbage Cooling Liquid
Parsley-Pumpkin Oil
Pumpkin portions
Pumpkin Bushi Paste
Kelp-Quince Butter
Pumpkin Seed Fudge
Koji-Tomato Sauce
Chives

Duck Brain Tempura and Duck Heart Tartare

For the duck brain tempura: A feathered duck head is trimmed to open the skull. The brain is removed and the skull is then cleaned and lined with beeswax.

Roasted duck carcasses are simmered in chicken stock. The stock is strained, then reduced to a glaze, which is mixed with BBQ duck garum and blueberry reduction.

The duck brain is brined, halved, coated in tempura batter, and fried. The fried brain is seasoned with the glaze and duck marinade, skewered with a duck feather, and served in the duck skull.

For the duck heart tartare: Duck beaks are cleaned and lined with beeswax. Lightly cooked eggs are blended with brined gooseberries, lacto-fermented koji water, and lemon juice, and the paste is emulsified with brown butter. Duck hearts are cold-smoked, cut into tiny dice, and lightly dressed with koji oil.

A duck beak is filled with a layer of the diced duck heart, a layer of the brown butter emulsion, and a final layer of the diced duck heart. The second duck beak is placed on top.

The duck brain tempura and duck heart tartare are served together on a cloth-lined basket.

DUCK BRAIN TEMPURA

ARCTIC THYME SPICE MIX
Arctic thyme leaves
Toasted coriander seeds
Toasted juniper berries

TEMPURA BATTER
Tipo "00" flour
Cornstarch
Potato starch
Baking powder
Arctic Thyme Spice Mix
Salt
Ethanol (96% ABV)
White wine vinegar
Sparkling water
Rye whiskey

DUCK BRAIN BRINE
Filtered water
Salt
Arctic thyme leaves
Toasted yellow mustard seeds
Toasted fennel seeds
Toasted star anise
Toasted coriander seeds

DUCK BRAIN
Duck head
Duck Brain Brine

DUCK MARINADE
Lemon thyme leaves
Cep Oil*
Spruce Wood Oil*
Juniper skins
Arctic thyme leaves
Brine from Salted Unripe Plums*

BLUEBERRY REDUCTION
Blueberries

LIGHT CHICKEN STOCK
Whole chickens

DUCK GLAZE BASE
Light Chicken Stock
Duck carcasses

DUCK GLAZE
Duck Glaze Base
BBQ Duck Garum*
Blueberry Reduction

TO FINISH THE DUCK BRAIN
TEMPURA
Duck Brain
Rice flour
Tempura Batter
Grapeseed oil
Duck Glaze
Duck Marinade

DUCK HEART TARTARE

BROWN BUTTER EMULSION
Eggs
Lacto Koji Water* (made with Øland
    Wheat Koji*)
Lemon juice
Brown Butter*
Salted Green Gooseberry Capers*
    (drained)

DUCK BEAKS
Duck skulls (reserved from preparing
    Duck Brain)
Beeswax

DUCK HEARTS
Duck hearts
Koji Oil*
Beeswax

TO FINISH THE DUCK HEART
TARTARE
Freshly toasted black peppercorns
Duck Heart
Duck Beaks
Brown Butter Emulsion

Pumpkin Ragout

Slices of butternut squash are cooked with hazelnut and squirrel garum oil, then sandwiched between two pieces of beeswax and cooked until the wax is very soft and infuses the squash with its flavor. The butternut squash is then cut into thin strips.

A small decorative pumpkin is hollowed out to make a bowl with a lid; both pieces are lined with beeswax.

Morels preserved in cep oil are lightly grilled, glazed with mushroom fudge, dusted with mushroom powder, and sprinkled with dried carrot flowers.

Morita chiles, grasshoppers, and garlic are browned in oil, then blended into a paste and emulsified with some olive oil. The paste is seasoned with grasshopper garum and potato stock reduction and mixed with roasted kelp oil.

Five grilled morels are arranged in the bottom of the pumpkin bowl and each is topped with a piece of semi-dried tomato, a piece of semi-dried lacto-fermented plum, and a lavender bud. The butternut squash strips are stacked and arranged in the bowl between the ingredients. The dish is warmed and dressed with hazelnut and squirrel garum oil and brushed with morita chile paste. Bee pollen and a sprinkling of salt finish the dish.

HAZELNUT AND SQUIRREL GARUM
OIL
Skinned hazelnuts
Squirrel Garum*

PUMPKIN
Butternut squash
Hazelnut and Squirrel Garum Oil
Sugar
Salt
Beeswax

REDUCED MUSHROOM-KELP
BROTH
Mushroom-Kelp Broth*

MUSHROOM FUDGE
Butter
Reduced Mushroom-Kelp Broth*
Cep Oil*

MUSHROOM POWDER
Dried ceps
Dried morels

PRESERVED MORELS
Morel mushrooms
Cep Oil*

GRILLED MORELS
Preserved Morels
Mushroom Fudge
Mushroom Powder
Seeded Dried Carrot Flowers*

SEMI-DRIED CHERRY TOMATOES
Ripe yet firm cherry tomatoes
Koji Oil*
Noma honey

SEMI-DRIED LACTO PLUMS
Lacto Plums*

MORITA CHILE PASTE
Seeded morita chile
Grasshoppers
Thinly sliced garlic
Olive oil
Grapeseed oil
Grasshopper Garum*
Potato Stock Reduction*
Salt
Roasted Kelp Oil*

TO FINISH
Decorative pumpkin
Beeswax
Grilled Morels
Semi-Dried Cherry Tomato halves
Semi-Dried Lacto Plums, diced
Lavender buds
Pumpkin stacks (5 slices in each)
Hazelnut and Squirrel Garum Oil
Bee pollen
Salt
Morita Chile Paste

Fallow Deer Broth

A broth is made by simmering dashi, fresh ceps, moss, toasted juniper, and fine shavings of deer bushi and then infusing the liquid with fresh juniper and Douglas fir branches.

A serving bowl is seasoned with small drops of cep oil and Douglas fir oil, and a mix of seasonal leaves is arranged in the bowl. The deer broth is poured into the bowl and the dish is finished with a generous spritzing of Douglas fir water spray.

DOUGLAS FIR WATER SPRAY
Douglas fir needles
Filtered water

DEER BUSHI BROTH BASE
Shaved Fallow Deer Bushi*
Cold-Infused Dashi*
Ceps
Moss
Toasted juniper wood
Salt

DEER BUSHI BROTH
Deer Bushi Broth Base
Fresh juniper berries
Fresh Douglas fir branches
White Wine Reduction*
Salt

TO FINISH
Cep Oil*
Douglas Fir Oil*
Seasonal leaves
Douglas Fir Water Spray
Deer Bushi Broth

Ceps and Hazelnuts

Fresh hazelnuts are blended with some water, ground, and strained to produce fresh hazelnut milk.

Fresh hazelnut halves are arranged in a serving bowl and the hazelnut milk is poured over them. Very fine slices of fresh ceps are shingled on top and seasoned with cold-infused kelp salt, and the dish is finished with slices of white truffle.

FRESH HAZELNUT MILK
Fresh hazelnuts
Filtered water

TO FINISH
Fresh hazelnuts
Fresh Hazelnut Milk
Ceps
Cold-Infused Kelp Salt*
White truffle
Salt

Sika Roast

Wild deer scraps and bones are deeply roasted and then simmered with kelp and black peppercorns to make a stock. The stock is reduced to a glaze. Mushroom-kelp broth and truffle juice are reduced to make a sauce and finished with brown butter and chopped black truffles.

The wild deer is grilled over hot charcoal while being brushed with the deer glaze, then carved into portions and served with the truffle sauce.

WILD DEER
Wild sika deer

DEER STOCK
Wild sika deer scraps and bones
Black peppercorns
Kelp

DEER GLAZE
Deer Stock
Blueberry Reduction*
Yeast Broth Reduction*
Smoked Butter*

TRUFFLE SAUCE
Reduced Mushroom-Kelp Broth*
Truffle juice
Brown Butter*
Black truffle
White wine vinegar
White Wine Reduction*

TO FINISH
Wild Deer
Deer Glaze
Salt
Toasted black peppercorns
Truffle Sauce

Duck Fat and Spruce Æbleskiver

Æbleskiver batter is simmered in smoked duck fat until fully cooked, crisp, and caramelized on the surface. The æbleskiver is brushed with linseed fudge, drizzled with roasted duck garum, and sprinkled generously with picked pine needles.

PINE NEEDLES
Pine shoots

ÆBLESKIVER BATTER
Cream
Egg yolks
Tipo "00" flour
Salt
Melted butter
Egg whites
Sugar

SMOKED DUCK FAT
Duck fat

LINSEED OIL
Linseeds

LINSEED FUDGE
Roasted Kelp Salt*
Celery Juice Reduction*
Linseed Oil
Cep Oil*
Brown Butter*

TO FINISH
Æbleskiver Batter
Smoked Duck Fat
Linseed Fudge
Roasted Duck Garum*
Pine Needles

Bear Baba

Lightly cooked egg yolks are cured in beef garum, then whisked until smooth and seasoned with whisky vinegar, Danish whisky, smoked butter, more beef garum, and salt to make a sauce.

Roasted bear meat is simmered in dashi with dried ceps, lemon thyme, juniper wood, and apples. The broth is strained, reduced, and then further reduced with cep oil to a thick and fudgy caramel.

A bear consommé is made from chicken stock and dashi clarified with brined bear meat, egg whites, and celery, and finished with rice fava shoyu and chicken wing garum. The consommé is reduced by half.

Chickens and ducks are simmered to make a stock, which is strained and left to settle. The fat is skimmed off the surface of the stock and reserved. The stock is reduced to a light glaze. The glaze is then mixed with some of the reserved fat, brought to a boil, and left to cool until a skin forms on top. The skin is delicately transferred from the saucepan to parchment and the parchment is placed in a skillet, where the skin is cooked until it begins to crisp but is still malleable. The skin is punched into discs and slightly dehydrated to keep it crisp.

Æbleskiver batter is cooked in bear fat until crisp and caramelized. The top of the æbleskiver is sliced off and the interior is soaked with reduced bear consommé. The cut surface of the cake is brushed with whisky–egg yolk sauce, then spread with arctic thyme marinade and topped with a spoonful of lovage and parsley leaves cooked in an elderflower emulsion, which are piped with a dot of bear caramel. The duck skin disc is brushed with bear fat and decorated with a fanciful stenciled bear head made with grated pumpkin bushi and bear spice mix. The bear caramel is painted on to make the bear's eyes. The duck skin disc is placed on the æbleskiver, which is served in a wicker basket with a small spoonful of bear caramel on the side.

ÆBLESKIVER BATTER
Cream
Egg yolks
Tipo "00" flour
Salt
Melted butter
Egg whites
Sugar

BEAR SPICE BRINE
Salt
Filtered water
Toasted coriander seeds
Toasted black peppercorns
Toasted juniper berries
Fennel seeds
Green aniseeds
Angelica seeds
Cardamom
Bay leaves
Dried ceps
Thyme sprigs
Lemon thyme sprigs

CHICKEN STOCK
Whole chickens
Chicken wings
Filtered water
Bay leaves
Celery

BEAR CONSOMMÉ
Bear meat (ideally with a high meat-to-fat ratio)
1% salt brine
Bear Spice Brine
Egg whites

Chopped celery
Cold-Infused Dashi*
Chicken Stock
Fava Rice Shoyu*
Chicken Wing Garum*

WHISKY–EGG YOLK SAUCE
Eggs
Beef Garum*
Whisky Vinegar*
Melted Smoked Butter*
Danish whisky
Beef Garum*
Salt

ARCTIC THYME MARINADE
Lemon thyme leaves
Cep Oil*
Spruce Wood Oil*
Juniper skins
Arctic thyme leaves
Liquid from Salted Green Gooseberry Capers*

BEAR FAT
Bear fat

DUCK SKINS
Whole chickens
Whole ducks
Chicken wings
Duck fat
Filtered water

CRISPY DUCK SKIN DISC
Duck Skin

BEAR CARAMEL
Bear meat (ideally with a high meat-to-fat ratio)
Cold-Infused Dashi*
Dried ceps
Lemon thyme sprigs
Juniper wood
Whole apples
Cep Oil*

ELDERFLOWER EMULSION BASE
Lacto Koji Water* (made with Øland Wheat Koji*)
Smoked Tomato Water* (smoked twice with hay)
Butter
Elderflower Oil*
Salt
Xantana

ELDERFLOWER EMULSION
Elderflower Emulsion Base
Filtered water

METTE-JUNIPER SPICE MIX
Toasted juniper berries
Toasted black peppercorns
Toasted coriander seeds
Toasted cardamom
Dried Ginger*
Freeze-dried black currants
Freeze-dried lingonberries
Fennel seeds

Dried ceps
Roasted Yeast*
Salt

TONI SPICE MIX
Dried Lacto Plum Skins*
Dried rose petals
Dried Horseradish*
Dried ceps
Roasted Kelp*
Toasted black peppercorns
Grated pumpkin bushi

BEAR SPICE MIX
Mette-Juniper Spice Mix
Toni Spice Mix

TO FINISH
Æbleskiver Batter
Bear Fat
Lovage leaves
Parsley leaves
Elderflower Emulsion
Bear Consommé
Whisky-Egg Yolk Sauce
Arctic Thyme Marinade
Bear Caramel
Grated pumpkin bushi
Bear Spice Mix

New Season Hazelnuts and Caviar

Chestnuts are roasted in brown butter, further cooked, and puréed. Fresh hazelnuts are brined, peeled, and sliced thin.

The chestnut purée is piped onto a serving plate and salted fresh hazelnut slices are arranged upright on the purée. A dollop of whipped cream is placed in the center of the plate and topped with caviar. The hazelnuts are generously dressed with hazelnut oil.

CHESTNUT PURÉE
Chestnuts
Brown Butter*
Filtered water
Salt

SALTED FRESH HAZELNUTS
Fresh hazelnuts
8% salt brine

TO FINISH
Rossini Baerii caviar
Whipped cream
Chestnut Purée
Salted Fresh Hazelnuts
Hazelnut Oil*

Cured Duck and Pickled Partridge Egg

Duck breasts are cured for about three weeks in salt, sugar, and arctic thyme. Partridge eggs are cooked and then pickled in elderberry balsamic vinegar flavored with spices and herbs. Lightly cooked egg yolks cured in beef garum are blended with smoked butter whey and kimchi tamari to make a sauce.

A pickled partridge egg is dressed with the smoked egg yolk sauce and draped with three slices of cured duck breast. The duck and egg are basted with warm Nordic seaweed spice butter and ancho chile oil, then skewered with a fresh carrot flower.

CURED DUCK BREAST
Duck crowns
Salt
Muscovado sugar
Sodium nitrite
Arctic thyme leaves

PICKLED PARTRIDGE EGG
Partridge eggs
White wine vinegar
Filtered water
Elderberry Balsamic Vinegar*
Toasted juniper berries
Toasted coriander seeds
Toasted green cardamom pods
Carrot flower seeds
Arctic thyme leaves
Angelica seeds
Salt

CURED EGG YOLKS
Eggs
Beef Garum*

SMOKED EGG YOLK SAUCE
Cured Egg Yolks
Smoked Butter Whey*
Kimchi Tamari*
Salt

NORDIC SEAWEED SPICE MIX
Toasted coriander seeds
Yellow mustard seeds
Arctic thyme leaves
Dried ceps
Roasted Yeast*
Fennel seeds
Salt
Koji Flour*
Roasted Kelp Powder*

NORDIC SEAWEED SPICE BUTTER
Butter
Nordic Seaweed Spice Mix
Maitake Garum*
Chicken Wing Garum*
Peaso Water Reduction*
Roasted Kelp Salt*
Seeded morita chile
Seeded ancho chile

TO FINISH
Cured Duck Breast
Koji Oil*
Pickled Partridge Egg
Smoked Egg Yolk Sauce
Nordic Seaweed Spice Butter
Ancho Chile Oil*
Carrot flower

Roast Waterfowl and Foraged Plate

Roast Waterfowl

To make the hazelnut feather, flatbread dough is rolled thin, cut into a feather shape, and baked. Truffles are blended with mushroom kelp broth, lacto-fermented cep water, and celery reduction and then emulsified with yeast oil and cep oil to create a thick, creamy purée. The feather is piped with soft cheese and layered with the truffle purée and sliced truffles. Vegetable fudge is piped on either side of the center quill, and finely julienned fresh hazelnuts are positioned to replicate the barbs of the feather.

Fresh truffles are sliced, brushed with cep oil, and spritzed with lacto-fermented cep water and then layered with baby spinach and truffle purée to create a truffle millefeuille.

A wild duck breast crown is cooked over charcoal until deeply caramelized, then finished with duck finishing glaze and sliced. The slices are spread with berry praline and sprinkled with chopped cold-smoked Madagascar peppercorns.

The duck is plated and a warm truffle sauce is ladled over. Grape leaves are spritzed with pine vinegar and arranged on the plate with the duck, along with the hazelnut feather and the truffle millefeuille. A foraged plate is served alongside.

Foraged Plate

Lemon verbena kombucha infused with fresh plums is mixed with quince juice and then infused with Douglas fir needles, pine shoots, green coriander seeds, and sea buckthorn berries. This plum-quince infusion is combined with pine vinegar and Douglas fir oil to make a vinaigrette.

The foraged items are arranged in a natural way on the plate, seasoned with salt, and dressed with the pine vinaigrette.

HAZELNUT FEATHER

MALT FLATBREAD FEATHER
Tipo "00" flour
Konini Flour*
Malt flour
Dried Rose Oil*
Butter
Salt
Kaelder Øl lager
Rolling flour

TRUFFLE PURÉE
Frozen summer truffles
Roasted Yeast Oil*
Cep Oil*
Mushroom-Kelp Broth*
Lacto Cep Water*
Celery Juice Reduction*

VEGETABLE FUDGE
Cucumber Juice Reduction*
Peaso Water Reduction*
Butter
Grapeseed oil

TO FINISH THE FEATHER
Malt Flatbread Feather
Troldhede Ask cheese
Fresh hazelnuts
Truffle Purée
Vegetable Fudge
Fresh truffle
Hazelnut Oil*
Salt

GRILLED WILD DUCK AND GARNISH

GRAPE LEAF COOKING LIQUID
Apple juice
Douglas Fir Oil*
Brine from Brined Japanese Quince*

GRAPE LEAVES
Danish grape leaves
Grape Leaf Cooking Liquid

TRUFFLE PURÉE
Summer truffles
Roasted Yeast Oil*
Cep Oil*
Mushroom-Kelp Broth*
Lacto Cep Water*
Celery Juice Reduction*

TRUFFLE MILLEFEUILLE
Fresh autumn/winter truffles
Truffle Purée
Spinach leaves
Lacto Cep Water,* in an atomizer
Cep Oil*

WILD DUCKS
Wild ducks
Lacto Koji Water* (made with Rice Koji*)
Filtered water

DUCK FINISHING GLAZE
Cep Tamari*
Ryeso Reduction*
Pine Dashi*

COOKED WILD DUCK BREAST
Blanched and aged duck breast crown
Douglas Fir Oil*
Duck Finishing Glaze

SMOKED MADAGASCAR PEPPER
Maitake Oil*
Madagascar peppercorns (voatsiperifery)

BERRY PRALINE
Freeze-dried black currants
Dried ceps
Söl
Madagascar peppercorns (voatsiperifery)
Black Currant Wood Oil*
Marigold Oil*

KANZURI OIL*

TRUFFLE SAUCE
Reduced Mushroom-Kelp Broth*
Truffle juice
Brown Butter*
Chopped black truffle
White wine vinegar
White Wine Reduction*

TO FINISH THE DUCK BREAST
Cooked Wild Duck Breast
Berry Praline
Smoked Madagascar Pepper
Grape Leaves
Pine Vinegar* spray
Hazelnut Feather
Truffle Millefeuille
Truffle Sauce

FORAGED PLATE

PLUM INFUSION
Lemon Verbena Kombucha*
Plum scraps

PLUM-QUINCE INFUSION
Plum Infusion
Quince Juice*

PINE INFUSION
Douglas fir needles
Pine shoots
Green coriander seeds
Unripe sea buckthorn berries
Plum-Quince Infusion

PINE VINEGAR
Douglas fir needles
White wine vinegar

PINE VINAIGRETTE
Pine Infusion
Pine Vinegar*
Douglas Fir Oil*

PEELED FRESH WALNUTS
Fresh walnuts

PEELED FRESH HAZELNUTS
Fresh hazelnuts

SALTED NOBLE FIR CONES
Noble fir cones
Filtered water
Salt

DRIED PLUMS
Large Danish Tophit plums

CANDIED PINE CONES
Jarred candied pine cones

TO FINISH
Peeled Fresh Walnut half
Peeled Fresh Hazelnut
Candied Pine Cone
Semi-Dried Mulberries*
Pine shoots
Coriander seeds
Unripe sea buckthorn berries
Salted Noble Fir Cones
Black currant shoots
Diced Santa Maria pear
Dried Plum
Pine Vinaigrette

Broth of Wild Fungi with Fresh Sumac

Mushroom broth and mushroom-chestnut broth are mixed with truffle juice and fresh ceps and then steeped with lovage and lemon thyme and seasoned with white wine. The broth is poured into a serving bowl over a whole sumac bud, and the dish is finished with cep oil and spruce wood oil.

MUSHROOM BROTH
Kelp
Dried ceps
Dried morels
Dried black trumpet mushrooms
Lacto Cep Water*
Freeze-dried lingonberries
Muscovado sugar
Filtered water
Cold-Infused Dashi*
Dried chanterelles
Dried Oyster Mushrooms*

MUSHROOM-CHESTNUT BROTH
Cold-Infused Dashi*
Ice-Clarified Tomato Water*
Lemon thyme
Dried Oyster Mushrooms*
Dried chanterelles
Dried ceps
Frozen chestnuts
Black Chestnuts*

TO FINISH
Mushroom Broth
Mushroom-Chestnut Broth
Truffle juice
Ceps
Lovage leaves
Lemon thyme leaves
White Wine Reduction*
Cep Oil*
Spruce Wood Oil*
Fresh sumac bud

Blackened Chestnut

Chestnuts are aged under vacuum until black, soft, and sweet. The flesh is removed and the shells are reserved. The flesh is cooked with dashi, then puréed with rabbit meat and cooked until the proteins set and the liquid separates, leaving a clarified broth. The rabbit broth is seasoned with oregano vinegar and set with gelatin, then poured into the reserved black chestnut shells.

The rabbit gel is seasoned with salt and hazelnut oil and topped with a slice of roasted chestnut.

BLACK CHESTNUT WATER
Black Chestnuts*
Cold-Infused Dashi*

RABBIT BROTH
Deboned rabbit flesh
Black Chestnut Water
White Wine Reduction*
Salt

RABBIT GEL
Rabbit Broth
Oregano Vinegar*
Gelatin
Salt

ROASTED CHESTNUT
Chestnuts
Brown Butter*
Salt

TO FINISH
Rabbit Gel
Black Chestnut
Roasted Chestnut slice
Hazelnut Oil*
Salt

Noble Fir Cone on the Cob

Noble fir cones are prepared by picking out the woody scales, pine nuts, and seed wings that sit between the scales of the cone. The cones are cut into smaller lengths, then marinated.

Forest skewers are fashioned from sharpened spruce or Douglas fir tips with flowering herbs tied on.

Pickled rose petals and marinated lacto-fermented cherry halves are slid between several scales of the fir cone. The cones are basted with smoked butter and grilled over hot charcoal, and the marinated pine shoots and black currant shoots are tucked between a few more scales. The forest skewers are speared into the ends of the chunk of fir cone and spruce fudge is spread all over it. The fir cone is dusted with woodruff and Japanese quince za'atar and spritzed with woodruff distillate.

PINE MARINADE
Noble fir cone scraps
Green gooseberries
Pine shoots
Unripe sea buckthorn berries
Douglas fir needles

PINE CONE
Noble fir cone
Pine Marinade

MARINATED PICKLED ROSE
PETALS
Pickled Rose Petals*
Pine Marinade

MARINATED LACTO CHERRIES
Lacto Cherries*
Pine Marinade

SPRUCE FUDGE
Cucumber Juice Reduction*
Peaso Water Reduction*
Butter
Spruce Wood Oil*

WOODRUFF DISTILLATE
Fresh woodruff leaves
Ethanol (60% ABV)

TOASTED BEECHNUTS
Beechnuts

ZA'ATAR BASE
Freeze-dried lingonberries
Freeze-dried rhubarb
Arctic thyme leaves
Toasted Beechnuts

WOODRUFF ZA'ATAR
Za'atar Base
Finely chopped Toasted Beechnuts
Finely chopped freeze-dried
  lingonberries
Ground dried yarrow flowers
Ground dried yarrow
Ground dried woodruff

WOODRUFF AND JAPANESE
QUINCE ZA'ATAR
Woodruff Za'atar
Dried Japanese Quince*
Salt

FOREST SKEWERS
Spruce tips
Douglas fir tips
Yarrow
Lemon thyme
Wood sorrel

MARINATED PINE SHOOTS
Pine shoots
Spruce Wood Oil*

TO FINISH
Pine Cone
Marinated Pickled Rose Petals
Marinated Lacto Cherries
Smoked Butter*
Marinated Pine Shoots
Black currant shoot halves
Forest Skewers
Spruce Fudge
Woodruff and Japanese Quince
  Za'atar
Woodruff Distillate

Pepper Meat

Wild boar back fat is salted, cold-smoked over hay, and then cured with star anise, juniper berries, ginger, black pepper, and coriander to make lardo.

Fresh sweet red peppers are roasted, gently crushed, and then hung to extract their juices, which are mixed with red pepper tamari, and then reduced to 20 degrees Brix.

More red peppers are grilled over hot charcoal to blacken their skins, then peeled and steamed. The flesh is dehydrated while alternately being brushed with smoked koji oil and red pepper tamari. The pepper pieces are rolled through a pasta machine to flatten them and then bathed in pepper reduction to create the "meat" portion of the red pepper meat.

The red pepper pieces are joined with strips of wild boar lardo and seasoned with salt and pepper meat spice mix.

LARDO SPICE MIX
Star anise
Juniper berries
Dried Ginger*
Toasted black peppercorns
Toasted coriander seeds

WILD BOAR LARDO
Wild boar back fat
Flake sea salt
Lardo Spice Mix

PEPPER REDUCTION
Sweet red peppers

RED PEPPER MEAT
Red bell peppers
Red Pepper Tamari*
Pepper Reduction
Smoked Koji Oil*

PEPPER MEAT SPICE MIX
Toasted juniper berries
Toasted black peppercorns
Toasted coriander seeds
Star anise petals
Arctic thyme leaves
Dried Ginger*
Salt

PEPPER GLUE
Rice flour
Cold-Infused Dashi*
Juice reserved from Pepper
   Reduction

TO FINISH
Wild Boar Lardo
Pepper Glue
Red Pepper Meat
Salt
Pepper Meat Spice Mix
Smoked Koji Oil*
Red Pepper Tamari*

Wild Boar Crisp

Potatoes are cooked with calcium chloride, then mashed into a dough and pressed into small potato tortillas. The tortillas are fried and topped with a layer of wild herbs that have been steamed with a koji emulsion and minced green gooseberries.

    The steamed herbs are dotted with green gooseberry seeds and smoked parsley purée, and curls of shaved wild boar lardo are loosely mounded on top. The dish is spritzed with Danish whisky and dusted with Canella spice blend.

LARDO SPICE MIX
Star anise
Juniper berries
Toasted black peppercorns
Toasted coriander seeds
Dried Ginger*

WILD BOAR LARDO
Wild boar back fat
Flake sea salt
Lardo Spice Mix

CANELLA SPICE BLEND
Toasted coriander seeds
Toasted black peppercorns
Toasted yellow mustard seeds
Arctic thyme leaves
Lacto Plum Skin Powder*
Noble Fir Salt*

PARSLEY PURÉE
Parsley leaves

SMOKED PARSLEY PURÉE
Strained Parsley Purée
Beef Garum*

POTATO TORTILLA
Potatoes
Calcium hydroxide

KOJI EMULSION
Butter
Lacto Koji Water* (made with Øland
    Wheat Koji*)
Xantana
Lemon juice
Filtered water

STEAMED HERBS
Koji Emulsion
Minced Salted Green Gooseberry
    Capers*
Goosefoot
Ground elder
Chickweed

TO FINISH
Potato Tortilla
Grapeseed oil
Steamed Herbs
Salted Green Gooseberry Caper*
    seeds
Smoked Parsley Purée
Wild Boar Lardo shavings
Danish whisky
Canella Spice Blend

Buttermilk Kombucha

Lightly sweetened green tea is combined with a small amount of kombucha and SCOBY starter. The mixture is fermented in a wide vessel so that a large SCOBY develops on the surface.

The SCOBY is simmered in sugar syrup to candy it and then cut into squares.

Buttermilk ice cream is piped into cherry-shaped molds and frozen. The ice cream cherries are topped with a leaf of Cuban oregano and a candied SCOBY square and then finished with a generous squeeze of black currant wood oil and some salt.

BUTTERMILK ICE CREAM
Buttermilk
Cream
Dextrose
Milk powder
Salt
Procrema

GREEN TEA SCOBY
Himalayan green tea
Filtered water
Sugar
Green tea kombucha (to backslop)
SCOBY starter

CANDIED SCOBY SQUARES
Sugar
Filtered water
Green Tea SCOBY

TO FINISH
Buttermilk Ice Cream
Cuban oregano leaves
Candied SCOBY Squares
Black Currant Wood Oil*
Salt

Saffron and Poppy Dessert

Layers of saffron ice cream separated by thin discs of tempered chocolate are piped into a wax bowl. The top of the ice cream is drizzled with a glaze made by flavoring poppy seed paste with licorice syrup and vanilla. The glaze is finished with a few drops of balsamic vinegar and adorned with anise hyssop flowers.

SAFFRON ICE CREAM
Milk
Cream
Dextrose
Noma honey
Milk powder
Trimoline
Saffron
Salt
Procrema

POPPY SEED PASTE
Black poppy seeds
Grapeseed oil

POPPY SEED GLAZE
Poppy Seed Paste
Grapeseed oil
Sweet licorice syrup
Vanilla bean

MEXICAN CHOCOLATE DISCS
Mexican chocolate

TO FINISH
Mexican Chocolate Discs
Saffron Ice Cream
Wax bowl
Poppy Seed Glaze
Italian balsamic vinegar
Anise hyssop flowers

Reindeer Marrow Fudge

Rendered reindeer bone marrow is cooked with sugars, cream, butter, and white chocolate into a bone marrow fudge.

White chocolate is slowly roasted until caramelized.

The bone marrow fudge is piped into the center of a split marrow bone, pieces of white chocolate are placed on top, and more fudge is piped on to fill the channel in the bone. The fudge is topped with crushed freeze-dried blueberries and marigold spice mix, which includes some intact marigold petals.

REINDEER BONE MARROW FAT
Reindeer bones
Ice water

BONE MARROW FUDGE
Sugar
Glucose syrup
Cream
Butter
Reindeer Bone Marrow Fat
White chocolate
Salt
Apple balsamic vinegar

MARIGOLD SPICE MIX
Toasted fennel seeds
Dried carrot seeds
Roseroot
Dried rose petals
Dried marigold flowers
Arctic thyme leaves

CARAMELIZED WHITE CHOCOLATE
White chocolate

TO FINISH
Reindeer bone
Bone Marrow Fudge
Freeze-dried blueberries
Marigold Spice Mix
Caramelized White Chocolate

Chocolate-Covered Moss

Reindeer moss is cleaned, dried, deep-fried, and then sprayed with melted Mexican chocolate.

Sugar is cooked until amber, Douglas fir needles and ants are added, and the caramel is allowed to set. The hardened caramel is then blended into a powder to make pine praline.

The chocolate moss is seasoned with pine salt and pine praline, piped with crème fraîche, and adorned with tiny pine shoots.

MELTED MEXICAN CHOCOLATE
Mexican 70% chocolate
Cocoa butter

CHOCOLATE MOSS
Reindeer moss
Grapeseed oil
Melted Mexican Chocolate

PINE PRALINE
Sugar
Douglas fir needles
Ants

CRÈME FRAÎCHE
Buttermilk
Cream

TO FINISH
Chocolate Moss
Crème Fraîche
Pine Praline
Pine Salt*
Pine shoot tips

Preserved Crab Apples and Autumn Leaf

Crab apples are preserved in a sugar syrup flavored with gooseberry, sea buckthorn, and green coriander seeds.

The backs of fresh crab apple leaves are brushed with multiple coats of carrot and sea buckthorn purée and spiced black currant purée. This purée is then dried and the leaf-shaped fruit leather is peeled off and brushed with toasted rose hip seed oil.

An anise hyssop leaf is adhered to the back of each fruit leather leaf, which are then arranged on a serving plate with two preserved crab apples dressed in a bit of their syrup.

PRESERVING SYRUP
Sugar
Filtered water
Freeze-dried gooseberries
Freeze-dried sea buckthorn berries
Green coriander seeds

PRESERVED CRAB APPLES
Crab apples
Preserving Syrup

SEA BUCKTHORN JUICE
Ripe sea buckthorn berries

CARROT JUICE
Carrots

CARROT AND SEA BUCKTHORN PURÉE
Sea Buckthorn Juice
Carrot Juice
Noma honey
Pectin

SPICED BLACK CURRANT PURÉE
Toasted coriander seeds
Toasted angelica seeds
Dried Ginger*
Juniper skins
Black currants
Muscovado sugar

TOASTED ROSE HIP SEED OIL
Rose hip seeds
Grapeseed oil

AUTUMN LEAF
Crab apple leaves
Carrot and Sea Buckthorn Purée
Spiced Black Currant Purée
Toasted Rose Hip Seed Oil

TO FINISH
Anise hyssop leaf
Preserved Crab Apples

Duck Fat Duck Feet

Smoked duck fat, butter, and cream are cooked with sugar, glucose syrup, and salt. The sweetness is balanced by apple balsamic vinegar, and more heat transforms it all into a caramel.

The caramel is poured into candy molds shaped like duck feet and allowed to set. The caramels are enrobed in bitter chocolate and then frozen. Just before service, the caramels are seasoned with salt and served.

SMOKED DUCK FAT
Duck fat

DUCK FAT CARAMEL
Sugar
Glucose syrup
Cream
Butter
Smoked Duck Fat
Salt
Apple balsamic vinegar
Oialla 100% chocolate
Cocoa butter

TO FINISH
Duck Fat Caramel duck feet
Salt

Cardamom and Poppy Seed Dessert

White currant juice and cardamom oil are emulsified, then folded with whipped cream, egg whites, and sugar to create a yogurt mousse. The mousse is drizzled with more cardamom oil and dressed with poppy seed glaze at the table.

CARDAMOM OIL
Green cardamom pods
Grapeseed oil

WHITE CURRANT EMULSION
Cardamom Oil
White Currant Juice*
Gelatin

YOGURT MOUSSE
Yogurt
Cream
Gelatin
Egg whites
Sugar
White Currant Emulsion

POPPY SEED PASTE
Black poppy seeds
Grapeseed oil

POPPY SEED GLAZE
Poppy Seed Paste
Grapeseed oil
Sweet licorice syrup
Vanilla bean

TO FINISH
Cardamom Oil
Yogurt Mousse
Poppy Seed Glaze

Sweet Blueberries with Ants

Blueberry sorbet, ant paste, and walnut praline are piped into a ring mold and studded with peeled walnut pieces. The surface of the sorbet is dusted with blueberry powder and ants are scattered over the top. The sorbet is ringed with seasoned walnut oil and leaves of wood sorrel.

BLUEBERRY PURÉE
Wild blueberries
Freeze-dried blueberries

INVERTED BIRCH SYRUP
Birch syrup

BLUEBERRY SORBET
Blueberry Purée
Filtered water
Inverted Birch Syrup
Green coriander seeds
Castor sugar
Procrema

WALNUT PRALINE
Walnuts
Sugar
Filtered water
Yeast Garum*

ANT PASTE
Ants
Meadowsweet Oil*
Muscovado sugar
Green coriander seeds

SEASONED WALNUT OIL
Walnut Oil*
Roasted Kelp Salt*
Salt

BLUEBERRY POWDER
Freeze-dried blueberries
Freeze-dried black currants
Freeze-dried sea buckthorn berries
Dried rose petals
Dried Ginger*

PEELED WALNUTS
Fresh walnuts

TO FINISH
Peeled Walnut
Blueberry Sorbet
Ant Paste
Walnut Praline
Seasoned Walnut Oil
Blueberry Powder
Ants
Wood sorrel leaves

Chestnut Ice Cream Sandwich

Chestnuts and water are blended and the liquid strained. This chestnut milk is then reduced for up to two days until thick, then further reduced until it begins to caramelize and thicken. The mixture is beaten in a mortar and pestle to smooth and aerate the texture of the mochi. The chestnut mochi is flattened into a thin sheet using a pasta roller and then a black currant leaf is pressed onto the surface so the mochi takes on the impression of the veining from the leaf. The edges are trimmed into a leaf shape.

To build the ice cream sandwich, chestnut praline is piped around the perimeter of one mochi leaf in successive rounds to build up a border. A fine layer of milk ice cream is piped over the uncovered surface of the leaf, followed by a layer of blueberry reduction. Semi-dried black currants and black currant shoots are placed on top, followed by another layer of milk ice cream. A second mochi leaf is gently pressed on top, using a final piping of chestnut praline so the two leaves adhere and enclose the fillings. To finish, the ice cream sandwich is quickly torched to soften its appearance, brushed with black currant wood oil, and nestled among real leaves.

CHESTNUT MOCHI
Chestnuts
Filtered water

CHESTNUT MOCHI LEAF
Chestnut Mochi
Black currant leaf

CHESTNUT PRALINE BASE
Chestnuts
Cream
Muscovado sugar

CHESTNUT PRALINE
Chestnut Praline Base
Roasted Kelp Salt*
Cream
Muscovado sugar
Vanilla bean

MILK ICE CREAM
Milk
Cream
Dextrose
Honey
Milk powder
Trimoline
Salt
Procrema

SEMI-DRIED BLACK CURRANTS
Black currants
Koji Oil*

BLUEBERRY REDUCTION
Blueberries

TO FINISH
Chestnut Mochi Leaf
Chestnut Praline
Blueberry Reduction
Semi-Dried Black Currants
Black currant shoots
Milk Ice Cream
Black Currant Wood Oil*

FOREST

Pine Fudge

Sugars, condensed milk, and smoked butter are cooked into a fudge, which is flavored with pine vinegar and Douglas fir needles and poured into pine cone molds. The molded fudge halves are decorated with pine shoots and joined with ant paste to form a whole pine cone shape. The fudge pine cones are finished with powdered dried Douglas fir needles.

ANT PASTE
Ants
Pine shoots
Meadowsweet Oil*
Muscovado sugar

PINE FUDGE
Condensed milk
Demerara sugar
Glucose syrup
Smoked Butter*
Salt
Pine Vinegar*
Douglas fir needles
Ant Paste
Pine branch

TO FINISH
Pine Fudge
Dried Douglas Fir Powder*

Waffle with Candied Cloudberries

Waffle batter flavored with meadowsweet oil and spruce wood oil is cooked in a waffle iron over a hot grill. The waffle is served with cloudberry mousse topped with cloudberries candied with birch syrup.

WAFFLE BATTER
Double cream
Tipo "00" flour
Salt
Meadowsweet Oil*
Spruce Wood Oil*

CLOUDBERRY PULP
Frozen cloudberries
Birch syrup

CLOUDBERRY MOUSSE
Whipped cream
Cloudberry Pulp
Birch syrup

CANDIED CLOUDBERRIES
Frozen cloudberries
Birch syrup

TO FINISH
Waffle Batter
Cloudberry Mousse
Candied Cloudberries

Foraging and discovery   Mette Søberg

My happiest food memories from childhood are all about anticipation: Going to the docks with my parents to buy the first lumpfish, then later that night eating the roe with a good loaf of bread. The first potatoes dug up from the garden. The first summer-ripe strawberries.

When I joined Noma, I was assigned to the foraging team. It was late summer; everything was coming out of the ground. As a native of Copenhagen, I thought I knew the places. Brøndby Beach was where I had spent summer vacations, but with a professional forager as guide, I came to see it as a market garden. He just pointed in every direction, naming all the things that were edible. I felt a whole new world opening up.

At Noma, we get to share that sense of discovery, opening minds while we fill bellies with food that is delicious, playful—and sometimes a little provocative. I am now the head of the test kitchen, where recipes take shape through a process of experimentation, obsession, and play. I still start some of my workdays with a bike ride to a beach or a municipal park, where I might forage for something that makes it onto our menu that very same night. Of course, even the seemingly simplest dish requires that touch of fermentation, or a drop of an oil that took twenty hours to extract.

It might seem as if the wildness of our ingredients and the precision of the techniques we use to prepare them are opposites—pristine nature on one side, human ingenuity on the other. But it's often the strangeness of an ingredient that fuels creativity. When I'm presented with something I've never cooked with before, I need to discover everything about it. I want to try out a million things. I get to dream on a blank page.

Since the move to our new location, we close the restaurant three times a year, change the ceramic, devise new drink pairings, and create an entire menu from scratch. What we've discovered is that however much you think you know about food, once you force yourself to create a meal with a single seasonal flow of ingredients—with only plants, or only seafood, or only game and mushrooms—you feel like a beginner again.

My favorite season is summer, when we design a menu drawn from the plant kingdom. It's the most fun to put together, but also challenging. You don't want guests to go home hungry, feeling they were served only flowers and leaves. But there's also the risk of overcompensating by making each dish extra rich in umami. When you're working with protein, it's not difficult to get people to sense the value of something—everyone knows a steak is expensive. Vegetable season at Noma is also a chance to challenge people's perception of luxury.

Each menu needs one truly iconic dish. In the summer that could be flatbreads that look like butterflies, or a vegetarian shawarma made from celeriac. It could be the brain of a wild bird served in its skull. It's true, our food can provoke. But it's never our goal to shock, or even to educate people. Instead, I hope that guests leave the restaurant a little more open. Having had reindeer brain or moose testicles, perhaps on their next trip to the butcher they try liver or sweetbreads instead of the usual chop.

But novel ingredients and new techniques are not enough. For a restaurant to practice the openness it preaches, it needs to also bring fresh ideas to how it treats its own people. When I first told my parents I wanted to be a chef, they voiced concerns. They had heard of the industry's reputation for fostering abusive work conditions. Now I look at my newborn son and vow that if he should ever choose this career, he should be able to do so free of fear. I'm glad that with initiatives like the MAD Academy, the restaurant industry is expanding the sustainability ethos to human resources. That's

FORAGING AND DISCOVERY

Clockwise from above: The fluid line between dining room and kitchen; treasures from the ocean; a just-foraged hen of the woods mushroom.

important, because creativity is also a resource that can be overfarmed.

Ours will always be an industry where people work long days and invest a lot of energy and passion. What matters to me is not so much the hours but building a culture of respect and mutual accountability. Most people enter this business very young; you absorb management styles as you work your way up the hierarchy. More than in other professions, your personality is created while you are on the job, so it can be difficult to rethink how you might want things to be. But as people with different backgrounds enter the industry, I am seeing a big shift toward a more holistic culture.

At Noma, we are committed to refilling the well of inspiration. And we invite everyone, no matter their role, to take part in the creative process. The test kitchen is always open for team members to pop in with feedback and suggestions. And we reach out to them: If we're working on a recipe based on kimchi, we might seek advice from a Korean colleague. A big part of my job is to make mistakes. Creativity is about producing the 999 failures, as well as the one thing that will become a massive success.

Even in the old Noma, we had a system for nourishing innovation across the whole team. Saturday Night Projects were regular gatherings—held late, after the restaurant had closed—where team members showcased their inventions. This might be a new dish or technique, or a fresh take on plating and presentation. It was a way to give everyone a sense of ownership over the menu. And people developed a habit of using all their senses, which made for a better product.

The future that I'd like to help build is really a return: a return to food that is about fun and about bringing people together. Everyone knows how powerfully new flavors and new smells help us connect with an environment and its people when we are in a new country. At Noma, we serve a bit of adventure and homecoming in every bite.

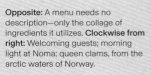

Opposite: A menu needs no description—only the collage of ingredients it utilizes. **Clockwise from right:** Welcoming guests; morning light at Noma; queen clams, from the arctic waters of Norway.

Ocean

January through April

Sea Snail Broth

A sea snail broth is made from smoked turbot bones, lemon thyme, dried mushrooms, and kelp. The broth is strained and simmered with green gooseberries, ginger, and more dried mushrooms until reduced by half, then clarified using egg whites and infused with lemon thyme and lemon verbena.

This broth is mixed with dashi and liquid reserved from cooking sea snails in koji oil and arctic thyme, then seasoned with Mexican oregano, maitake and parsley oils, and ancho angelica spiced butter. The broth is served in a sea snail shell to which tiny oxalis flowers have been affixed with strawberry paste. A few small drops of parsley oil finish the dish.

SEA SNAIL COOKING LIQUID
Sea snails
Arctic thyme
Koji Oil*

COLD-SMOKED MAITAKE
Maitake mushrooms

SMOKED FISH BROTH
Turbot bones
Cold filtered water
Lemon thyme
Dried ceps
Dried morels
Kelp
White Wine Reduction*

SECOND INFUSION
Freeze-dried green gooseberries
Dried Ginger*
Cold-Smoked Maitake
Dried ceps

CLARIFICATION
Egg whites

THIRD INFUSION
Lemon thyme sprigs
Lemon verbena sprigs

ANCHO ANGELICA SPICE MIX
Toasted seeded ancho chile
Toasted yellow mustard seeds
Toasted black peppercorns
Toasted coriander seeds
Dried Horseradish*
Dried Ginger Skins*
Juniper berries
Dried angelica seeds

ANCHO ANGELICA SPICED
BUTTER
Smoked Butter*
Ancho Angelica Spice Mix
Maitake Garum*
Chicken Wing Garum*
Peaso Water Reduction*
Roasted Kelp Salt*

SEA SNAIL BROTH
Sea Snail Cooking Liquid
Cold-Infused Dashi*
Smoked Fish Broth
Mexican oregano leaves
Maitake Oil*
Ancho Angelica Spiced Butter
Parsley Oil*
White wine vinegar
Salt

ROSEROOT SPICE MIX
Dried roseroot
Dried carrot flower seeds
Toasted fenugreek
Toasted coriander seeds
Fennel seeds
Arctic thyme

STRAWBERRY PASTE
Roseroot Spice Mix
Koji Oil*
Halved red strawberries

TO FINISH
Yellow oxalis flowers
White oxalis flowers
Pink oxalis flowers
Oyster leaf flowers
Lemon thyme flowers
Strawberry Paste
Sea snail shell
Parsley Oil*
Sea Snail Broth

Trout Roe and Broccoli

Broccoli stems are sliced thin, cooked, and then marinated in parsley oil. Koji water and yeast broth are emulsified with butter and sea lettuce oil and seasoned with roasted kelp salt and smoked seaweed shoyu to make a sauce.

Trout roe is lightly cooked and brined, then folded with an egg yolk sauce and roasted kelp salt. The roe is surrounded by shingled slices of broccoli stem, topped with more roasted kelp salt, and dressed with the sea lettuce and yeast sauce and droplets of rose oil.

EGG YOLK SAUCE
Eggs
Kimchi Tamari*
Beef Garum*
Smoked Butter Whey*

SEA LETTUCE OIL
Dried Sea Lettuce*
Grapeseed oil

SEA LETTUCE AND YEAST SAUCE
Lacto Koji Water* (made with Øland
  Wheat Koji*)
Yeast Broth*
Butter
Sea Lettuce Oil
Roasted Kelp Salt*
Smoked Seaweed Shoyu*
Xantana

BROCCOLI STEMS
Broccoli
Parsley Oil*

TROUT ROE
6% salt brine
2% salt brine
Trout roe sac

TO FINISH
Trout Roe
Egg Yolk Sauce
Roasted Kelp Salt*
Broccoli Stems
Sea Lettuce and Yeast Sauce
Rose Oil*

Drunken Flower Pickle

White currant juice and elderflower syrup are infused with caraway and lovage, seasoned with lacto-fermented cep water, and blended with elderflower oil to make a sauce.

Orange carrots, white carrots, white pearl onions, and kohlrabi are cooked in a mix of dashi, spruce wood oil, white currants, sea buckthorn, Douglas fir needles, and herbs. Purple carrots are cooked in berry juice, herbs, and Douglas fir needles.

All the vegetables are cut into small teardrops, which are arranged in a flower pattern in a serving bowl along with rehydrated red currants topped with lemon thyme leaves. The vegetable "flower petals" are generously spritzed with black currant wood water spray, and the dish is lightly strewn with a variety of herbs, flowers, shoots, and seeds. The white currant and elderflower sauce is spooned into the bowl to finish.

WHITE CURRANT AND
ELDERFLOWER SAUCE
Filtered water
White Currant Juice*
Elderflower Syrup*
White wine vinegar
Lacto Cep Water*
Fresh caraway
Lovage leaves
Elderflower Oil*

VEGETABLE COOKING LIQUID
Lemon verbena leaves
Lemon thyme leaves
Rose geranium
Douglas fir needles
Unripe sea buckthorn berries
White currants
Cold-Infused Dashi*
Spruce Wood Oil*

ORANGE CARROT
Large orange carrot
Vegetable Cooking Liquid

WHITE CARROT
Large white carrot
Vegetable Cooking Liquid

WHITE PEARL ONIONS
Large white pearl onions
Vegetable Cooking Liquid

KOHLRABI
Kohlrabi
Vegetable Cooking Liquid

PURPLE CARROTS
Large purple carrot
Aronia berry juice
Black currants
Lemon thyme leaves
Geranium leaves
Douglas fir needles

REHYDRATED RED CURRANTS
Semi-Dried Red Currants*
Rose Kombucha*

BLACK CURRANT WOOD WATER
SPRAY
Filtered water
Black currant wood
Pine shoots

TO FINISH
Rehydrated Red Currants
Lemon thyme leaves
Kohlrabi pieces
Orange Carrot pieces
Purple Carrot pieces
White Carrot pieces
White Pearl Onion pieces
Unripe sea buckthorn berry halves
Small pine shoots
Fennel top
Salted Black Currant Caper* halves
Fresh angelica buds
Green coriander seeds
Fresh nasturtium seeds
Black currant shoots
Dried bluebells
Dried Carrot Flower*
Dried arctic thyme
Black Currant Wood Water Spray
White Currant and Elderflower Sauce

Fossilized Shrimp

Grey shrimp are halved and cooked in oil, with a weight pressing them flat, until crisp.

Chickens and ducks are simmered to make a stock, which is strained and left to settle. The fat is skimmed off and reserved, and the stock is reduced to a light glaze. The glaze is mixed with some of the reserved fat, brought to a boil, and left to cool until a skin forms on top. The skin is delicately transferred from the saucepan to parchment and the parchment is placed in a skillet, where the skin cooks until it begins to crisp.

The shrimp are laid onto the duck skin before it is fully crisped and topped with a parchment square. A saucepot is set on top to fuse the shrimp into the duck skin. The duck skin is brushed with rose oil just before serving.

CRISPY GREY SHRIMP
Grey shrimp
Grapeseed oil

DUCK SKINS
Whole chickens
Whole ducks
Chicken wings
Duck fat
Filtered water

TO FINISH
Crispy Grey Shrimp
Duck Skin
Rose Oil*

Squid and Roasted Kelp Butter

Center-cut portions of squid are cooked in spruce wood oil and then cut into strips. The strips are shingled on each other, forming a rectangle, which is loosely rolled onto a black currant wood mat and basted in warm roasted kelp butter.

ROASTED KELP BUTTER
Roasted Kelp Salt*
Butter

SQUID
Large Danish squid
Spruce Wood Oil*

TO FINISH
Squid
Roasted Kelp Butter

Norwegian Queen Clam

A queen scallop is presented still attached to the half shell, with its roe nestled next to it, seasoned with just a few grains of salt. The diner uses the top shell to scrape the scallop from the bottom shell.

QUEEN CLAM
Live queen scallop
Salt

Horse Mussel Stew

Lightly brined horse mussels are cured between kelp sheets and then diced.

Plum kernel–infused milk, cream, and buttermilk are cultured with rennet and steamed to make a fresh cheese.

Fresh maitake mushrooms are cold-smoked and sautéed in brown butter until crisp. The cooked mushrooms are dried and then finely chopped.

The diced horse mussel flesh is sautéed, flambéed with vermouth, and cooked with dried lacto-fermented plums and the cold-smoked maitakes. The mussels, plums, and mushrooms are folded with horse mussel stew base.

The horse mussel stew is spooned into a horse mussel shell and topped with pickled chanterelles and fried sourdough bread crumbs. A spoonful of the plum kernel fresh cheese is nestled next to the stew.

LACTO PLUM GLAZE
Mushroom-Kelp Broth*
Beef Garum*

DRIED LACTO PLUMS
Lacto plum halves (without skins)
Lacto Plum Glaze

LACTO PLUM AND TOMATO
REDUCTION
Lacto Plum Juice*
Ice-Clarified Tomato Water*
Kelp
Dried Ginger*

HORSE MUSSEL STEW BASE
Roasted Kelp Salt*
Green coriander seeds
Tomato Water Reduction*
Celery Juice Reduction*
Fennel Juice Reduction*
Lacto Plum and Tomato Reduction
Butter

COLD-SMOKED MAITAKE
Maitake mushrooms (in palm-size
  clusters)
Brown Butter*

FRIED SOURDOUGH BREAD
CRUMBS
Sourdough bread (crusts removed)
Butter

HORSE MUSSELS
Horse mussels
Salt brine
Large sheets of kelp

PLUM KERNEL FRESH CHEESE
Milk
Cream
Plum kernels
Buttermilk
Rennet

HORSE MUSSEL STEW
Butter
Diced Horse Mussels
Dry vermouth
Cold-Smoked Maitake
Dried Lacto Plums
Horse Mussel Stew Base
Diced Horse Mussel adductors

TO FINISH
Horse mussel shell
Horse Mussel Stew
Pickled Chanterelle* halves
Fried Sourdough Bread Crumbs
Plum Kernel Fresh Cheese

Surf and Turf

Raw Skagen shrimp topped with roasted kelp salt are nestled next to a quenelle of bleak roe that's been lightly brined and cured in egg white garum. Seasoned cream surrounds the shrimp and roe, flavored with droplets of horseradish juice. The dish is finished with quartered rose hips dressed with sloeberry paste and a few drops of toasted hay oil.

PEELED SKAGEN SHRIMP
Fresh Skagen shrimp

BLEAK ROE
Bleak roe
Egg White Garum*
2% salt brine

SLOEBERRY PASTE
Salted Sloeberry* flesh
Spruce Wood Oil*
Yeast Broth Reduction*

SEASONED ROSE HIP
Peeled and seeded rose hip
Sloeberry Paste
Toasted Hay Oil*

SEASONED CREAM
Cream
Lacto Koji Water* (made with
  Rice Koji*)

TO FINISH
Peeled Skagen Shrimp
Roasted Kelp Salt*
Seasoned Rose Hip quarters
Seasoned Cream
Bleak Roe
Horseradish juice

Best of Mussel

Blue mussels are steamed and the fleshy cheeks are carved off and reserved. The remaining mussel meat is cooked in smoked butter until caramelized, then blended with the smoked butter and lacto-fermented koji water to make a smooth mussel purée.

The mussel cheeks are piped with the mussel purée, layered, and arranged in mussel shells that have been brushed with roasted kelp oil. The dish is finished with melted butter, salt, and a spritz of lacto-fermented koji water.

MUSSELS
Blue mussels

MUSSEL PURÉE
Mussel guts
Smoked Butter*
Lacto Koji Water* (made with Øland
  Wheat Koji*)

TO FINISH
Roasted Kelp Oil*
Mussel cheeks
Mussel Purée
Melted butter
Salt
Lacto Koji Water* (made with Øland
  Wheat Koji*)

Apple and Oyster

Sloeberries are blended with cold-infused jasmine tea and birch syrup. The juice is strained and set with gelatin.

Peeled Gala apples are cooked in apple cooking tea and then cooked again with the melted sloeberry marinade. The marinade is strained, poured over the cooled apples, and allowed to set once more.

Two spoonfuls of the gelled sloeberry marinade are placed onto a serving plate. A raw oyster is halved and placed on the gel, and thin slices of the cooked apple, brushed with gooseberry praline, are laid on top of the oyster halves and seasoned with roasted kelp salt. The dish is finished with jasmine and gooseberry broth and droplets of fresh koji oil.

APPLE COOKING TEA
Cold-Infused Jasmine Tea*
Plum kernels
Freeze-Dried Gooseberry Powder*
Rose pulp (reserved from making
   Rose Oil*)

SLOEBERRY MARINADE
Sloeberries
Cold-Infused Jasmine Tea*
Birch syrup
Gelatin

POACHED APPLE
Gala apples
Apple Cooking Tea
Sloeberry Marinade

GOOSEBERRY PRALINE
Juniper skins
Lemon thyme leaves
Freeze-Dried Gooseberry Powder*
Black Currant Wood Oil*

JASMINE AND GOOSEBERRY
BROTH
Cold-Infused Jasmine Tea*
Freeze-dried green gooseberries

TO FINISH
Gigas oyster
Gelled Sloeberry Marinade
Poached Apple slices
Gooseberry Praline
Roasted Kelp Salt*
Jasmine and Gooseberry Broth
Fresh Barley Koji Oil*

Cod Tongue

A cod tongue, still attached to the bone, is cooked with Douglas fir oil, then breaded and fried. The fried tongue is spread with a bit of lacto-fermented green strawberry paste, garnished with wasabi flowers, and served with a wedge of Japanese quince.

EGG WHITE MIX
Egg whites
Egg White Garum*

BREADED COD TONGUE
Douglas Fir Oil*
Cod heads
Rice flour
Egg White Mix
Panko

LACTO GREEN STRAWBERRY
PASTE
Lacto Green Strawberries*
Douglas Fir Oil*

TO FINISH
Grapeseed oil
Breaded Cod Tongue
Lacto Green Strawberry Paste
Wasabi flowers
Japanese quince

Sea Urchin and Pumpkin

Crown prince pumpkin is cooked with walnut oil, sliced thin, and cut into lens shapes. Cooked kelp is cut into lens shapes and split to create thinner pieces.

Sea urchin tongues are seasoned with chicken wing garum and shingled inside a serving bowl with slices of salted fresh hazelnut, pumpkin, and kelp. A dot of rose fudge joins each ingredient and a piece of roasted kelp salt tops each urchin tongue. The dish is finished with seasoned cream and droplets of rose oil.

SEA URCHIN
Sea urchins
2% salt brine

CROWN PRINCE PUMPKIN
Crown Prince pumpkin
Walnut Oil*

SALTED FRESH HAZELNUTS
Fresh hazelnuts
8% salt brine
Hazelnut Oil*

ROSE FUDGE
Cucumber Juice Reduction*
Peaso Water Reduction*
Butter
Rose Oil*

SEASONED CREAM
Cream
Brine from Brined Japanese Quince*

TO FINISH
Sea urchins
Crown Prince Pumpkin
Salted Fresh Hazelnuts
Rose Fudge
Kelp (reserved from making
    Mushroom-Kelp Broth*)
Roasted Kelp Salt*
Chicken Wing Garum*
Walnut Oil*
Seasoned Cream
Rose Oil*

Sea Cucumber

Sea cucumbers are cleaned and butchered to remove their gonads and produce an even sheet of flesh; the gonads are reserved. The flesh is dried until crisp and then deep-fried until puffed but still flat. The gonads are also dried until caramelized and sweet.

Ice-clarified mussel juice is reduced until viscous, then spread into a thin layer and dried until the mussel caramel is completely crisp.

Whipped cream is dolloped in a serving bowl and seasoned with roasted kelp salt. The sea cucumber crisp, sea cucumber gonads, and mussel caramel are broken into shards of varying sizes and arranged in the whipped cream. The dish is finished with oyster garum and horseradish juice.

MUSHROOM STOCK
Filtered water
Dried black trumpet mushrooms
Dried ceps
Kelp

SEA CUCUMBER CRISPS
Live sea cucumber
Mushroom Stock
Grapeseed oil

SEA CUCUMBER GONADS
Sea cucumber gonads

ICE-CLARIFIED MUSSEL JUICE
Mussels
Filtered water

MUSSEL CARAMEL
Ice-Clarified Mussel Juice

TO FINISH
Sea Cucumber Crisps
Mussel Caramel
Sea Cucumber Gonads
Horseradish Oil*
Whipped cream
Roasted Kelp Salt*
Oyster Garum*
Horseradish juice

Sea Snail–Stuffed Tomato Skewer

Sea snail meat and arctic thyme are simmered in dashi until greatly reduced; the concentrated broth is strained.

Two semi-dried cherry tomatoes are stuffed with lingonberry paste, smoked parsley purée, green coriander seeds, and morita chile paste; one tomato also gets lemon thyme leaves.

Two more tomatoes are stuffed with Japanese quince paste. Then the lingonberry paste–stuffed tomatoes are inserted into the quince paste–stuffed tomatoes. The double-stuffed tomatoes are slid onto a skewer fashioned from a sea snail shell.

To finish, the skewers are warmed, bathed in a spoonful of hot sea snail broth, dotted with Japanese quince paste, and adorned with half a black currant shoot.

MUSTARD SPICE MIX
Fennel seeds
Yellow mustard seeds
Coriander seeds
Seeded pasilla chile
Freeze-dried gooseberries
Black peppercorns
Juniper berries

SUNFLOWER SEED PASTE
Sunflower seeds
Brown Butter*
Ginger Powder*
Mustard Spice Mix
Celery Juice Reduction*
Peaso Water Reduction*
Roasted Kelp Salt*
Kohlrabi Shoyu*

MUSHROOM SPICE MIX
Arctic thyme
Yellow mustard seeds
Coriander seeds
Fennel seeds
Dried ceps
Dried morels

FRIED PARSLEY
Parsley leaves
Grapeseed oil

FRIED OREGANO
Oregano leaves
Grapeseed oil

LINGONBERRY PASTE
Freeze-dried rhubarb
Freeze-dried lingonberries
Cold-Infused Dashi*
Mushroom Spice Mix
Koji Oil*
Fried Parsley
Fried Oregano
Sunflower Seed Paste

PARSLEY PURÉE
Parsley leaves

SMOKED PARSLEY PURÉE
Strained Parsley Purée
Beef Garum*

JAPANESE QUINCE PASTE
Japanese quince
Butter
Dried Carrot Flowers*

MORITA CHILE PASTE
Seeded morita chile
Garlic, soaked in water overnight
Koji Oil*
Smoked Koji Oil*
Smoked Seaweed Shoyu*
Peaso Water Reduction*
Roasted Kelp Salt*
Chicken Wing Garum*
Fresh Corn Miso*

SEA SNAIL BROTH
Sea snails
Cold-Infused Dashi*
Arctic thyme

TO FINISH
Lingonberry Paste
Smoked Parsley Purée
Green coriander seeds
Morita Chile Paste
Lemon thyme leaves
Black currant shoot halves
Semi-Dried Tomatoes*
Sea Snail Broth
Japanese Quince Paste

Squid and Seaweed Butter

Thinly sliced squares of squid are brushed with spruce wood oil and briefly cooked.

The squid trimmings are grilled with smoked koji oil over charcoal, blended with dashi, and cooked; the liquid is then frozen and strained as it thaws to clarify. This clarified grilled squid broth is combined with Nordic shoyu, chicken wing garum, peaso water reduction, berry spice, and roasted kelp salt, then blended with melted butter to make squid and seaweed sauce.

The squid squares are folded into a diamond shape, arranged on a black currant wood mat, and briefly heated. Each diamond is dolloped with horseradish and sea buckthorn paste and then sauced, tableside, with squid and seaweed sauce.

RAW SQUID
Danish squid
Spruce Wood Oil*

HORSERADISH AND SEA
BUCKTHORN PASTE
Seeded unripe sea buckthorn berries
Grated fresh horseradish
Yeast Broth Reduction*
Black Currant Wood Oil*
Black currant shoots

GRILLED SQUID BROTH
Smoked Koji Oil*
Squid trimmings
Cold-Infused Dashi*

BERRY SPICE
Dried Horseradish*
Dried Ginger*
Arctic thyme
Toasted coriander seeds
Toasted angelica
Toasted fennel seeds
Dried Strawberries*

SQUID AND SEAWEED SAUCE
Butter
Nordic Shoyu*
Chicken Wing Garum*
Peaso Water Reduction*
Berry Spice
Roasted Kelp Salt*
Grilled Squid Broth

TO FINISH
Squid
Horseradish and Sea Buckthorn
  Paste
Squid and Seaweed Sauce

Lumpfish Roe, Elm Seeds, and Grilled Ramsons

Lightly cooked and raw egg yolks are cured in beef garum and whisked with smoked butter whey and more beef garum to make a sauce.

Scallops are puréed and then dried until caramelized and crisp like a chip. The scallop chips are processed into a powder, which is blended with oil and beeswax to make scallop fudge.

Lumpfish roe is gently folded into the egg yolk sauce and spooned into the serving dish. Roasted kelp salt is folded into the middle of the roe and egg yolk sauce. A rose and yeast sauce is spooned around the roe, and rose oil and elm seeds are sprinkled on top.

Ramsons are brushed with smoked butter and grilled over hot charcoal until caramelized and slightly crisp but juicy. The grilled ramsons are dressed with warm scallop fudge, smoked butter, horseradish juice, and salt and served alongside the dressed lumpfish roe.

EGG YOLK SAUCE
Eggs
Beef Garum*
Smoked Butter Whey*

ROSE AND YEAST SAUCE
Lacto Koji Water* (made with Øland
 Wheat Koji*)
Yeast Broth*
Butter
Rose Oil*
Xantana

LUMPFISH ROE
2% salt brine
Lumpfish roe

SCALLOP FUDGE
Scallops
Grapeseed oil
Beeswax

TO FINISH
Lumpfish Roe
Egg Yolk Sauce
Roasted Kelp Salt*
Rose and Yeast Sauce
Rose Oil*
Elm seeds
Young ramsons
Scallop Fudge
Horseradish juice
Clarified Smoked Butter*

Ling Liver

Ling cod liver is brined with herbs, spices, shallots, and kelp, cold-smoked, and cooked confit with Nordic seaweed spice mix and ancho chile.

Raw and lightly cooked egg yolks are cured in beef garum and then whisked with smoked butter whey to make a sauce.

Koji cake is brushed with Nordic koji butter, caramelized over hot charcoal, sliced, and piped with koji fudge.

The ling liver confit is sliced, brushed with ling liver glaze, dressed with the egg yolk sauce, and draped over the grilled koji cakes. The liver and koji are seasoned with smoked maitake oil and morita and ancho chile oil, and dusted with ancho chile powder and Nordic seaweed spice mix before being arranged in a serving bowl dressed with plate glaze.

NORDIC SEAWEED SPICE MIX
Toasted coriander seeds
Yellow mustard seeds
Arctic thyme
Dried ceps
Roasted Yeast*
Fennel seeds
Salt
Koji Flour*
Roasted Kelp Powder*

NORDIC KOJI BUTTER
Butter
Lacto Koji Water* (made with
   Rice Koji*)
Cold-Infused Dashi*
Double Algae Vinegar*
Chicken Wing Garum*
Roasted Kelp Salt*
Nordic Seaweed Spice Mix

KOJI CAKE
Koji*

SPICED BRINE
Dried Ginger Skins*
Dried chamomile
Arctic thyme
Dried angelica buds
Dried fennel seeds
Black peppercorns
Juniper berries
Coriander seeds
Salt
Lemon thyme sprigs
Shallots
Kelp
Filtered water

CONFIT OIL
Grapeseed oil
Smoked Butter*
Nordic Seaweed Spice Mix
Seeded ancho chile

CONFIT LING COD LIVER
Whole ling cod liver
Filtered water
Ice
Salt
Spiced Brine
Confit Oil

EGG YOLK SAUCE
Eggs
Beef Garum*
Smoked Butter Whey*

KOJI FUDGE
Cucumber Juice Reduction*
Peaso Water Reduction*
Butter
Koji Oil*

ANCHO CHILE POWDER
Ancho chiles

LING COD LIVER GLAZE
Mushroom-Kelp Broth*
Yeast Broth*

SMOKED MAITAKE OIL
Maitake mushroom
Cep Oil*
Brown Butter*

TO FINISH
Koji Cake
Nordic Koji Butter
Koji Fudge
Confit Ling Cod Liver
Ling Cod Liver Glaze
Egg Yolk Sauce
Smoked Maitake Oil
Morita Chile Oil*
Ancho Chile Oil*
Ancho Chile Powder
Nordic Seaweed Spice Mix

Mushroom Scented with King Crab

Lion's mane mushrooms are brushed with glaze and grilled over hot charcoal, then threaded onto a Douglas fir skewer.

KING CRAB AND MUSHROOM GLAZE
Mushroom-Kelp Broth*
Yeast Broth*
Brown Butter*
King Crab Garum*

LION'S MANE MUSHROOM
Lion's mane mushroom

TO FINISH
Lion's Mane Mushroom
Douglas fir skewer
King Crab and Mushroom Glaze

Grilled Sole

Lightly aged whole Dover sole is tied between black currant wood branches and gently grilled over charcoal. The fish is glazed with roasted kelp butter during cooking and then smoked over Douglas fir branches.

The darkened skin is removed and the fish is filleted into portions, glazed with warm roasted kelp butter, and served on a black currant wood mat.

ROASTED KELP BUTTER
Roasted Kelp Salt*
Butter

GRILLED DOVER SOLE
Large sole
Black currant wood branches
Roasted Kelp Butter
Douglas fir branches

Seaweed Flatbread

Cod roe is lightly salted and cold-smoked over hay, then blended with lemon juice and emulsified with oil and brown butter. More roe is folded into the emulsion.

Irish moss is cooked with mushroom-kelp broth.

Lightly cooked ovals of sugar kelp are coated in tempura batter, deep-fried, and showered with lemon verbena, oregano, and oxalis. Dots of parsley paste, sliced salted green gooseberries, a piping of cod roe emulsion, and a dusting of samphire and plankton powder dress the crisp as well. The crisps are arranged on a napkin with Mexican oregano leaves, marinated sea lettuce, Irish moss, and Japanese quince sliced into fans.

SUGAR KELP CRISP
Fresh sugar kelp

ARCTIC THYME SPICE MIX
Arctic thyme
Toasted coriander seeds
Toasted juniper berries

TEMPURA BATTER
Tipo "00" flour
Cornstarch
Potato starch
Baking powder
Arctic Thyme Spice Mix
Salt
Ethanol (96% ABV)
White wine vinegar
Sparkling water
Rye whiskey

PARSLEY PASTE
Parsley leaves
Yeast Broth Reduction*
Roasted Kelp Salt*
Parsley Oil*

SMOKED COD ROE
Fresh cod roe
Salt

COD ROE EMULSION
Grapeseed oil
Melted Brown Butter*
Smoked Cod Roe
Lemon juice
Salt

SAMPHIRE AND PLANKTON POWDER
Dried Samphire*
Plankton powder

MARINATED SEA LETTUCE
Sea lettuce
Ice-Clarified Mussel Juice*

DILUTE MUSHROOM-KELP BROTH
Mushroom-Kelp Broth*
Filtered water

IRISH MOSS
Mushroom-Kelp Broth*
Irish moss
Dilute Mushroom-Kelp Broth

JAPANESE QUINCE FANS
Japanese quince

TO FINISH
Sugar Kelp Crisp
Tempura Batter
Grapeseed oil
Oregano leaves
Lemon verbena leaves
Green oxalis clusters
Parsley Paste
Seeded Salted Green Gooseberry
 Capers*
Cod Roe Emulsion
Samphire and Plankton Powder
Mexican oregano leaves
Marinated Sea Lettuce
Irish Moss
Japanese Quince Fans
Cracked toasted black peppercorns

Cured Perch

Perch fillets are lightly brined with seaweed, spices, and herbs, then cured in a mixture of fresh corn miso, kelp powder, dashi, coriander seeds, and smoked seaweed shoyu. A butter sauce is made from reduced mushroom-kelp broth, smoked seaweed shoyu, and roasted kelp salt.

The cured perch fillets are cut into bite-size pieces, skewered onto Douglas fir toothpicks, dressed with the smoked shoyu kelp butter sauce, and served on fresh sugar kelp.

SPICED BRINE
Filtered water
Kelp
Söl
Fine salt
Dried Ginger Skins*
Coriander seeds
Angelica buds
Parsley
Lemon thyme leaves

PERCH
Whole perch

RAW KELP POWDER
Kelp

CORN MISO CURE
Fresh Corn Miso*
Raw Kelp Powder
Cold-Infused Dashi*
Toasted coriander seeds
Smoked Seaweed Shoyu*

CURED PERCH
Perch fillets
Corn Miso Cure

SMOKED SHOYU KELP BUTTER
SAUCE
Butter
Roasted Kelp Salt*
Smoked Seaweed Shoyu*
Mushroom-Kelp Broth*

TO FINISH
Cured Perch
Douglas fir toothpicks
Smoked Shoyu Kelp Butter Sauce
Fresh sugar kelp

Apple and Trout Roe

Lacto-fermented plums are glazed with a reduction of mushroom-kelp broth and beef garum, dried until chewy, and cut into tiny dice. Maitake mushrooms are cold-smoked and lightly roasted in brown butter until crispy, then dehydrated and finely chopped into a crumble.

The lacto-fermented plums and cold-smoked maitakes are combined with cooked grains, pickled chanterelles, and a stew base made by emulsifying butter into muddled green coriander seed, roasted kelp salt, celery and fennel reductions, and lacto plum and tomato reduction. A tiny dice of fresh apple is folded into this ragout.

A lightly steamed whole apple is hollowed out and filled with the ragout. The layer of ragout is topped with trout roe that has been lightly cured in kelp and trout bushi dashi. The top of the apple is repositioned, and the apple is lightly steamed.

APPLE VESSEL
Apples, with stems and leaves
    attached

KELP AND TROUT BUSHI DASHI
Golden Trout Bushi*
Cold-Infused Dashi*

TROUT ROE
2% salt brine
Trout roe sac
Kelp and Trout Bushi Dashi

LACTO PLUM GLAZE
Mushroom-Kelp Broth*
Beef Garum*

DRIED LACTO PLUMS
Lacto Plums* (without skins)
Lacto Plum Glaze

LACTO PLUM AND TOMATO
REDUCTION
Lacto Plum Juice*
Ice-Clarified Tomato Water*
Kelp
Dried Ginger*

COLD-SMOKED MAITAKE
Maitake mushrooms
Brown Butter*

GRAIN MIX
Spelt
Emmer
Konini wheat
Mustard seeds

STEW BASE
Roasted Kelp Salt*
Green coriander seeds
Celery Juice Reduction*
Fennel Juice Reduction*
Lacto Plum and Tomato Reduction
Xantana
Butter

TO FINISH
Grain Mix
Stew Base
Dried Lacto Plums
Pickled Chanterelles*
Cold-Smoked Maitake
Apple brunoise
Apple Vessel with lid
Trout Roe

Cod Roe Waffle

Buckwheat-corn waffles are cooked in brown butter. Grapeseed oil and smoked butter are infused with Nordic seaweed spice and ancho chile to make confit oil.

Cod roe is soaked in a spiced brine, lightly cured in a barley koji paste, and then gently cooked in the confit oil with juniper berries. The confited cod roe is sliced into thin rounds.

The waffle is brushed with hazelnut oil and piped with veg fudge and smoked egg yolk paste. The cod roe slices are laid on top and dressed with hazelnut oil, morita chile oil, and koji-cep glaze.

Pumpkin and sunflower seeds from savory granola along with lemon thyme leaves and black currant caper halves are arranged around the edges of the waffle.

BUCKWHEAT-CORN WAFFLE
Buckwheat flour
Tipo "00" flour
Baking powder
Salt
Roasted Kelp Powder*
Cream
Buttermilk
Egg
Fresh Corn Miso*
Melted butter
Brown Butter*

NORDIC SEAWEED SPICE
Toasted coriander seeds
Yellow mustard seeds
Arctic thyme
Dried ceps
Roasted Yeast*
Fennel seeds
Salt
Koji Flour*
Roasted Kelp Powder*

SPICED BRINE
Juniper berries
Coriander seeds
Lemon thyme sprigs
Kelp
Roasted Kelp*
Salt
Filtered water

CONFIT OIL
Grapeseed oil
Smoked Butter*
Nordic Seaweed Spice
Seeded ancho chile

KOJI CURE
Salt
Filtered water
Barley Koji*

CONFIT COD ROE
Whole cod roe
Spiced Brine
Koji Cure
Confit Oil
Juniper berries

KOJI-CEP GLAZE
Butter
Lacto Koji Water* (made with Øland
  Wheat Koji*)
Cep and Birch Bark Vinegar*
Roasted Kelp Salt*
Smoked Seaweed Shoyu*

VEG FUDGE
Cucumber Juice Reduction*
Peaso Water Reduction*
Butter
Grapeseed oil

CURED EGG YOLKS
Eggs
Beef Garum*

SMOKED EGG YOLK PASTE
Cured Egg Yolks
Smoked Butter Whey*
Cep Tamari*
Dashi Reduction*
Salt

SAVORY GRANOLA
Pheasant-Spice Oil*
Toasted coriander seeds
Toasted sunflower seeds
Toasted pumpkin seeds
Toasted black peppercorns
Lemon thyme sprig
Shallot
Seeded ancho chile

LAPSANG SOUCHONG–BLACK
CURRANT TEA
Cold-Infused Dashi*
Cold-Infused Tarry Lapsang
  Souchong Tea*
Black currant shoots

SOAKED BLACK CURRANT
CAPERS
Salted Black Currant Capers*
Lapsang Souchong–Black Currant
  Tea

TO FINISH
Buckwheat-Corn Waffle
Veg Fudge
Smoked Egg Yolk Paste
Roasted Kelp Salt*
Confit Cod Roe slices
Hazelnut Oil*
Morita Chile Oil*
Koji-Cep Glaze
Pumpkin seeds from Savory Granola
Sunflower seeds from Savory
  Granola
Lemon thyme leaves
Soaked Black Currant Caper halves

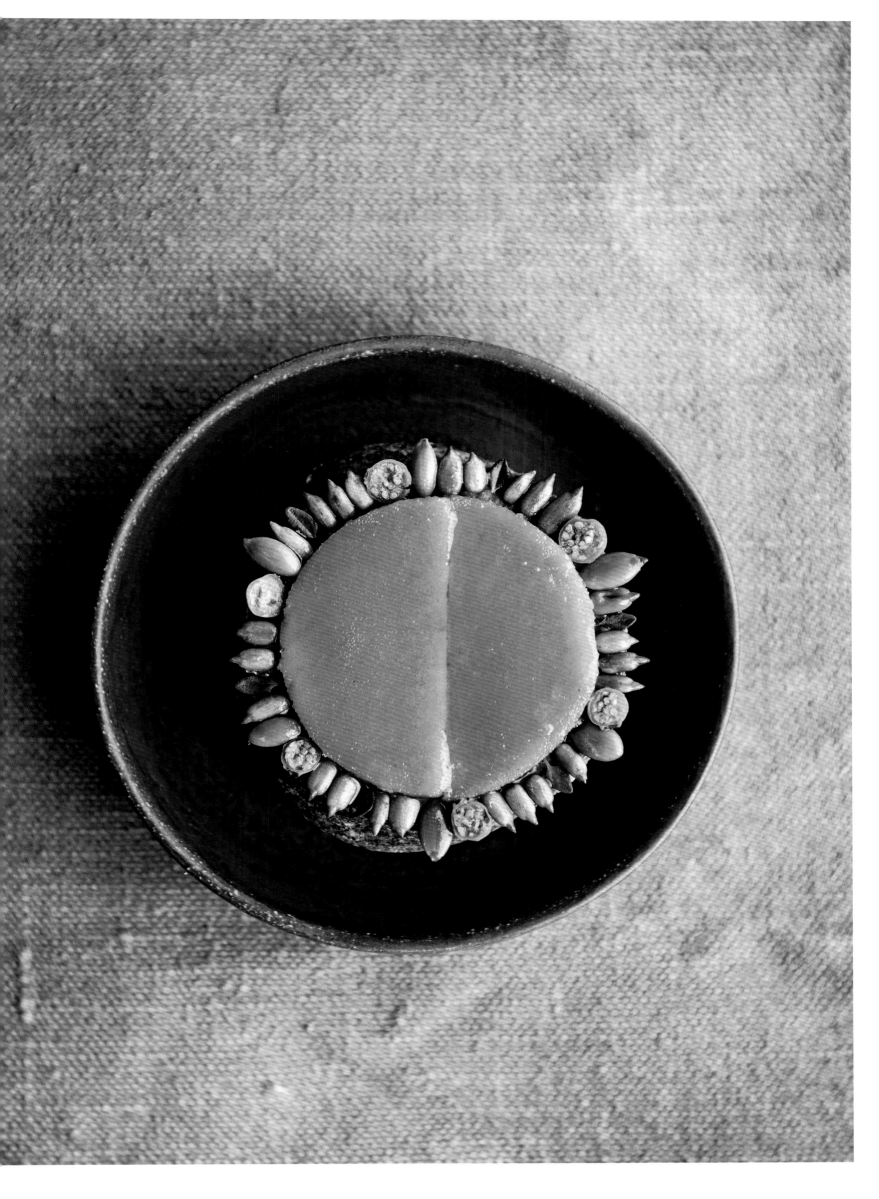

Shrimp and Dried Fruits

Raw shrimp and lacto-fermented koji water are blended and cooked until the proteins set and separate from the liquid. The clarified liquid is reduced to make a shrimp and koji reduction.

Melted butter is cooked with dried Skagen shrimp tails and dried roses. The mixture is blended and the shrimp butter is strained and reserved.

Chicken stock is reduced to a light glaze, then mixed with some of the fat reserved from making the stock, brought to a boil, and left to cool until a skin forms on top. The skin is delicately transferred from the saucepan to parchment and the parchment is placed in a skillet, where the skin is cooked until it begins to crisp. The partially crisp skin is cut into a round and dried, then brushed with the shrimp butter.

Dried Skagen shrimp tails are cooked with shrimp butter and spices and then worked in a mortar and pestle with lemon thyme, fennel reduction, tomato powder, and more butter to make a shrimp fudge.

Raw peeled Norwegian shrimp tails are arranged in the bottom of a lidded serving bowl with a selection of fruits and pickled chanterelles that have been brushed with oils and dried until chewy. Ice-cold broth is spooned around the shrimp and fruit, and a shrimp and chicken skin is dusted with lacto mirabelle and samphire powder and placed on top.

The lid is set on the bowl and blanched Norwegian shrimp heads piped with shrimp fudge are placed on the lid.

GREEN STRAWBERRY AND HONEY GLAZE
Lacto Green Strawberry* juice
Noma honey

SHRIMP AND KOJI REDUCTION
Lacto Koji Water* (made with Barley Koji*)
Peeled Skagen shrimp

ICE-CLARIFIED MUSSEL JUICE
Mussels
Filtered water

GOOSEBERRY AND MUSSEL BROTH
Green Gooseberry Water*
Ice-Clarified Mussel Juice
Black Currant Wood Oil*

DRIED SKAGEN SHRIMP TAILS
Skagen shrimp

SHRIMP BUTTER
Butter
Dried Skagen Shrimp Tails
Dried roses

SHRIMP AND CHICKEN SKINS
Whole chickens
Chicken wings
Filtered water
Shrimp Butter

LACTO MIRABELLE AND SAMPHIRE POWDER
Dried Samphire*
Dried Lacto Mirabelle Plum Skins*

PEELED NORWEGIAN SHRIMP
Fresh Norwegian shrimp

DANISH CURRY POWDER
Toasted yellow mustard seeds
Toasted coriander seeds
Toasted fennel seeds
Saffron
Sumac powder
Horseradish Powder*
Ginger Powder*
Vinegar powder

SHRIMP FUDGE
Dried Skagen Shrimp Tails
Shrimp Butter
Butter
Danish Curry Powder
Dried Ginger*
Fennel Juice Reduction*
Roasted Kelp Salt*
Lemon thyme leaves
Dried Tomato Powder*

TO FINISH
Dried Tomatoes (one with koji oil and one with chamomile oil)
Dried Lacto Mirabelle Plums* (with either koji oil or verbena oil)
Dried Lacto Plum* slices
Shrimp and Koji Reduction
Peeled Norwegian Shrimp
Dried Green Gooseberries
Dried Red Gooseberries
Dried Strawberry* slices
Dried Lacto Green Strawberries
Dried Pickled Chanterelles
Gooseberry and Mussel Broth
Shrimp and Chicken Skin
Lacto Mirabelle and Samphire Powder
Peeled Norwegian shrimp heads
3% salt brine
Shrimp Fudge

Mussel and Caviar

Dried sea lettuce and oil are blended and strained. Dashi, mushrooms, lemon thyme, and ice-clarified tomato water are cooked to make a broth.

The bottom of a lidded serving bowl is lined with citrus seaweed and other seaweeds are mounded in the bowl.

Blue mussels are briefly steamed and their fleshy "cheeks" are carved off and stacked. The stacks of mussel meat are placed in an empty mussel shell and seasoned with walnut oil, and a row of caviar is spooned along the edge of the mussels.

The seaweed-filled bowl is heated, and the mushroom and seaweed broth and a bit of the sea lettuce oil are poured into the bowl. The filled mussel shell is gently squeezed shut and positioned on the bed of seaweed, and the bowl is covered with its lid. When the diner lifts the lid, the mussel opens, as if it's just been steamed, to reveal the mussel meat and caviar.

SEA LETTUCE OIL
Dried Sea Lettuce*
Grapeseed oil

MUSHROOM AND
SEAWEED BROTH
Cold-Infused Dashi*
Fresh maitake mushrooms
Dried chanterelles
Lemon thyme leaves and tender
  stems
Ice-Clarified Tomato Water*

SEAWEED BED
Spaghetti seaweed, bladderwrack,
  or other long-stranded seaweed
  varieties
Citrus seaweed (*Flustra foliacea*)

MUSSELS
Blue mussels

TO FINISH
Mussel cheeks
Rossini Baerii caviar
Walnut Oil*
Mushroom and Seaweed Broth
Sea Lettuce Oil

Barbecued King Crab

King crab is cold-smoked until the shells are almond-scented. The body and legs are divided. The collars are mopped with a glaze of chicken wing garum, cucumber reduction, and smoked butter as they cook over hot charcoal until touched with color. The shell and meat are cut into portions, with the meat arranged neatly inside the clean body shell.

The crab legs are hot-smoked over birch bark, bathed in smoked butter, and then charcoal-grilled. The meat is freed from the leg shell, then nestled back in place, this time brushed with a glaze of deeply reduced chicken stock, ryeso water, and mushroom-kelp broth.

A tiny spoonful of ant paste, made with ants, berry spice, and black currant wood oil, and droplets of horseradish emulsion are spread onto the meat, and the top shell is set on top to form a lid to encase it all.

The crab collar is dressed with a warm sauce of mushroom-kelp broth, truffle juice, brown butter, and black truffle. The crab leg joins the collar on the plate and a sea snail shell filled with more horseradish emulsion is served alongside.

HORSERADISH EMULSION
Cold-Infused Dashi*
Koji Oil*
Horseradish juice

LIGHT CHICKEN STOCK
Whole chickens

CHICKEN GLAZE
Light Chicken Stock
Chicken carcasses

CRAB GLAZE
Ryeso Water*
Mushroom-Kelp Broth*
Chicken Glaze

COLD-SMOKED KING CRAB
King crab

BERRY SPICE
Toasted coriander seeds
Toasted fennel seeds
Toasted angelica
Dried Horseradish*
Dried Ginger*
Arctic thyme
Dried Strawberries*

ANT PASTE
Ants
Berry Spice
Black Currant Wood Oil*

COLLAR GLAZE
Chicken Wing Garum*
Cucumber Juice Reduction*
Smoked Butter*

TRUFFLED COLLAR SAUCE
Reduced Mushroom-Kelp Broth*
  (reduced to 43 °Bx)
Truffle juice
Brown Butter*
Chopped black truffle
White wine vinegar
White Wine Reduction*

HOT-SMOKED KING CRAB LEG
Birch bark
Cold-Smoked King Crab legs
Smoked Butter*

BARBECUED KING CRAB COLLAR
Cold-Smoked King Crab collar
Collar Glaze

TO FINISH
Hot-Smoked King Crab Leg
Smoked Butter*
Barbecued King Crab Collar
Truffled Collar Sauce
Crab Glaze
Ant Paste
Horseradish Emulsion

Fjæsing

Fjæsing is filleted, leaving the fillets attached at the tail, and briefly cured in a fermented koji cure.

Cod mousse is piped onto one fillet; the two fillets are sandwiched back together and the skin side is brushed with koji butter. The fish is rolled, steamed, and split in half lengthwise along the fillet to reveal the strata of the fillet and the cod mousse. This cut face is brushed with fresh barley koji butter and spread with veggie XO sauce.

Conical cabbage leaves are blanched in spiced and herbed cooking liquid, then brushed with parsley oil and dressed with vinaigrette.

Mustard-koji sauce is blended until foamy. The plate is dressed with the sauce and the fish is arranged on one side. A dressed cabbage leaf is rolled up and set on the other side.

COD MOUSSE
Cod
Egg whites
Potato starch
Salt
Double cream
Crème fraîche

FERMENTED KOJI CURE
Koji* (any type)
Filtered water
Salt

STUFFED FJÆSING
Whole fjæsing (greater weever)
Fermented Koji Cure
Cod Mousse
Fresh Barley Koji Butter*

VEGGIE XO SAUCE
Pumpkin bushi
Dried Rose Oil*
Morita Chile Oil*
Kanzuri Oil*
Semi-Dried Tomatoes*
Madagascar peppercorns
  (voatsiperifery)

MUSTARD-KOJI SAUCE
Lacto Koji Water* (made with Barley
  Koji*)
Ice-Clarified Tomato Water*
White Currant Juice*
Butter
Fresh Mustard Seed Oil*

CABBAGE BLANCHING LIQUID
Filtered water
Salt
Barley Koji*
Lovage sprigs
Lemon thyme sprigs
Parsley
Kelp
Juniper berries
Coriander seeds
Fennel seeds
Black peppercorns

CABBAGE VINAIGRETTE
White Currant Juice*
Horseradish juice
Black Currant Wood Oil*
Japanese Quince Juice*

TO FINISH
Stuffed Fjæsing
Fresh Barley Koji Butter*
Veggie XO Sauce
Mustard-Koji Sauce
Spidskål conical cabbage
Cabbage Blanching Liquid
Parsley Oil*
Cabbage Vinaigrette
Cold-Infused Kelp Salt*

Stuffed Clams

Black currant wood oil is mixed with reduced cucumber juice, reduced peaso water, and butter to make a fudge. The fudge is whipped until nicely aerated and then piped into clean clam shells and frozen.

Steamed Venus clams are nestled into four clam shells and moistened with their cooking liquid.

The frozen aerated clam shells are seasoned with rose oil and dusted with Danish curry powder, and both types of clam are set on a plate lined with empty clam shells.

VENUS CLAMS
Venus clams
Lacto Koji Water* (made with Øland
  Wheat Koji*)
Koji Oil*

DANISH CURRY POWDER
Toasted yellow mustard seeds
Toasted coriander seeds
Toasted fennel seeds
Saffron
Sumac powder
Horseradish Powder*
Ginger Powder*
Vinegar powder

BLACK CURRANT WOOD FUDGE
Cucumber Juice Reduction*
Peaso Water Reduction*
Butter
Black Currant Wood Oil*

AERATED CLAMS
Medium clam shells
Black Currant Wood Fudge

TO FINISH
Steamed Venus Clams
Clam shells
Reserved clam cooking liquid
Aerated Clams
Rose Oil*
Danish Curry Powder

Marinated Mussel

Lightly cooked blue mussel cheeks are stacked and arranged on one half of a mussel shell, then seasoned with hazelnut oil and mussel cooking liquor. Thinly sliced salted fresh hazelnuts are shingled on top.

    More mussel cheeks are stacked in the other half of the mussel shell, seasoned with Douglas fir oil, and garnished with pepper söl, a vinegared pine cone, and a few drops of mussel liquor. The mussels are served in a bowl of Irish moss.

SALTED FRESH HAZELNUTS
Fresh hazelnuts
8% salt brine
Hazelnut Oil*

MUSSELS
Blue mussels

VINEGARED PINE CONE
Jarred candied pine cones
Pine Vinegar*

TO FINISH
Mussel cheeks
Hazelnut Oil*
Sliced Salted Fresh Hazelnuts
Douglas Fir Oil*
Pepper söl
Vinegared Pine Cone
Reserved mussel cooking liquid
Irish moss

Sea Snail Salad

Dried shrimp are cooked in butter with spices, then ground in a mortar and pestle with garlic, dried tomato and lemon thyme powders, kelp salt, and fennel reduction to make a paste. The shrimp paste is blended with freeze-dried rhubarb, cucumber-kelp broth, fried herbs, chile no chile powder, and koji oil to create a rhubarb paste.

 Sea snails are cooked in koji oil with arctic thyme, then sliced very thin. The snail slices are spread with the rhubarb paste and seasoned with chicken wing garum, horseradish juice, and hot chile no chile butter. The slices are then tossed with a selection of herbs spritzed with pine vinegar. The salad is arranged in a beeswax bowl and topped with more herbs and pickled rose petals that have been brushed with a dashi reduction.

CHILE NO CHILE POWDER
Horseradish Powder*
Yellow mustard seeds
Dried Ginger Skins*
Black peppercorns
Toasted coriander seeds

CHILE NO CHILE BUTTER
Smoked Butter*
Chile No Chile Powder

DANISH CURRY POWDER
Toasted yellow mustard seeds
Toasted coriander seeds
Toasted fennel seeds
Saffron
Sumac powder
Horseradish Powder*
Ginger Powder*
Vinegar powder

DRIED SHRIMP
Skagen shrimp

LEMON THYME POWDER
Bunches of lemon thyme

SHRIMP PASTE
Garlic
Butter
Dried Shrimp
Ginger Powder*
Danish Curry Powder
Dried Tomato Powder*
Lemon Thyme Powder
Kelp Salt*
Fennel Juice Reduction*

FRIED PARSLEY
Parsley leaves
Grapeseed oil

FRIED LOVAGE
Lovage leaves
Grapeseed oil

RHUBARB PASTE
Freeze-dried rhubarb
Cucumber-Kelp Broth*
Fried Parsley
Fried Lovage
Chile No Chile Powder
Shrimp Paste
Salt
Koji Oil*

SEA SNAILS
Sea snails
Salt
Arctic thyme
Koji Oil*
Rhubarb Paste
Chile No Chile Butter

DRIED PICKLED ROSE PETALS
Cold-Infused Dashi*
Pickled Rose Petals*

HERBS
Soft thyme leaves
Soft lemon thyme leaves
Soft oregano leaves
Marjoram leaves
Lemon verbena leaves
Small wasabi leaves
Wasabi flowers
Green coriander seed halves
Soft lovage leaves
Soft parsley leaves

TO FINISH
Sea Snails
Chicken Wing Garum*
Horseradish juice
Pine Vinegar*
Herbs
Chile No Chile Butter
Dried Pickled Rose Petals

Sea Urchin and Ancient Grains

Small rectangles of koji cake are brushed with melted koji butter and grilled over charcoal. A sauce is made by whisking raw and lightly cooked egg yolks that have been cured in beef garum and seasoned with smoked butter whey. The egg yolk sauce and a bit of koji fudge are piped onto the koji cake; a sea urchin tongue is placed on top and seasoned with pine vinegar, horseradish juice, and chicken wing garum.

A bit more of the koji fudge and the egg yolk sauce is dotted onto the sea urchin tongue, along with roasted kelp salt.

SEA URCHIN
Sea urchins
2% salt brine

EGG YOLK SAUCE
Eggs
Beef Garum*
Smoked Butter Whey*

KOJI FUDGE
Cucumber Juice Reduction*
Peaso Water Reduction*
Butter
Koji Oil*

NORDIC SEAWEED SPICE MIX
Toasted coriander seeds
Yellow mustard seeds
Arctic thyme
Dried ceps
Roasted Yeast*
Fennel seeds
Salt
Koji Flour*
Roasted Kelp Powder*

KOJI BUTTER
Butter
Lacto Koji Water* (made with Øland
    Wheat Koji*)
Cold-Infused Dashi*
Double Algae Vinegar*
Chicken Wing Garum*
Nordic Seaweed Spice Mix

KOJI CAKE
Koji*

TO FINISH
Koji Cake
Koji Butter
Koji Fudge
Sea Urchin
Pine Vinegar*
Horseradish juice
Chicken Wing Garum*
Roasted Kelp Salt*
Egg Yolk Sauce

Sea Snail and
Venus Clam Skewer

Sea snails are cooked with koji oil; the cooking liquid is reserved and the snail meat is sliced.

Venus clams are sautéed in smoked butter, lemon thyme, and whisky. The Venus clam tongues are removed and the clam bellies are returned to the cooking liquid, which is simmered a bit longer for more flavor.

Egg yolks, the clam cooking liquid, and saffron are cooked over gentle heat until light and fluffy. Söl oil is whisked in to emulsify, as you would to make a hollandaise, and the sauce is lightened with whipped cream to make a sauce mousseline.

Slices of sea snail, clams, preserved truffle slices, and salted noble fir scales are threaded onto a skewer made from a sea snail shell. The skewer is warmed in reserved sea snail liquid seasoned with more clam cooking liquid, then spritzed with some pine vinegar and lightly coated with the sauce mousseline.

SEA SNAILS
Sea snails
Ice
Koji Oil*

VENUS CLAMS AND VENUS CLAM
COOKING LIQUID
Venus clams
Smoked Butter*
Lemon thyme
Danish whisky

SÖL AND SAFFRON SAUCE
MOUSSELINE
Saffron
Egg yolks
Venus Clam Cooking Liquid
Cold-Infused Kelp Salt*
Söl Oil*
Butter whey
Whipped cream

TO FINISH
Sea Snail slices
Large Venus clams
Venus Clam Cooking Liquid
Söl and Saffron Sauce Mousseline
Preserved Truffle* slices
Salted Noble Fir Cone* scales
Pine Vinegar*

OCEAN

Frozen Kombucha Salad

Rose and kiwi kombuchas are frozen in a mold to create a shell.

Softened söl is steeped in cold-infused Hojicha tea until very tender, then marinated with söl oil and seasoned with morita chile oil and salt. Freeze-dried black currant halves are marinated in black currant leaf oil, and a marjoram leaf is placed on each half. Basil and coriander leaves are marinated in marigold oil.

The frozen kombucha shell is filled with a spoonful of berry praline. The söl, black currant halves, basil leaves, and coriander leaves are layered into a stack and placed atop the berry praline.

KOMBUCHA SHELL
Rose Kombucha*
Kiwi Kombucha*

COLD-INFUSED HOJICHA TEA
Hojicha tea
Cold water

TENDER SÖL
Cold-Infused Hojicha Tea
Dried Danish söl

BERRY PRALINE
Freeze-dried black currants
Dried ceps
Söl
Madagascar peppercorns
 (voatsiperifery)
Black Currant Wood Oil*
Marigold Oil*
Kanzuri Oil*

HERB SALAD STACK
Basil leaves
Coriander leaves
Marigold Oil*
Tender Söl
Söl Oil*
Morita Chile Oil*
Freeze-dried black currant halves
Black Currant Leaf Oil*
Marjoram leaves

TO FINISH
Kombucha Shell
Berry Praline
Herb Salad Stack

Langoustine and Douglas Fir

Langoustine heads are roasted in butter with kelp and Douglas fir needles until caramelized. The langoustine butter is strained off and reserved.

Langoustine tails are smoke-grilled over charcoal and Douglas fir branches and then brushed with the langoustine butter. The tail meat is removed from the shell, glazed with more langoustine butter, and brushed with a grilled lemon thyme and kelp paste.

Langoustine heads are split and the brains are carefully removed, then mixed with chopped claw meat and seasoned with langoustine butter. This brain paste is spread inside the langoustine heads, which are seared in clarified butter until golden and seasoned with grilled lemon thyme and kelp paste.

The stuffed split head is served with the grilled tail, which is skewered with a Douglas fir branch and dusted with oxalis and pine powder.

DRIED OXALIS POWDER
Oxalis

OXALIS AND PINE POWDER
Dried Oxalis Powder
Dried Douglas Fir Powder*

SMOKED KELP
Kelp (reserved from making
  Cold-Infused Dashi*)

GRILLED LEMON THYME AND
KELP PASTE
Roasted Kelp Salt*
Finely chopped Smoked Kelp
Grilled Lemon Thyme*
Yeast Broth Reduction*
Lemon Thyme Oil*

LANGOUSTINE BUTTER
Halved langoustine heads
Langoustine claws
Butter
Kelp
Douglas fir needles

LANGOUSTINE
Extra-large langoustines
Douglas fir branches

LANGOUSTINE HEADS
Extra-large langoustine heads
Langoustine Butter

TO FINISH
Extra-large langoustine tail, tied
Douglas fir branches
Langoustine Butter
Stuffed Langoustine Head halves
Clarified butter
Grilled Lemon Thyme and Kelp Paste
Douglas fir skewer
Oxalis and Pine Powder

Crab Flatbread

A dough is rolled thin and cut into a crab shape. The flatbread is fried until puffed and brown, and a cavity is cut out of the belly area.

Lacto-fermented plums are glazed with a reduction of mushroom-kelp broth and beef garum, dried until chewy, and cut into tiny dice.

Maitake mushrooms are cold-smoked, lightly roasted in brown butter until crispy, dehydrated, and finely chopped into a crumble.

The flesh and juices from the head of a brown crab are gently cooked to create a paste.

The lacto-fermented plums and cold-smoked maitakes are combined with the crab head paste, chopped grains, pickled chanterelles, and a stew base made by emulsifying butter into muddled green coriander seed, roasted kelp salt, celery and fennel reductions, and lacto plum and tomato reduction. Chopped fresh parsley is folded into this ragout.

The ragout is spooned into the belly cavity of the crab flatbread. The layer of ragout is topped with picked crabmeat and a few drops of rose oil, and the flatbread is served with a piece of brown crab roe.

MALT FLATBREAD
Tipo "00" flour
Koji Flour*
Malt flour
Dried Rose Oil*
Butter
Salt
Kaelder Øl lager
Grapeseed oil

CHOPPED GRAINS
Spelt
Barley
Emmer
Konini wheat
Mustard seeds

CRAB HEAD PASTE
Brown crab

LACTO PLUM GLAZE
Mushroom-Kelp Broth*
Beef Garum*

DRIED LACTO PLUMS
Lacto Plums* (without skins)
Lacto Plum Glaze

LACTO PLUM AND TOMATO
REDUCTION
Lacto Plum Juice*
Ice-Clarified Tomato Water*
Kelp
Dried Ginger*

COLD-SMOKED MAITAKE
Maitake mushrooms
Brown Butter*

STEW BASE
Roasted Kelp Salt*
Green coriander seeds
Celery Juice Reduction*
Fennel Juice Reduction*
Lacto Plum and Tomato Reduction
Xantana
Butter

TO FINISH
Female brown crab (with roe,
    if available)
Chopped Grains
Crab Head Paste
Stew Base
Dried Lacto Plums
Pickled Chanterelles*
Cold-Smoked Maitake
Finely chopped parsley
Rose Oil*

Shrimp Mousse

Raw skagen shrimp are blended with cream and rose oil and then folded with whipped cream to make a mousse. The mousse is aerated and frozen under vacuum, then sliced into rectangular portions.

Dried mirabelle plum blossoms are steamed with oil and infused, and the oil is strained.

A spoonful of this mirabelle blossom oil is added to the serving plate, along with roasted kelp salt, horseradish juice, and skinned toasted beechnuts. One side of the frozen aerated shrimp mousse receives a dusting of powdered lacto-fermented plum skin. The mousse is then placed atop the other elements, undusted-side up.

PEELED SKAGEN SHRIMP
Raw Skagen shrimp

AERATED SHRIMP MOUSSE
Peeled Skagen Shrimp
Cream
Rose Oil*
Salt
Whipped cream

MIRABELLE BLOSSOM OIL
Dried mirabelle plum blossoms
Grapeseed oil

TOASTED BEECHNUTS
Beechnuts

TO FINISH
Mirabelle Blossom Oil
Roasted Kelp Salt*
Horseradish juice
Toasted Beechnuts
Aerated Shrimp Mousse
Lacto Plum Skin Powder*
Salt

Crab Gel

A cleaned beach crab shell is double-dipped in beeswax.

Stone crabs are lightly steamed; their meat is picked out and blended to create a purée, which is cooked until the proteins set and the liquid separates. The clarified liquid is mixed with gelatin and seasoned with a touch of pickled rose petal vinegar, then poured into the crab shell and chilled to set.

The crab gel is seasoned with spruce wood oil and topped with salted noble fir cone scales, roasted kelp salt, and horseradish cream.

CRAB SHELL
Small beach crab
Beeswax

CRAB BROTH
Stone crabs
Filtered water

CRAB GEL
Crab Broth
Gelatin
Pickled Rose Petal* vinegar
Salt
Crab Shell

HORSERADISH CREAM
Cream
Fresh horseradish
Horseradish juice

TO FINISH
Crab Gel
Salted Noble Fir Cone* scale halves
Spruce Wood Oil*
Roasted Kelp Salt*
Horseradish Cream

Cod Head Roast

Cod heads are butchered to produce multiple sections, each with a portion of meat and a piece of bone. The cod sections are bathed in spiced salt brine and cured in a chicken wing garum and koji cure, then briefly cooked.

Seaweed flatbread dough is rolled thin, cut into rectangles, brushed with smoked butter, and grilled until crisp.

A thin batter made with dried sea lettuce, rice flour, kelp salt, spirulina, and other seasonings is slowly fried in koji and lovage oils until crisp.

The cod head pieces, except for the throat and eye socket, are brushed with cod head glaze and broiled, then brushed with lemon thyme paste.

The cod throat and eye socket pieces are glazed in a pan with chicken garum–mushroom base and smoked butter until caramelized and sticky.

The seaweed flatbread is brushed with roasted kelp oil, spread with cep crème fraîche, and dotted with chanterelle umami paste and wasabi paste. Bits of sea lettuce crisp are added and the glazed throat and eye socket meat is arranged on top. The flatbread is garnished with wasabi flowers.

The glazed cod head pieces are arranged on a towel-lined basket and the dish is accompanied by ramekins of ant paste condiment, horseradish emulsion, and Danish curry powder.

BLACK TRUMPET MUSHROOM WATER
Dried black trumpet mushrooms
Muscovado sugar
Filtered water
Freeze-dried gooseberries

BLACK TRUMPET MUSHROOM REDUCTION
Black Trumpet Mushroom Water
Ryeso*
Sweet Koji Water Reduction*
Dryad Saddle Garum*
Potato Stock Reduction*
Birch syrup

CHICKEN GARUM-MUSHROOM BASE
Chicken Wing Garum*
Black Trumpet Mushroom Reduction
White Wine Reduction*
Lacto Cep Water*

CHICKEN WING GARUM AND KOJI CURE
Barley Koji*
Cold-Infused Dashi*
Chicken Wing Garum*

KOJI SALT
Koji* (any type)
Filtered water
Salt

CHILE NO CHILE POWDER
Horseradish Powder*
Yellow mustard seeds
Dried Ginger Skins*
Black peppercorns
Toasted coriander seeds

TOGARASHI POWDER
Chile No Chile Powder
Whole dried shrimp
Dried Samphire*
Koji Salt

BUTCHERED COD HEAD
Cod head
Spiced Brine
Chicken Wing Garum and Koji Cure

NORDIC PUNCH
Toasted green cardamom pods
Toasted juniper berries
Toasted coriander seeds
Roasted Yeast*
Ginger Powder*
Koji Flour*

SPICED FENNEL STOCK REDUCTION
Fennel bulb
Cold-Infused Dashi*
Dried roses
Douglas fir branch
Juniper wood
Toasted coriander seeds
Toasted caraway
Toasted rose hip seeds
Douglas fir needles
Lemon thyme leaves
Kelp
Togarashi Powder
Koji Oil*

GRILLED AND MARINATED LEMON THYME
Lemon thyme
Yeast Broth Reduction*
Smoked Butter*

COD HEAD GLAZE
Chicken Garum-Mushroom Base
Spiced Fennel Stock Reduction
Grilled and Marinated Lemon Thyme
Lemon thyme leaves
Xantana
Smoked Butter*

CHANTERELLE UMAMI PASTE
Pickled Chanterelles*
Peaso Water Reduction*
Roasted Kelp Salt*
Sweet Awamori Koji Water Reduction*

SPICED BRINE
Filtered water
Kelp
Söl
Fine salt
Dried Ginger Skins*
Coriander seeds
Angelica buds
Parsley
Lemon thyme leaves

LEMON THYME PASTE
Lemon thyme leaves
Yeast Broth Reduction*
Peaso Water Reduction*
Koji Oil* (made with Awamori Koji*)
Kelp Salt*
Lemon juice

RAW KELP POWDER
Kelp

SEAWEED FLATBREAD
Tipo "00" flour
Raw Kelp Powder
Spirulina powder
Beer
Roasted Kelp Oil*
Butter
Salt

SEA LETTUCE BATTER SEASONING
Dried Ginger*
Dried Douglas fir needles
Dried angelica seeds

SEA LETTUCE BATTER
Dried Sea Lettuce*
Filtered water
Kelp Salt*
Sea Lettuce Batter Seasoning
Rice flour
Spirulina powder

SEA LETTUCE CRISP
Koji Oil*
Lovage Oil*
Sea Lettuce Batter

CEP CRÈME FRAÎCHE
Cep Oil*
Crème fraîche
Lemon juice
Salt

KELP AND SAFFRON POWDER
Koji Flour*
Roasted Kelp Powder*
Kelp Salt*
Saffron

WASABI PASTE
Lemon thyme leaves
Grated Nordic wasabi
Yeast Broth Reduction*
Lemon Thyme Oil*

ANT PASTE CONDIMENT
Ants
Koji Oil* (made with Awamori Koji*)
Danish Curry Powder
Nordic Punch

HORSERADISH EMULSION
Peaso Water*
Koji Oil*
Horseradish juice

DANISH CURRY POWDER
Toasted yellow mustard seeds
Toasted coriander seeds
Toasted fennel seeds
Saffron
Sumac powder
Horseradish Powder*
Ginger Powder*
Vinegar powder

TO FINISH
Butchered Cod Head
Cod Head Glaze
Lemon Thyme Paste
Cod throat and eye socket pieces
Chicken Garum-Mushroom Base
Smoked Butter*
Seaweed Flatbread
Roasted Kelp Oil*
Cep Crème Fraîche
Chanterelle Umami Paste
Wasabi Paste
Sea Lettuce Crisp
Wasabi flowers
Horseradish juice
Lemon juice
Kelp and Saffron Powder
Ant Paste Condiment
Horseradish Emulsion
Danish Curry Powder

Caviar and Kelp

Braised kelp is cut into rounds and the rounds are split into thin, flexible discs. The kelp discs are cut in half, brushed with roasted kelp oil, and rolled into tiny cones. The cones are arranged on a serving plate, alternating with toasted beechnuts. A scoop of caviar anchors the center of the dish, and the plate is dressed with lacto koji butter sauce and a few drops of hazelnut oil.

BRAISED KELP CONES
Kelp (reserved from making
  Mushroom-Kelp Broth*)
Roasted Kelp Oil*

TOASTED BEECHNUTS
Beechnuts

LACTO KOJI BUTTER SAUCE
Lacto Koji Water* (made with Øland
  Wheat Koji*)
Butter
Filtered water
Xantana

TO FINISH
Braised Kelp Cones
Toasted Beechnuts
Rossini Gold caviar
Lacto Koji Butter Sauce
Hazelnut Oil*

Tender Squid

Extra-large squid are cleaned and peeled, cured with kelp, scored on both sides, and cut into small pieces.

The squid pieces are immersed in plum kernel water to warm them, and then brushed on one side with fresh barley koji butter, ant paste, and two drops of squid garum. The other side is brushed with more fresh barley koji butter, dusted with squid spice mix, and finished with mussel-squid reduction.

SQUID
Extra-large Danish squid
Kelp sediment (reserved from making
  Roasted Kelp Oil*)

SQUID SPICE MIX
Pumpkin bushi
Madagascar peppercorns
  (voatsiperifery)
Cold-Infused Kelp Salt*
Dried ceps

ANT PASTE
Koji Oil* (made with Rice Koji*)
Ants

MUSSEL-SQUID REDUCTION
Ice-Clarified Mussel Juice*
Pine Dashi*
Squid Garum*
Aquavit-Seawater Vinegar*
Fresh Barley Koji Butter*

TO FINISH
Squid
Plum Kernel Water*
Squid Spice Mix
Ant Paste
Squid Garum*
Mussel-Squid Reduction
Fresh Barley Koji Butter*

Lobster with Fragrant Flowers

Smoked fish broth base is made by simmering cold-infused dashi with caramelized shallots deglazed with white wine, along with deeply smoked and roasted cod bones and cod heads. Butter and elderflower peaso are emulsified into the broth base to make a smoked fish beurre blanc.

Danish lobster is cooked and cleaned, and the head separated and reserved, with brains and roe intact. The tail and claw meat is removed from the shell.

To finish, hot and foamy smoked fish beurre blanc is generously spooned onto the plate, a butter-warmed half lobster tail and claw meat are arranged on the sauce and salted, and a few peeled Swedish grapes coated in elderflower oil are scattered over the sauce. A sorrel leaf is spritzed with sorrel juice spray and tucked in between the lobster pieces, and the dish is garnished with petals and blossoms from several seasonal flowers.

SMOKED FISH BROTH BASE
Cod bones
Cod heads
Large shallots
White wine
Cold-Infused Dashi*

PEELED SWEDISH GRAPES
Swedish green grapes
Elderflower Oil*

SMOKED FISH BEURRE BLANC
Butter
Elderflower Peaso*
Smoked Fish Broth Base
White Wine Reduction*
White wine vinegar

COOKED DANISH LOBSTER
Danish blue lobster

SORREL JUICE SPRAY
Sorrel leaves

TO FINISH
Smoked Fish Beurre Blanc
Butter
Cooked Danish Lobster
Salt
Peeled Swedish Grapes
Sorrel leaves
Sorrel Juice Spray
Seasonal blossoms

Seaweed and Shrimp Salad

Skagen shrimp are blended with cream and folded with more whipped cream to create an aerated mousse, which is then frozen and cut into cubes.

Sugar kelp is cooked in ice-clarified mussel juice, tomato water, lemon juice, and sugar kelp marinade until tender, then torn into small pieces and dressed with more sugar kelp marinade.

The serving bowl is swiped with seasoned parsley purée. Three cubes of shrimp mousse are arranged in the bowl, seasoned with roasted kelp salt and shrimp garum, and draped with pieces of cooked sugar kelp.

AERATED SHRIMP MOUSSE
Skagen shrimp
Cream
Salt
Whipped cream

SUGAR KELP MARINADE
White Currant Juice*
Koji Oil*
Rose Oil*

MARINATED SUGAR KELP
Dried sugar kelp
Ice-Clarified Mussel Juice*
Ice-Clarified Tomato Water*
Lemon juice
Sugar Kelp Marinade

PARSLEY PURÉE
Parsley leaves

SEASONED PARSLEY PURÉE
Parsley Purée
Smoked Seaweed Shoyu*
Parsley Oil*
Peaso Water Reduction*
Fava Rice Shoyu*
Salt

TO FINISH
Aerated Shrimp Mousse
Shrimp-Tarry Lapsang Souchong
  Garum*
Marinated Sugar Kelp
Roasted Kelp Salt*
Seasoned Parsley Purée

Scallop Steak

Live Norwegian scallops are removed from their shells and gently torn into portions and dressed with kelp butter. The sauced scallop is seasoned with crushed black pepper and black currant wood oil, then placed on a black currant wood mat brushed with more black currant wood oil, along with a little pile of horseradish paste, a slice of the abductor muscle, and a piece of the scallop roe seasoned with horseradish oil and cold-infused kelp salt. The black currant wood mat is presented on a piece of sugar kelp.

HORSERADISH PASTE
Grated fresh horseradish
Horseradish Oil*

KELP BUTTER
Roasted Kelp Salt*
Filtered water
Butter

SUGAR KELP MAT
Dried or fresh sugar kelp

TO FINISH
Live Norwegian scallop with roe
Kelp Butter
Toasted black peppercorns
Black currant wood mat
Black Currant Wood Oil*
Horseradish Paste
Horseradish Oil*
Cold-Infused Kelp Salt*
Sugar Kelp Mat

Smoked Fish Broth

Cold-smoked turbot bones, dried mushrooms, kelp, and lemon thyme are simmered to make a broth. The broth is strained, simmered with freeze-dried green gooseberries, dried ginger, cold-smoked maitake, and dried ceps, then clarified with egg whites. This clarified broth is then infused with lemon thyme and lemon verbena.

Two cod eyes and a fin are cold-smoked and arranged in a serving bowl, along with a few drops of maitake oil and a bouquet of wild herbs. The hot smoked fish broth is poured into the bowl at the table.

COLD-SMOKED MAITAKE
Maitake mushrooms

SMOKED FISH BROTH, FIRST
INFUSION
Turbot bones
Cold filtered water
Lemon thyme
Dried ceps
Dried morels
Kelp
White Wine Reduction*

SMOKED FISH BROTH, SECOND
INFUSION
Freeze-dried green gooseberries
Dried Ginger*
Cold-Smoked Maitake
Dried ceps

CLARIFICATION
Egg whites

SMOKED FISH BROTH, THIRD
INFUSION
Lemon thyme sprigs
Lemon verbena sprigs

COLD-SMOKED COD
Cod eye
Cod fin

HERB BOUQUET
Greek cress
Wild chervil
Yarrow sprigs

TO FINISH
Cold-Smoked Cod eye
Cold-Smoked Cod fin
Maitake Oil*
Herb Bouquet
Smoked Fish Broth

Grilled Lobster Head

Bunches of lemon thyme are brushed with smoked butter and grilled, and the leaves are picked from the stems. Fresh butter is infused with the grilled lemon thyme, then strained.

Danish blue lobster heads are trimmed to reveal the brains, which are brushed with grilled lemon thyme butter and gently grilled over indirect heat until set like a custard.

The lobster head is finished with rose butter and pasilla-morita chile paste.

CHARRED GARLIC CLOVES
Garlic

PASILLA-MORITA CHILE PASTE
Seeded pasilla chiles
Seeded morita chiles
Grapeseed oil
Charred Garlic Cloves
BBQ Duck Garum*
Egg White Garum*
Smoked Beef Garum*

GRILLED LEMON THYME BUTTER
Grilled Lemon Thyme*
Butter

ROSE BUTTER
Roasted Kelp Salt*
Yeast Broth Reduction*
Rose Oil*
Grilled Lemon Thyme Butter

TO FINISH
Danish blue lobster head
Grilled Lemon Thyme Butter
Pasilla-Morita Chile Paste
Rose Butter

Cod Collar Schnitzel

A cod head is butchered to obtain a cod collar with a length of bone attached, which is frenched. This piece is submerged in dashi brine and cold-smoked.

The smoked cod collar is dusted with rice flour, dipped in beer batter, and deep-fried in grapeseed oil, taking care to keep the bone free of batter and oil. The fried cod is seasoned with salt and rose spice mix. Crème fraîche is piped on the cod and topped with caviar.

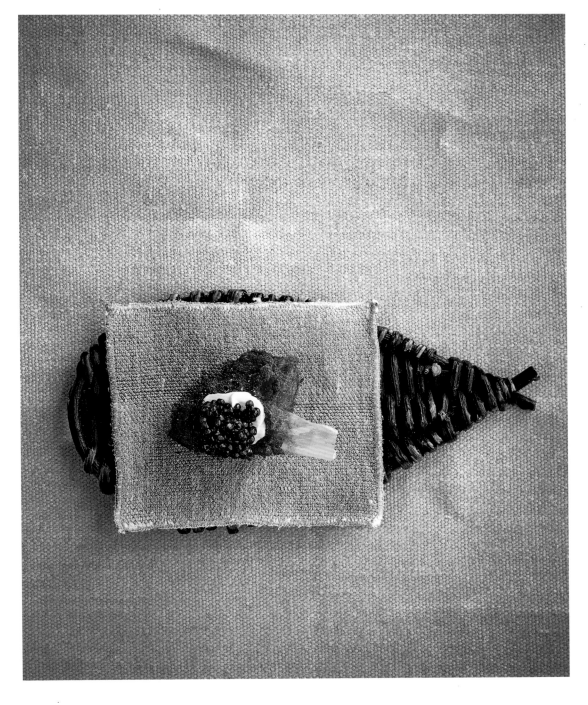

DASHI BRINE
Cold-Infused Dashi*
2% salt brine

COD COLLAR
Cod head
Dashi Brine

ROSE SPICE MIX
Roasted Kelp Powder*
Seeded morita chiles
Dried ceps
Dried rose petals
Dried Ginger*
Dried Horseradish*
Toasted black peppercorns
Toasted coriander seeds
Toasted fennel seeds

BEER BATTER
Rice flour
All-purpose flour
Baking powder
Roasted Kelp Flour*
Vodka
Noma honey
Beer (pilsner)

TO FINISH
Cod Collar
Rice flour
Beer Batter
Grapeseed oil
Salt
Rose Spice Mix
Crème fraîche
Black Label Rossini caviar

Perch Pepper Steak

Perch fillets are brined in spiced salt brine, marinated in a corn miso cure, and lacquered with warm smoked shoyu kelp butter sauce. The fillets are then showered with coarsely cracked black peppercorns and salt, and served on a piece of kelp. A ramekin of horseradish juice accompanies the perch.

SPICED BRINE
Filtered water
Kelp
Söl
Fine salt
Dried Ginger Skins*
Coriander seeds
Angelica buds
Parsley
Lemon thyme sprigs

PERCH
Whole perch

RAW KELP POWDER
Kelp

CORN MISO CURE
Fresh Corn Miso*
Raw Kelp Powder
Cold-Infused Dashi*
Toasted coriander seeds
Smoked Seaweed Shoyu*

CURED PERCH
Perch fillets
Corn Miso Cure

SMOKED SHOYU KELP BUTTER
SAUCE
Butter
Roasted Kelp Salt*
Smoked Seaweed Shoyu*
Mushroom-Kelp Broth*

TO FINISH
Cracked toasted black peppercorns
Cured Perch
Horseradish juice
Smoked Shoyu Kelp Butter Sauce
Soaked kelp (reserved from making
   Cold-Infused Dashi*)

King Crab Salad

Kale leaves are torn into pieces and fried until crisp. Baby Gem lettuce leaves are trimmed down almost to the ribs, which are cut into short pieces.

Sunflower seeds are roasted in butter with Danish curry powder and other seasonings, then ground into a paste. Freeze-dried rhubarb is rehydrated in dashi, seasoned with berry spice, and caramelized in koji oil. The caramelized rhubarb is blended with the sunflower seed paste and fried parsley to make king crab salad paste.

The lower joints of king crab legs are brushed with smoked butter and grilled briefly over hot charcoal. The meat is removed and piped with the king crab salad paste.

The leaves and tender stems of a variety of fresh herbs are tossed with green coriander seed halves and dressed with pine vinegar and horseradish juice.

The lettuce ribs are blanched in a koji emulsion, combined with the fried kale leaves and most of the crab, and dressed in hot melted spiced king crab butter. The dressed fresh herbs are added and everything is gently shaken to mix, then transferred to a serving dish in which a horn spoon has been placed. The salad is topped with the remaining crabmeat and select herb flowers and pretty tops.

SPICE MIX
Toasted coriander seeds
Toasted fennel seeds
Toasted yellow mustard seeds
Arctic thyme leaves
Dried Horseradish*

SPICED KING CRAB BUTTER
Smoked Butter*
Roasted Kelp Salt*
Spice Mix
Peaso Water Reduction*
King Crab Garum*

DANISH CURRY POWDER
Toasted yellow mustard seeds
Toasted coriander seeds
Toasted fennel seeds
Saffron
Sumac powder
Dried Horseradish*
Dried Ginger*
Vinegar powder

SUNFLOWER SEED PASTE
Sunflower seeds
Butter
Ginger Powder*
Danish Curry Powder
Celery Juice Reduction*
Dried Tomato Powder*
Roasted Kelp Salt*
Nordic Shoyu*
Salt

BERRY SPICE
Dried Horseradish*
Dried Ginger*
Arctic thyme leaves
Toasted coriander seeds
Toasted angelica seeds
Toasted fennel seeds
Dried Strawberries*

KING CRAB SALAD PASTE
Freeze-dried rhubarb
Cold-Infused Dashi*
Berry Spice
Koji Oil*
Fried Parsley Leaves
Sunflower Seed Paste

LEAVES AND FLOWERS
Soft parsley
Soft lovage
Oregano
Marjoram
Oxalis
Golden oxalis
Soft thyme
Chickweed
Lemon verbena
Watercress
Wasabi flowers
Green coriander seed halves

FRIED KALE
Green kale
Koji Oil*

KOJI EMULSION
Lacto Koji Water* (made with Øland
    Wheat Koji*)
Butter

KING CRAB LEG MEAT
Lower king crab legs
Smoked Butter*
King Crab Salad Paste

TO FINISH
King Crab Leg Meat
Baby Gem Lettuce Ribs
Koji Emulsion
Fried Kale
Spiced King Crab Butter
Leaves and flowers
Pine Vinegar*
Horseradish juice

Cod Bladder

Cod bladders are cooked with koji oil, Japanese quince brine, and dashi, then sliced into ribbons.

Pumpkin seeds are cooked with squid garum and then milled to extract their oil.

The ribbons of cod bladder are layered into a stack with Japanese quince paste and set on top of turnip brunoise dressed with the pumpkin seed and squid garum oil. The cod bladder is topped with rose hip quarters, slices of brined Japanese quince, and sea buckthorn berries. A sauce of clarified mussel cooking liquid and more Japanese quince brine is poured around the turnips and seasoned with mixed chile oil, pumpkin seed and squid garum oil, and some Jun spice mix.

COD BLADDER COMPRESSION
LIQUID
Brine from Brined Japanese Quince*
Cold-Infused Dashi*

COD BLADDERS
Cod bladders
Koji Oil*
Cod Bladder Compression Liquid

ICE-CLARIFIED MUSSEL JUICE
Mussels
Filtered water

MUSSEL AND QUINCE SAUCE
Ice-Clarified Mussel Juice*
Brine from Brined Japanese Quince*

TURNIP BRUNOISE
White turnip
Koji Oil*

JAPANESE QUINCE SLICES
Brined Japanese Quince*

ROSE HIP
Rose hip

MIXED CHILE OIL
Ancho Chile Oil*
Árbol Chile Oil*

PUMPKIN SEED AND SQUID
GARUM OIL
Pumpkin seeds
Squid Garum*

JUN SPICE MIX
Dried ceps
Dried chanterelles
Black peppercorns
Juniper berries
Angelica
Freeze-dried lingonberry
Coriander seeds
Arctic thyme
Roasted Kelp*

JAPANESE QUINCE PASTE
Japanese quince
Butter
Dried Carrot Flowers*

TO FINISH
Cod Bladders
Japanese Quince Paste
Turnip Brunoise
Pumpkin Seed and Squid Garum Oil
Mussel and Quince Sauce
Koji Oil*
Rose Hip quarters
Brined Japanese Quince* slices
Unripe sea buckthorn berries
Mixed Chile Oil
Jun Spice Mix

Whole Cooked Langoustine

A large Norwegian langoustine is carefully cut into pieces. The head, with brains intact, is steamed, the claws are blanched, the meat is removed from the legs, and the tail is tied to keep it straight. The claw meat is then removed from the shells and the head is trimmed to make the brains more accessible to the diner.

The tail is gently cooked in butter, and all the langoustine pieces, except the head, are brushed with fresh koji butter. The inside of the head is brushed with lango head butter and seasoned with morita chile oil and salt. All the pieces are arranged on a warm plate, and the claws and knuckles are seasoned with pine salt. A sea snail shell full of mussel garum sauce and a frozen quince wedge are served on a plate to the side.

MUSSEL GARUM SAUCE
Blue Mussel Garum*
Butter
White wine vinegar
Xantana

LANGO HEAD BUTTER
Dashi Reduction*
Yeast Broth Reduction*
Butter
Roasted Kelp Salt*

NORWEGIAN LANGOUSTINE
Live extra-large Norwegian
   langoustine

TO FINISH
Langoustine meat
Langoustine tail
Butter
Fresh Barley Koji Butter*
Lango Head Butter
Morita Chile Oil*
Salt
Pine Salt*
Mussel Garum Sauce
Japanese quince wedge (frozen)

Salt Cod Pie

Icelandic salt cod is soaked in water to remove excess salt, then cooked (with the skin) in sparkling water until soft. The cooking liquid is reserved. The softened cod and its skin are whipped with koji oil and cooking liquid as needed until emulsified.

Full-fat milk is reduced in a wide nonstick skillet until all that's left is a skin, which is slowly cooked until lightly caramelized. The caramelized milk skin is punched into a round to be used as the pie "crust."

Sliced leeks are shallow-steamed in salted water, then mixed with celery leaf oil, salt, and pepper. The caramelized milk skin is layered with some leek filling, whipped Icelandic salt cod, elderflower oil, and elderflower peaso mix, folded into a half circle, and fried until browned and puffed.

To finish, the pie is topped with oyster leaves affixed with a few dots of elderflower peaso mix.

WHIPPED ICELANDIC SALT COD
Icelandic salt cod
Filtered water
Sparkling water
Koji Oil*

CARAMELIZED MILK SKINS
3.5% milk

COOKED LEEKS
Leeks
.7% salt brine

LEEK FILLING
Cooked Leeks
Celery Leaf Oil*
Cracked toasted black peppercorns
Sea salt

ELDERFLOWER PEASO MIX
Elderflower Peaso*
Smoked Seaweed Shoyu*

SALT COD PIE
Caramelized Milk Skin
Cooked Leeks
Whipped Icelandic Salt Cod
Cracked toasted black peppercorns
Elderflower Oil*
Elderflower Peaso Mix
Flour slurry

TO FINISH
Salt Cod Pie
Oyster leaves
Elderflower Peaso Mix
Cracked toasted black peppercorns
Grapeseed oil

Crispy Sweet Shrimp

Dried meadowsweet, angelica seeds, rose hips, and red gooseberries
are cooked with chamomile oil into a compote, which is spread over a
shrimp-shaped stencil and dried into a fruit leather. The fruit leather
shrimp parts are assembled using a bit of rose hip flesh as an adhesive,
and juniper berry skins are cut to create the eyes. The fruit leather
shrimp shell is dried until crisp.

The crispy fruit leather shrimp shell is filled with marinated raw
Skagen shrimp cut into quarters, and the marinated shrimp are piped
with dots of plum and tomato paste and adorned with green coriander
seeds, oregano leaves, and fennel and parsley flowers. The shrimp shell
is brushed with black currant wood oil and arranged in a bowl lined
with dried Irish moss.

ROSE HIP FLESH
Rose hips

CRISPY SHRIMP LEATHER
Rose Hip Flesh
Red gooseberries
Chamomile Oil*
Dried meadowsweet
Dried angelica seeds
Juniper berries

SHRIMP MARINADE
Lemon thyme
Sunflower Seed and Beef Garum Oil*
Lemon Thyme Oil*
Roasted Kelp Salt*
Liquid from Salted Green
  Gooseberry Capers*
Arctic thyme

SEMI-DRIED LACTO PLUMS
Lacto Plums*
Koji Oil*

PLUM AND TOMATO PASTE
Semi-Dried Tomatoes*
Semi-Dried Lacto Plums

SKAGEN SHRIMP
Raw Skagen shrimp
Shrimp Marinade

TO FINISH
Crispy Shrimp Leather
Skagen Shrimp
Plum and Tomato Paste
Green coriander seed halves
Lemon thyme leaves
Small oregano leaves
Fennel flower crowns
Parsley flower florets
Black Currant Wood Oil*
Dried Irish moss

Gobble and Seaweeds

Gobble jelly is made from squid water mixed with salted sloeberry–
infused dashi and lightly set with kuzu and agar.

Crème fraîche is combined with a black currant and kelp reduction
and lightly set with gelatin.

Sugar kelp is cooked and torn into irregular shapes. Irish moss is
cooked in cucumber-kelp broth and then marinated in Nordic mette
paste, chicken wing garum, and kelp oil.

The black currant kelp crème fraîche is painted onto a serving bowl
in the shape of a jellyfish brain, and lumpfish roe is spread in a ring
around the jellyfish shape. A dome of gobble jelly is positioned over the
roe and two flat rounds of gobble jelly are laid onto the dome.

Arranged around the edge of the plate are pieces of steamed sugar
kelp seasoned with horseradish juice and kelp oil, and little clusters of
steamed Irish moss seasoned with horseradish juice, roasted kelp oil,
and chicken wing garum and spritzed with pine vinegar. More small
bunches of cleaned, but not dressed, seaweed varieties join the sugar
kelp and Irish moss around the plate, and the dish is finished with
lemon thyme–ant broth, black currant wood oil, and spritzes of pine
vinegar.

SQUID WATER
Filtered water
Danish squid

GOBBLE BASE LIQUID
Cold-Infused Dashi*
Pumpkin bushi
Salted Sloeberries*
White wine vinegar
Squid Water

GOBBLE JELLY
Gobble Base Liquid
Kuzu starch
Agar
Grapeseed oil

BLACK CURRANT AND KELP
REDUCTION
Filtered water
Kelp
Dried black trumpet mushrooms
Freeze-dried black currants
Dried juniper needles (with stem
  is fine)
Söl
Muscovado sugar
Freeze-dried blueberries
Freeze-dried blackberries
Freeze-dried gooseberries

BLACK CURRANT KELP CRÈME
FRAÎCHE
Black Currant and Kelp Reduction
Crème fraîche
Gelatin

SQUID PEASO WATER REDUCTION
Peaso Water*
Danish squid

STEAMED SUGAR KELP
Fresh sugar kelp
Peaso Water*
Crushed white currants
Sweet Koji Water Reduction*
Squid Peaso Water Reduction
Kelp Salt*

NORDIC METTE PASTE
Lemon thyme leaves
Sunflower Seed and Beef Garum Oil*
Lemon Thyme Oil*
Liquid from Salted Green
  Gooseberry Capers*
Kelp Salt*

STEAMED IRISH MOSS
Irish moss
Cucumber-Kelp Broth*
Nordic Mette Paste
Chicken Wing Garum*
Roasted Kelp Oil*

LEMON THYME-ANT BROTH
Filtered water
Lemon thyme leaves
Ants

LUMPFISH ROE
Salt brine
Lumpfish roe

TO FINISH
Steamed Irish Moss
Horseradish juice
Roasted Kelp Oil*
Chicken Wing Garum*
Pine Vinegar*
Steamed Sugar Kelp
Black Currant Kelp Crème Fraîche
Lumpfish Roe
Gobble Jelly semi-sphere
Gobble Jelly
Sea lettuce
Bloodred ribbed seaweed
  (Delesseria sanguinea)
Sea grass
Gaffeltang (Furcellaria lumbricalis)
Bladderwrack seaweed
Lemon Thyme-Ant Broth
Black Currant Wood Oil*

Mexican Oregano with Oyster Paste

Fresh gigas oysters are puréed and emulsified with parsley leaves and parsley oil, and freshened with a bit of lemon. The oyster liquor is strained and reserved.

Thick pieces of kombu are braised until just tender in a stock flavored with dried mushrooms, lacto-fermented cep water, lingonberries, and sugar. The kombu is cut into diamond shapes and dusted with a powder made from dried samphire, dried sea lettuce, and roasted kelp salt.

A Mexican oregano leaf is brushed on one side with the oyster emulsion and sprayed on the other with reserved oyster liquor. Rocks are arranged on the serving plate and the oregano leaf is placed on the rocks, with a dusted kombu diamond placed on either side of the spine. A dot of oyster emulsion is piped into the center of a rosette of oyster leaf plant, which then receives a drop of horseradish juice, a spray of oyster liquor, and a few grains of salt. The rosette is then positioned to look as if it is growing from under the rocks with other wild beach plants, such as purslane, ice plant, and beach mustard.

OYSTER EMULSION
Gigas oysters
Grapeseed oil
Parsley leaves
Parsley Oil*
Salt
Lemon juice

BRAISED KELP
Kelp reserved from Mushroom-Kelp
  Broth*

JUN-SAN-NORI POWDER
Roasted Kelp Salt*
Dried Sea lettuce*

BEACH PLANT POWDER
Dried Samphire*
Jun-San-Nori Powder

TO FINISH
Mexican oregano leaf
Oyster leaf rosette
Purslane
Ice plant
Beach mustard
Braised Kelp parallelograms
Beach Plant Powder
Oyster Emulsion
Beach horseradish leaves
Horseradish juice
Oyster liquor, in a spray bottle

Trout Roe and Beach Herbs

Egg yolks are cured in beef garum, then blended with smoked butter whey and kimchi tamari to make a sauce. Trout roe is lightly brined and then folded with the egg yolk sauce.

    Purslane tips are lightly sautéed in koji oil until tender.

    The roe is placed in a serving bowl and surrounded by a variety of seasonal beach greens that have been lightly dressed in juniper rose vinaigrette. Rose and yeast sauce is spooned around the trout roe, and the roe is decorated with marigold petals seasoned with roasted kelp salt and salt.

CURED EGG YOLKS
Eggs
Beef Garum*

EGG YOLK SAUCE
Cured Egg Yolks (passed)
Kimchi Tamari*
Smoked Butter Whey*
Beef Garum*
Salt

ROSE AND YEAST SAUCE
Lacto Koji Water* (made with Rice Koji*)
Yeast Broth*
Butter
Rose Oil*
Xantana

JUNIPER ROSE VINAIGRETTE
Maitake Garum*
Green coriander seeds
Juniper skins
Rose Oil*
Lemon juice

TROUT ROE
6% salt brine
2% salt brine
Trout roe sac

BEACH GREENS
Beach mustard leaves and flower
Purslane tips
Koji Oil*
Beach cress flowers
Chickweed
Yarrow flowers
Watercress
Ground elder
Wood sorrel

TO FINISH
Trout Roe
Egg Yolk Sauce
Roasted Kelp Salt*
Rose Oil*
Marigold (*Calendula officinalis*) petals
Beach Greens
Purslane tips
Koji Oil*
Juniper Rose Vinaigrette
Rose and Yeast Sauce
Salt

Trout Roe and Egg Yolk

Raw shrimp and lacto-fermented koji water are blended and cooked until the proteins set and separate from the liquid. The clarified liquid is reduced, then mixed with dashi to create a cure.

A few lightly cooked egg yolks are cured in the shrimp, koji, and kelp cure, and other yolks are cured between sheets of kelp. All the cured yolks are whisked with more of the cure until smooth to make a sauce.

The trout roe is lightly cured in dashi infused with golden trout bushi.

Peaso paste is piped onto a serving plate in a sea star shape and the outline is filled in with the egg yolk sauce. The trout roe is distributed over the surface and decorated with small shards of plum crisp, made by blending lacto-fermented plums and freeze-dried lingonberries and blueberries, spreading the paste thin, and drying it until crisp.

The sea star is finished with pumpkin seed oil.

PEASO PASTE
Peaso*
Roasted Kelp Salt*
Cold-Infused Dashi*
Peaso Water Reduction*

SHRIMP AND KOJI REDUCTION
Lacto Koji Water* (made with
   Barley Koji*)
Peeled Skagen shrimp

SHRIMP, KOJI, AND KELP CURE
Shrimp and Koji Reduction
Cold-Infused Dashi*

EGG YOLK SAUCE
Eggs
Shrimp, Koji, and Kelp Cure
Kelp

KELP AND TROUT BUSHI DASHI
Golden Trout Bushi*
Cold-Infused Dashi*

TROUT ROE
Trout roe sac
2% salt brine
Kelp and Trout Bushi Dashi

PLUM CRISP
Lacto Plums*
Freeze-dried lingonberries
Freeze-dried blueberries

TO FINISH
Trout Roe
Peaso Paste
Egg Yolk Sauce
Pumpkin Seed Oil*
Plum Crisp

Fried Grey Shrimp Ravioli

Sea lettuce is laid out, liberally lubricated with parsley-koji oil, and marinated under vacuum.

Freeze-dried gooseberries are steamed with koji oil, maitake garum, freeze-dried rhubarb, dashi, lemon verbena, and lemon thyme to confit.

Lightly cooked egg yolks are cured in beef garum and smoked seaweed shoyu, then whisked until smooth to make a paste.

Fjord shrimp are dredged in a seasoned mix of flours, fried until crisp, and seasoned with Jun spice mix.

A square sea lettuce sheet is spread with the cured egg yolk paste and then piped with ancho chile fudge. Two fried shrimp and two confit gooseberry halves are placed on the fudge and the sea lettuce is folded over to make a packet. The packet is trimmed and brushed with more parsley-koji oil.

PARSLEY-KOJI OIL
Koji Oil*
Parsley

SEA LETTUCE SHEET
Fresh sea lettuce
Parsley-Koji Oil

ANCHO CHILE FUDGE
Butter
Peaso Water Reduction*
Ancho Chile Oil*
Yeast Broth Reduction*

CONFIT GOOSEBERRIES
Freeze-dried gooseberries
Koji Oil*
Maitake Garum*
Freeze-dried rhubarb
Cold-Infused Dashi*
Lemon verbena leaves
Lemon thyme sprig

FLOUR MIX
Rice flour
Cornstarch
Potato starch
Baking powder
Roasted Kelp Powder*
Koji Flour*
Salt

CURED EGG YOLK PASTE
Beef Garum*
Smoked Seaweed Shoyu*
Eggs

JUN SPICE MIX
Dried ceps
Dried chanterelles
Black peppercorns
Juniper berries
Angelica buds
Freeze-dried lingonberry
Coriander seeds
Arctic thyme
Roasted Kelp Powder*

FRIED SHRIMP
Fjord shrimp
Flour Mix
Jun Spice Mix
Salt

TO FINISH
Sea Lettuce Sheet
Cured Egg Yolk Paste
Ancho Chile Fudge
Confit Gooseberries
Fried Shrimp
Ancho Chile Oil*
Parsley-Koji Oil

Crab and Seaweed Broth

Cold-smoked turbot bones, lemon thyme, dried mushrooms, and kelp are simmered to make a broth. The broth is strained, then simmered with freeze-dried green gooseberries, dried ginger, and more dried mushrooms until reduced by half, and finally clarified using egg whites. The clarified smoked fish broth is then infused with lemon thyme and lemon verbena.

Stone crabs are steamed and their meat puréed; the purée is cooked until the proteins set and the liquid separates, leaving a clarified broth.

The smoked fish broth and crab broth are combined and enriched with butter and cream, poured into a bowl filled with lemon thyme and seaweed, and spritzed with citrus seaweed distillate.

COLD-SMOKED MAITAKE
Maitake mushrooms

SMOKED FISH BROTH, FIRST
INFUSION
Turbot bones
Filtered water
Lemon thyme leaves
Dried ceps
Dried morels
Kelp
White Wine Reduction*

SMOKED FISH BROTH, SECOND
INFUSION
Freeze-dried green gooseberries
Dried Ginger*
Cold-Smoked Maitake
Dried ceps

CLARIFICATION
Egg whites

SMOKED FISH BROTH, THIRD
INFUSION
Lemon thyme sprigs
Lemon verbena sprigs

CLARIFIED CRAB STOCK
Stone crabs
Filtered water

CITRUS SEAWEED DISTILLATE
Citrus seaweed (*Flustra foliacea*)
Ethanol (60% ABV)

SEAWEED BED
Irish moss
Sea lettuce
Gaffeltang (*Furcellaria lumbricalis*)
Citrus seaweed (*Flustra foliacea*)
Lemon thyme

CRAB BROTH
Smoked Fish Broth
Clarified Crab Stock
White Wine Reduction*
Cream
Butter
Lemon juice
Salt

TO FINISH
Seaweed Bed
Citrus Seaweed Distillate
Crab Broth

Mussel Eye and Quail Egg

A large blue mussel is lightly steamed, removed from the shell, and then infused into cold-infused Lapsang souchong tea.

A pickled and smoked soft-boiled quail egg is warmed in melted butter, then one side is sliced to reveal the yolk.

Lovage and parsley leaves are gently wilted in smoked butter and kelp–Lapsang souchong tea until tender, then finely chopped.

The mussel is piped with smoked egg yolk paste and stuffed with a bit of the chopped greens, and the quail egg is tucked inside, with the yolk facing up. Cold-infused kelp salt and koji fudge are placed on either side of the quail egg, which is then seasoned with ancho chile paste.

A horse mussel shell is brushed with spiced smoked butter, with a bit more spooned into the center of the shell, and then generously dusted with cep and chanterelle spice mix. The stuffed mussel is placed on the spiced smoked butter.

STEAMED MUSSELS
Extra-large blue mussels
Lemon thyme sprigs
Cold-Infused Tarry Lapsang
  Souchong Tea*

QUAIL EGG PICKLING LIQUID
Apple balsamic vinegar
Cold-Infused Dashi*
Lemon thyme sprigs

SMOKED PICKLED QUAIL EGG
Quail eggs
Quail Egg Pickling Liquid

CURED EGG YOLKS
Eggs
Beef Garum*

SMOKED EGG YOLK PASTE
Cured Egg Yolks
Smoked Butter Whey*
Cep Tamari*
Dashi Reduction*
Salt

CEP AND CHANTERELLE SPICE
MIX
Dried ceps
Dried chanterelles
Toasted black peppercorns
Toasted juniper berries
Toasted angelica
Toasted coriander seeds
Toasted fennel seeds
Freeze-dried lingonberry
Freeze-dried green gooseberry
Arctic thyme
Dried Ginger*
Roasted Kelp Powder*
Salt

KOJI FUDGE
Cucumber Juice Reduction*
Peaso Water Reduction*
Butter
Koji Oil*

ANCHO CHILE PASTE
Grapeseed oil
Seeded morita chile
Seeded ancho chile
Roasted Kelp*
Chicken Wing Garum*
Red Pepper Tamari*

KELP–LAPSANG SOUCHONG TEA
Cold-Infused Tarry Lapsang
  Souchong Tea*
Cold-Infused Kelp Salt*

SPICED SMOKED BUTTER
Smoked Butter*
Smoked Mussel Shoyu*
Cep and Chanterelle Spice Mix

TO FINISH
Steamed Mussel
Smoked Pickled Quail Egg
Smoked Egg Yolk Paste
Koji Fudge
Ancho Chile Paste
Cold-Infused Kelp Salt*
Smoked Butter*
Parsley leaves
Lovage leaves
Kelp–Lapsang Souchong Tea
Spiced Smoked Butter
Cep and Chanterelle Spice Mix
Horse mussel shell

Raw Seafood Plate

Mussels are steamed in white wine and the broth is lightly set with gelatin, frozen, and then strained as it thaws to clarify. Sugar kelp is cooked in the ice-clarified mussel broth until tender, then torn into squares.

Slices of live Norwegian scallop and its roe are arranged on a serving plate and topped with a dot of black currant wood fudge. Fresh Skagen shrimp are nestled among the scallop slices and topped with a small pile of horseradish paste. Pieces of sugar kelp are tucked between the seafood, ice-clarified mussel broth is spooned around the seafood, and a few drops of koji and horseradish oils finish the dish.

ICE-CLARIFIED MUSSEL JUICE
Mussels
White wine
Gelatin

BLACK CURRANT WOOD FUDGE
Cucumber Juice Reduction*
Peaso Water Reduction*
Butter
Black Currant Wood Oil*

HORSERADISH PASTE
Grated fresh horseradish
Horseradish Oil*
Salt

PEELED SKAGEN SHRIMP
Fresh Skagen shrimp

COOKED SUGAR KELP
Dansk Tang sugar kelp
Ice-Clarified Mussel Juice

TO FINISH
Live Norwegian scallop with roe
Black Currant Wood Fudge
Peeled Skagen Shrimp
Horseradish Paste
Cooked Sugar Kelp
Ice-Clarified Mussel Juice
Lemon juice
Salt
Koji Oil*
Horseradish Oil*

Grilled Lobster and Roses

Wild beach rose petals and pieces of lightly cooked lobster meat are threaded onto a skewer made from black currant wood, then brushed with grilled lemon thyme butter and gently cooked over charcoal to warm. The skewer is then brushed with a rose butter made by emulsifying roasted kelp salt and yeast broth reduction with rose oil and grilled lemon thyme butter.

COOKED DANISH LOBSTER
Danish blue lobster

GRILLED LEMON THYME BUTTER
Grilled Lemon Thyme*
Butter

ROSE BUTTER
Roasted Kelp Salt*
Yeast Broth Reduction*
Rose Oil*
Grilled Lemon Thyme Butter

TO FINISH
Black currant wood skewer
Cooked Danish Lobster pieces
  (a mix of tail, claw, and knuckle)
Wild beach rose petals
Salt
Grilled Lemon Thyme Butter
Rose Butter

Fresh Oyster Marinated in Tomato Water

A Gigas oyster is presented on the half-shell nestled into a loose spiral of gracilaria seaweed layered on bladderwrack seaweed. The oyster is seasoned with cracked black pepper and fennel flowers and a nasturtium blossom is tucked into its shell. A tomato half and some beach cress flowers are served with the oyster. Diners are invited to squeeze the tomato juice onto the oyster and then follow their oyster with a bite of the beach cress.

RAW OYSTER
Gigas oyster

TO FINISH
Raw Oyster
Nasturtium flower
Cracked toasted black peppercorns
Fennel flowers
Organic Danish beefsteak tomato
   half
Beach cress flowers
Bladderwrack seaweed
Gracilaria seaweed

Crab Flask

Stone crabs are lightly cooked; the crabmeat is blended into a purée, and the purée is cooked until the proteins set and the liquid separates, leaving a clarified broth.

The crab shells are trimmed so that two shells fit together perfectly; the shell pair is then sealed with wax and tied together to form a flask.

The clarified crab broth is combined with shrimp garum, cold-infused Hojicha tea, smoked kelp vinegar, and cep oil and chilled. Just before serving, the broth is muddled with black currant shoots, warmed, strained, and poured into the crab flasks.

COLD-INFUSED HOJICHA TEA
Hojicha tea
Filtered water

CRAB BROTH
Stone crabs
Filtered water

CRAB FLASK
Stone crab heads

TO FINISH
Crab Broth
Shrimp-Tarry Lapsang Souchong
 Garum*
Cold-Infused Hojicha Tea
Black currant shoots
Smoked Kelp Vinegar*
Cep Oil*
Crab Flask

Stone Crab with Hazelnuts

Lightly cooked stone crab meat is blended into a purée and cooked until the proteins set and the liquid separates, leaving a clarified broth. The broth is mixed with shrimp garum and fresh koji butter and reduced until syrupy.

Fresh hazelnuts are blended with some water, ground, and strained to produce fresh hazelnut milk.

The cold-infused Lapsang souchong and jasmine teas are infused with kelp and then steeped with barley koji, rose pulp, and lemon thyme. The liquid is put into an atomizer.

Cooked stone crab meat and roe are arranged in a serving bowl and seasoned with fresh barley koji oil, shrimp garum, and droplets of the crab reduction. A few flakes of cold-infused kelp salt are sprinkled onto the crab and fresh hazelnut milk is spooned around it. To finish, the dish is spritzed with the Lapsang souchong and jasmine tea spray.

CRAB BROTH
Stone crabs
Filtered water

CRAB REDUCTION
Crab Broth
Shrimp–Tarry Lapsang Souchong
 Garum*
Fresh Barley Koji Butter*

FRESH HAZELNUT MILK
Hazelnuts
Filtered water

LAPSANG SOUCHONG AND
JASMINE TEA SPRAY
Cold-Infused Tarry Lapsang
 Souchong Tea*
Cold-Infused Jasmine Tea*
Kelp
Barley Koji*
Rose pulp (reserved from making
 Rose Oil*)
Lemon thyme leaves
Salt

STONE CRAB
Stone crab

TO FINISH
Stone Crab
Fresh Barley Koji Oil*
Shrimp–Tarry Lapsang Souchong
 Garum*
Crab Reduction
Cold-Infused Kelp Salt*
Fresh Hazelnut Milk
Lapsang Souchong and Jasmine
 Tea Spray

Seafood Platter, Part 1

A queen clam is sliced in half; the roe is removed and also halved. Each clam half is spread with vegetable fudge and the roe halves are set on top. The clam pieces are placed back in the clean bottom shell and the other shell half is placed on top.

A mahogany clam is cleaned; the muscle is sliced thin and repositioned in the shell. The clam is scattered with salted green gooseberries, pickled black currant shoots, black currant buds, and salted black currant capers and dotted with black currant wood fudge. Ice-clarified mussel juice and black currant wood oil are dripped into the shell, and the top of the clam shell is put in place to close.

The queen clam and mahogany clam are served on ice.

VEGETABLE FUDGE
Cucumber Juice Reduction*
Peaso Water Reduction*
Butter
Grapeseed oil

BLACK CURRANT WOOD FUDGE
Cucumber Juice Reduction*
Peaso Water Reduction*
Butter
Black Currant Wood Oil*

ICE-CLARIFIED MUSSEL JUICE
Mussels
White wine

TO FINISH
Queen clam
Vegetable Fudge
Mahogany clam
Salted Green Gooseberry Capers*
Pickled Black Currant Shoots*
Black currant buds
Salted Black Currant Caper* halves
Black Currant Wood Fudge
Ice-Clarified Mussel Juice
Black Currant Wood Oil*

Seafood Platter, Part 2

A gigas oyster is blanched in the shell and then shucked, sliced into thirds, and put back in the half shell. A spoonful of gooseberry compote is nestled next to the oyster meat, and Icelandic wasabi is grated on top of the compote. Wood sorrel is arranged on the compote and the oyster is garnished with oxalis flowers.

Two sea urchin tongues are arranged in a cleaned and trimmed sea urchin shell. The tongues are spread with rose fudge and peeled pumpkin seeds are shingled on top. Cream and rose oil are drizzled around the sea urchin tongues and pumpkin seeds inside the shell.

The oyster and sea urchin are served on an ice plate.

GOOSEBERRY COMPOTE
Lacto Green Gooseberries*
Parsley Oil*

ROSE FUDGE
Cucumber Juice Reduction*
Peaso Water Reduction*
Butter
Rose Oil*

PEELED PUMPKIN SEEDS
Fresh Hokkaido pumpkin seeds
Rose Oil*

SEA URCHIN
Sea urchins
2% salt brine

TO FINISH
Gigas oyster
Gooseberry Compote
Icelandic wasabi root
Wood sorrel bunches
Oxalis flowers
Sea Urchin tongues
Rose Fudge
Peeled Pumpkin Seeds
Cream
Rose Oil*

Venus clams are steamed in cucumber juice seasoned with coriander seed, dried angelica, and lemon thyme. Sea buckthorn, juniper berries, angelica, green coriander, pine shoots, and Douglas fir needles are muddled together with mirabelle plum juice to make a sauce for the clams. The trimmed steamed clams are placed upright in a clam shell on some purslane leaves, with more purslane in between the clams. The shell is filled with the Venus clam sauce.

Carpet clams are cooked in clarified fennel juice, sliced into pieces, and arranged along the lip of a carpet clam shell. The center of the shell is filled with cooked mixed grains that have been folded with koji fudge. Oxalis leaves top the grains and a sorrel and clam sauce is piped into the shell.

Razor clam grains are folded with some hazelnut fudge and chopped razor clam skirts and then spooned into an empty razor clam shell. The grains are dressed with a few dots of hazelnut marinade. Sliced razor clam flesh is alternately shingled with thin slices of salted fresh hazelnuts.

A cleaned cockle shell is filled with five little piles of cooked barley and Kamut. Each grain pile is topped with a slice of cockle belly, foot, and skirt. The cockle stacks are seasoned with a drop of Douglas fir oil and a bit of salt made by drying the brine used to preserve noble fir cones. Some cockle cream sauce is piped into the cockle shell.

The Venus clam, carpet clam, razor clam, and cockle are served on ice with a wedge of Japanese quince.

VENUS CLAMS

CLARIFIED CUCUMBER JUICE
Cucumbers

CLAM COOKING LIQUID
Clarified Cucumber Juice
Coriander seeds
Dried angelica buds
Lemon thyme sprigs

MIRABELLE MARINADE
Ice-Clarified Mirabelle Plum Juice*
Unripe sea buckthorn berries
Juniper berries
Angelica buds
Green coriander seeds
Pine shoots
Douglas fir needles

STEAMED VENUS CLAMS
Venus clams
Clam Cooking Liquid

VENUS CLAM SAUCE
Mirabelle Marinade
Spruce Wood Oil*

TO FINISH THE VENUS CLAMS
Purslane leaves
Steamed Venus Clams
Venus Clam Sauce

CARPET CLAMS

KOJI FUDGE
Cucumber Juice Reduction*
Peaso Water Reduction*
Butter
Koji Oil*

CARPET CLAM GRAINS
Kamut
Konini wheat
Koji Fudge

CLARIFIED FENNEL JUICE
Fennel bulbs

CARPET CLAMS
Carpet clams
Clarified Fennel Juice

SHEEP SORREL JUICE
Sheep sorrel

SORREL AND CLAM SAUCE
Carpet clam liquor (reserved from opening the cooked clams)
Sheep Sorrel Juice

TO FINISH THE CARPET CLAMS
Carpet Clams
Carpet clam shell
Carpet Clam Grains
Green oxalis leaves
Sorrel and Clam Sauce

RAZOR CLAMS

RAZOR CLAM GRAINS
Spelt
Emmer
Konini wheat
Mustard seeds

HAZELNUT FUDGE
Cucumber Juice Reduction*
Peaso Water Reduction*
Butter
Hazelnut Oil*

HAZELNUT MARINADE
Lemon thyme leaves
Hazelnut and Lobster Garum Oil*
Lemon Thyme Oil*
Liquid from Salted Green Gooseberry Capers*
Roasted Kelp Salt*

SALTED FRESH HAZELNUTS
Fresh hazelnuts
8% salt brine
Hazelnut Oil*

TO FINISH THE RAZOR CLAMS
Razor Clam Grains
Hazelnut Fudge
Hazelnut Marinade
Whole razor clam

NORWEGIAN COCKLES

COCKLE GRAINS
Barley
Kamut

NORWEGIAN COCKLES
Norwegian cockles

COCKLE CREAM SAUCE
Cream
Cockle juice (reserved from opening the Norwegian cockles)

TO FINISH THE NORWEGIAN COCKLES
Cockle Grains
Cockle belly
Cockle foot
Cockle skirt
Douglas Fir Oil*
Noble Fir Salt*
Cockle Cream Sauce

TO FINISH THE SEAFOOD PLATTER
Japanese quince
Venus Clam
Carpet Clam
Razor Clam
Norwegian Cockle

Saffron and Löjrom Custard

Egg yolk sauce is made by curing raw and lightly cooked egg yolks in chicken wing garum and beef garum. The cured yolks are whisked with clarified smoked butter and smoked butter whey until smooth.

Venus clams are steamed in lacto-fermented koji water, butter, and lemon thyme, and then simmered with water to create a broth. The broth is then steeped with toasted saffron. The clam broth is blended with whole eggs to make a custard base, which is steamed in individual serving bowls to create a soft custard. Egg yolk sauce is piped over the surface of the custard, seasoned with roasted kelp salt and toasted black pepper, and completely covered with Kalix löjrom.

VENUS CLAM AND SAFFRON
BROTH
Venus clams
Lacto Koji Water* (made with
 Rice Koji*)
Butter
Lemon thyme sprigs
Filtered water
Saffron

CLAM AND SAFFRON CUSTARD
BASE
Cold Venus Clam and Saffron Broth
Eggs

SMOKED BUTTER AND WHEY
Butter
Toasted Hay*

EGG YOLK SAUCE
Eggs
Beef Garum*
Chicken Wing Garum*
Clarified Smoked Butter*
Smoked Butter and Whey

KALIX LÖJROM
Kalix löjrom (vendace roe)
Filtered water

TO FINISH
Clam and Saffron Custard Base
Egg Yolk Sauce
Roasted Kelp Salt*
Kalix Löjrom
Cracked toasted black peppercorns

Oyster and Caviar Éclair

A classic pâte à choux is piped into small éclair shapes and baked.

Whipped cream is piped into the éclair shells through the bottom, and the tops of the éclairs are dipped into an oyster and parsley emulsion.

To finish, the éclair is dressed with a scoop of caviar and two pieces of roasted kelp salt.

ÉCLAIR DOUGH
Milk
Cold filtered water
Butter
Tipo "00" flour
Eggs
Salt
Sugar

OYSTER EMULSION
Shucked Gigas oysters
Grapeseed oil
Parsley leaves
Parsley Oil*
Lemon juice

TO FINISH
Éclair Dough
Oyster Emulsion
Whipped cream
Roasted Kelp Salt*
Osetra caviar

Sweet Quince Amazake
and Oyster

Oysters are puréed with oyster liquor and some dashi, and the purée is cooked until the proteins set and the liquid separates, leaving a clarified broth.

The clarified oyster broth is reduced with roasted kelp salt and peaso water reduction until it has the texture of soft caramel.

Gigas oyster shells are marinated in quince juice to neutralize any seafood flavors. A shell is partially filled with quince amazake ice cream, spread to mimic an actual oyster. Elderflower oil is drizzled around the ice cream and the ice cream is dressed with pinches of spirulina powder and dots of the oyster kelp caramel. A thin layer of broken quince honey gel is piped over the surface and the dish is finished with two big pinches of grated pumpkin bushi and served on a plate dressed with fresh seaweed.

QUINCE AMAZAKE BASE
Quince
Rice Amazake*

QUINCE AMAZAKE ICE CREAM
Quince Amazake Base
Milk
Cream
Dextrose
Milk powder
Salt
Procrema

OYSTER BROTH
Gigas oysters
Oyster liquor
Cold-Infused Dashi*

OYSTER KELP CARAMEL
Oyster Broth
Roasted Kelp Salt*
Peaso Water Reduction*

QUINCE HONEY GEL
Quince Juice*
Noma honey
Gelatin

MARINATED GIGAS OYSTER SHELL
Quince Juice*
Gigas oyster shells

ICE CREAM-STUFFED GIGAS
SHELL
Marinated Gigas Oyster Shell
Quince Amazake Ice Cream

TO FINISH
Ice Cream-Stuffed Gigas Shell
Oyster Kelp Caramel
Quince Honey Gel
Elderflower Oil*
Spirulina powder
Pumpkin bushi
Fresh Gaffeltang and gracilaria
   seaweeds

Candied Mushroom Tart

A cream tartelette shell is made by dipping a ladle into cream and then into liquid nitrogen to freeze it. A second tartelette shell is made in the same way and then coated in berry spice and stacked on the first cream shell.

Dried pumpkin seeds, dried ceps, and sugar are ground in a mill and then blended with spruce wood oil and parsley oil to make a praline. The praline is piped into the berry spice–coated tartelette shell. Two pickled chanterelles that have been candied in birch syrup are tucked into the tart, which is served on a cold stone.

CREAM TARTELETTE SHELL
Cream

PUMPKIN SEED PRALINE
Pumpkin seed pulp (reserved from
    making Pumpkin Seed Oil*)
Dried ceps
Muscovado sugar
Spruce Wood Oil*
Parsley Oil*
Cold-Infused Kelp Salt*

BERRY SPICE
Freeze-dried black currants
Freeze-dried blueberries
Dried rose petals
Dried Ginger*

CANDIED CHANTERELLES
Pickled Chanterelles*
Filtered water
Birch syrup

TO FINISH
Cream Tartelette Shell
Pumpkin Seed Praline
Berry Spice
Candied Chanterelles

Chocolate-Covered Fish Skin

Cod skins are lightly brined, blanched in spiced cooking liquid, dehydrated, and then deep-fried until puffed and crisp.

The fried skins are enrobed in tempered chocolate. The chocolate-coated fish skin is sprinkled with toasted fennel seed, arctic thyme, licorice powder, and salt and served with a dagger.

COOKING LIQUID
Filtered water
White wine vinegar
Salt
Coriander seeds
Juniper berries
Arctic thyme

COD SKIN
Fresh cod skins
2% salt brine
Cooking Liquid
Grapeseed oil

TEMPERED CHOCOLATE
70% chocolate
Cocoa butter

CHOCOLATE-COVERED SKINS
Cod Skins
Tempered Chocolate
Toasted fennel seeds
Arctic thyme
Raw licorice powder
Flake sea salt

TO FINISH
Chocolate-Covered Skin

Sheep's Yogurt Mousse with Salted Berries

Fresh noble fir cones are frozen, thawed, and then juiced. The pine juice is mixed with white currant juice, pine brine, and sugar syrup to make a sauce.

Individual scales from a fresh noble fir cone are infused with candied pine cone syrup.

The sheep's yogurt mousse is centered in a bowl and surrounded by a selection of fruits that have been dried with a bit of koji oil until lightly chewy. The mousse is topped with squares of aronia kelp, compressed noble fir cone scales, candied pine cones, angelica, green coriander seeds, and black currant shoots, and finished with the white currant sauce and droplets of black currant wood oil.

SHEEP'S YOGURT MOUSSE
Sheep's-milk yogurt
Double cream
Gelatin
Egg whites
Sugar

SEMI-DRIED RED GOOSEBERRIES
Red gooseberries
Koji Oil*

SEMI-DRIED GREEN GOOSEBERRIES
Green gooseberries
Koji Oil*

SEMI-DRIED LACTO MIRABELLE PLUMS
Lacto Mirabelle Plums*
Koji Oil*

SEMI-DRIED LACTO CHERRIES
Lacto Cherries*
Koji Oil*

SEMI-DRIED DANISH KIWIS
Danish kiwis
Black Currant Leaf Oil*

WHITE CURRANT SAUCE
White Currant Juice*
Noble fir cones
Brine reserved from Salted Noble Fir Cones* (made using 6% salt brine)
Simple syrup

COMPRESSED NOBLE FIR CONE SCALES
Freshly frozen noble fir cone
Candied pine cone syrup
Filtered water

TO FINISH
Sheep's Yogurt Mousse
Semi-Dried Red Gooseberries
Semi-Dried Green Gooseberries
Semi-Dried Lacto Mirabelle Plums
Semi-Dried Lacto Cherries, with the stem off
Semi-Dried Danish Kiwis
Aronia Kelp*
Compressed Noble Fir Cone Scales
Jarred candied pine cone halves
Freshly frozen angelica halves
Green coriander seed halves
Black currant shoot halves
White Currant Sauce
Black Currant Wood Oil*

Crispy Sugar Kelp and
Plum Kernel Mousse

Sugar kelp is steamed in cooking tea, cut into natural leaf shapes, brushed with clarified butter, and dusted with confectioners' sugar. The kelp is then baked and dehydrated until crisp.

A plum kernel mousse is made with yogurt, plum kernel cream, and Swiss meringue.

A slab of the plum kernel mousse is seasoned with Douglas fir oil, pine salt, and plum reduction and then sandwiched between two pieces of the crispy sugar kelp.

COOKING TEA
Pine Dashi*
Cold-Infused Jasmine Tea*
Noma honey

CRISPY SUGAR KELP
Dried sugar kelp
Cooking Tea
Clarified butter
Confectioners' sugar

PLUM KERNEL CREAM
Plum kernels
Cream

SWISS MERINGUE
Egg whites
Sugar
Filtered water

PLUM KERNEL MOUSSE
Yogurt
Plum Kernel Cream
Gelatin
Swiss Meringue

TO FINISH
Crispy Sugar Kelp
Plum Kernel Mousse
Pine Salt*
Douglas Fir Oil*
Plum Reduction*

Chilled Sweet Cloudberry Soup

Cloudberries and Douglas fir needles are made into a sorbet and frozen in sea snail–shaped molds. Cloudberry juice and purée are blended to make cloudberry soup. Yogurt is frozen, then blended so that it has the texture of snow.

Candied cloudberries and some cloudberry purée are placed in a serving bowl. Yogurt snow is mounded in the center, and cloudberry soup is poured around it. The sorbet sea snails and some candied pine cones are placed on the snow, and the soup is drizzled with rose oil to finish.

CANDIED CLOUDBERRIES
Frozen cloudberries
Birch syrup

REDUCED CLOUDBERRY JUICE
Cloudberry pulp
Filtered water

SEA BUCKTHORN JUICE
Ripe sea buckthorn berries

CLOUDBERRY PURÉE
Leftover cloudberry pulp
Noma honey
Sea Buckthorn Juice

YOGURT SNOW
Yogurt

SEA SNAIL CLOUDBERRY SORBET
Cloudberry Purée
Douglas fir needles
Glucose syrup
Trimoline

CLOUDBERRY SOUP
Reduced Cloudberry Juice
Cloudberry Purée

TO FINISH
Candied Cloudberries
Cloudberry Purée
Yogurt Snow
Cloudberry Soup
Rose Oil*
Sea Snail Cloudberry Sorbet
Jarred candied pine cones

Plankton Mousse Cake

Flour, cornstarch, milk powder, sugar, and salt are mixed with melted butter, crumbled onto a baking sheet, and baked until dry. The milk crumb is blended with black currant wood oil and butter to create a glaze.

Plankton-infused cream is whipped, folded with crème fraîche and Italian meringue, and set with gelatin to make a plankton mousse.

A sponge cake flavored with black currant wood oil is cut into a round, spread with dried plum paste, and layered with the plankton mousse. The whole cake is coated in the black currant wood glaze. More glaze is shaped in decorative shell molds, dusted with rose berry ginger powder, and used to decorate the top of the cake.

BLACK CURRANT WOOD OIL
SPONGE
Sugar
Eggs
Egg yolks
Black Currant Wood Oil*
Lemon juice
Tipo "00" flour
Baking powder

DRIED DANISH TOPHIT PLUMS
Danish Tophit plums

DRIED PLUM PASTE
Dried Danish Tophit Plums
Aronia Kelp*
Black Currant Leaf Oil*
Black currant shoots
Plum aquavit

MILK CRUMB
Milk powder
Tipo "00" flour
Sugar
Melted butter
Cornstarch
Salt

BLACK CURRANT WOOD GLAZE
Milk Crumb
Black Currant Wood Oil*
Butter

ROSE BERRY GINGER POWDER
Freeze-dried black currants
Freeze-dried lingonberry
Freeze-dried sea buckthorn berries
Dried roses
Ginger Powder*

ITALIAN MERINGUE
Sugar
Egg whites

PLANKTON MOUSSE
Plankton powder
Cream
Gelatin
Crème fraîche
Italian Meringue

TO FINISH
Black Currant Wood Oil Sponge
Dried Plum Paste
Plankton Mousse
Black Currant Wood Glaze
Rose Berry Ginger Powder

Oyster Caramel

Sugar kelp is simmered in sugar syrup, cut into rounds, and dried between two tart molds to create a crisp tart shell.

Oysters are puréed and then cooked until the proteins set and separate from the liquid. The clarified liquid is reduced to a thick paste, spread thin, and dried until hardened like caramel.

Whipped cream is dolloped into the center of a sugar kelp tart shell and then generously dusted with pine praline. A shard of oyster caramel is placed atop the cream.

SUGAR SYRUP
Muscovado sugar
Filtered water

SUGAR KELP TART SHELL
Sugar Syrup
Sugar kelp
Filtered water

PINE PRALINE
Sugar
Douglas fir needles
Ants

OYSTER CARAMEL
Oysters

TO FINISH
Sugar Kelp Tart Shell
Cream
Pine Praline
Oyster Caramel

Mussel Ice Cream Sandwich

Conference pears are aged and caramelized under vacuum for two months, then dried until sticky. The black pears are blended with Conference pear purée and dried into a thin fruit leather, which is draped over mussel shells to shape.

An ice cream is made with smoked cream and roasted kelp and beeswax caramel. Roasted beet juice is reduced with kelp, then mixed with freeze-dried black currants and green gooseberry water and set with pectin.

Bilberry crisp ingredients are cooked and rolled thin, then mussel shell shapes are cut out and baked until dry.

The fruit leather mussel shells are filled with the roasted kelp salt and beeswax ice cream and a small indentation is scooped out of the center of the ice cream. The beet reduction is piped into the center of the ice cream.

A bilberry crisp is dusted with black currant and licorice powder, piped with salted licorice syrup, and seasoned with roasted kelp salt. The seasoned crisp is sandwiched between two ice cream–filled fruit leather mussel shell halves. The ice cream sandwich is served on a rock plate.

ROASTED KELP AND BEESWAX
CARAMEL
Roasted Kelp Salt*
Cane sugar
Cream
Roasted Kelp*
Beeswax cut into small chunks

ROASTED KELP SALT AND
BEESWAX ICE CREAM
Smoked cream
Milk
Trimoline
Egg yolks
Roasted Kelp and Beeswax Caramel
Roasted Kelp Salt*

CONFERENCE PEAR PURÉE
Peeled Conference pears
Freeze-dried gooseberries

BLACK PEAR LEATHER MUSSELS
Dried Black Pears*
Conference Pear Purée
Roasted Kelp*
Roasted Kelp Oil*
Roasted Kelp Salt and Beeswax Ice
Cream

BEET REDUCTION
Cylindra beets
Kelp
Freeze-dried black currants
Green Gooseberry Water*
Pectin

BLACK CURRANT AND LICORICE
POWDER
Freeze-dried black currants
Fine licorice powder

BILBERRY CRISP
Butter
Glucose syrup
Filtered water
70% chocolate
Sugar
Pectin
Bilberry powder

TO FINISH
Black Pear Leather Mussels
Beet Reduction
Bilberry Crisp
Black Currant and Licorice Powder
Roasted Kelp Salt*
Salted licorice syrup

Sea Star Caramel

Carrot and sea buckthorn purée and black currant purée are mixed together and painted into a sea star mold to create a sea star shell.

Cardamom-scented cream is cooked with sugar, butter, and sweet licorice syrup to make a toffee. The toffee is poured into the sea star shell and cooled until set.

The toffee side of the sea star is dipped into saffron glaze; the tips of the star's arms are dusted with cardamom seed powder and the center is dusted with cloudberry powder. The sea star is presented on a plate of dried Irish moss.

SEA BUCKTHORN JUICE
Ripe sea buckthorn berries

CARROT JUICE
Carrots

CARROT AND SEA BUCKTHORN
PURÉE
Sea Buckthorn Juice
Carrot Juice
Noma honey
Pectin

BLACK CURRANT PURÉE
Black currants
Muscovado sugar

SEA STAR SHELL
Carrot and Sea Buckthorn Purée
Black Currant Purée

CARDAMOM TOFFEE SEA STAR
BASE
Castor sugar
Glucose syrup
Cream
Green cardamom pods
Butter
Salt
White wine vinegar
Sweet licorice syrup

SAFFRON GLAZE
Confectioners' sugar
Milk powder
Cocoa butter
Saffron powder
Soy lecithin

CARDAMOM SEED POWDER
Green cardamom seeds

CLOUDBERRY POWDER
Cloudberry pulp

GLAZED SEA STAR
Cardamom Toffee Sea Star Base
Saffron Glaze

TO FINISH
Glazed Sea Star
Cardamom Seed Powder
Cloudberry Powder
Dried Irish moss

HOW TO

RETAIN

YOUR

SPARKLE

D. SHRIG 2022

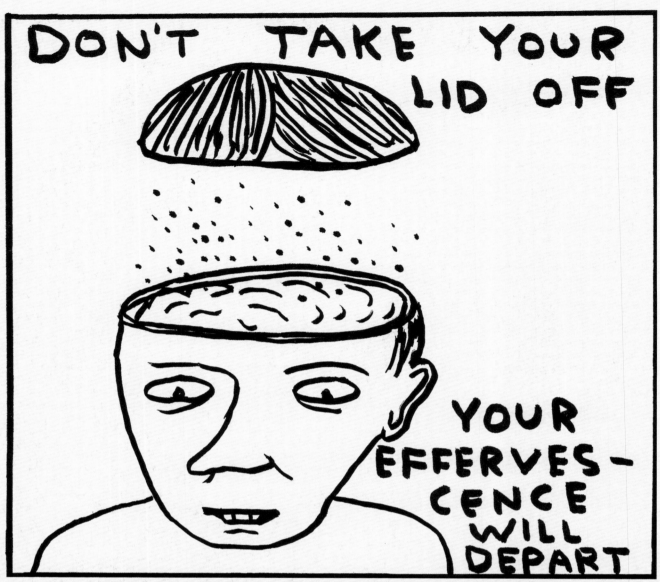

REMEMBER:
THE NEW YOU IS
CONTAINED INSIDE
THE OLD YOU

RELEASE
THE
NEGATIVE
GASES

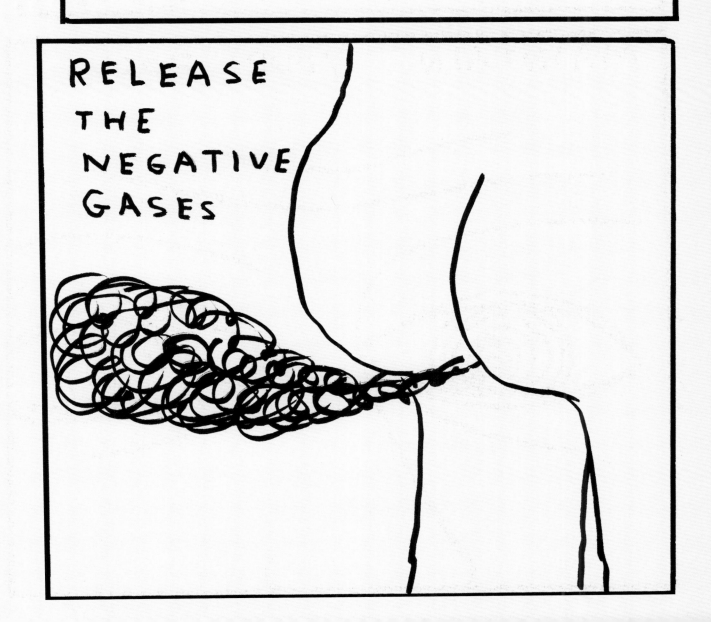

DON'T READ THE REVIEWS

THE CRITICS ARE MORONS

JUST GET ON WITH IT

WHATEVER IT IS

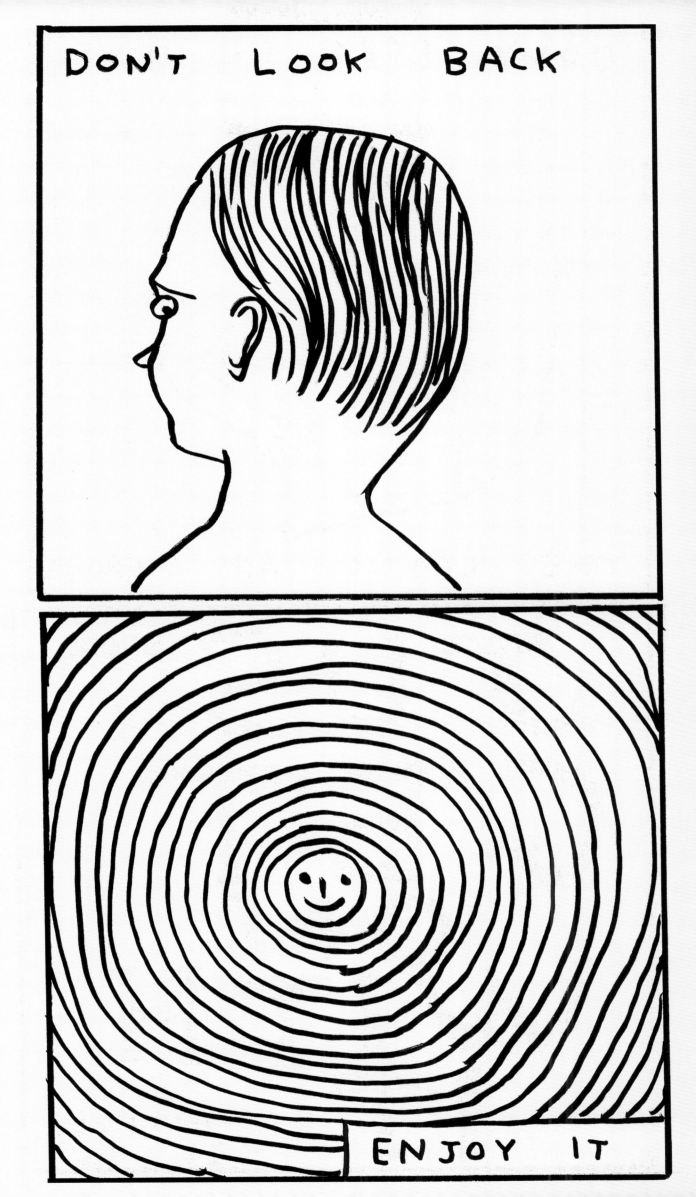

Broths, Waters, Juices, and Teas

Cold-Infused Dashi
1 liter cold filtered water
60 grams kelp

Place the water and kelp in an airtight container and let stand in the fridge to infuse overnight (or at minimum 8 hours). Strain through a fine-mesh nylon sieve. Reserve in an airtight container in the fridge.

Cucumber-Kelp Broth
3 grams angelica
15 grams juniper berries
10 grams arctic thyme
100 grams Dried Cucumber (page 349)
300 grams kelp
5 liters filtered water
2 liters Cold-Infused Dashi (above)

Place all the ingredients in a pot and bring to a boil, then *barely* simmer it for 2 days. Should the water level get too low, top it off with fresh water. Let cool, then strain the liquid through a conical strainer and again through a fine-mesh nylon sieve. Reserve in an airtight container in the fridge.

Mushroom-Kelp Broth
MUSHROOM KELP
250 grams thick center pieces of kelp
125 grams dried ceps
65 grams dried morels
35 grams dried black trumpet mushrooms
500 grams Lacto Cep Water (page 344)
25 grams freeze-dried lingonberries
125 grams muscovado sugar
5 liters filtered water

MASTER STOCK
250 grams thin outer pieces of kelp
125 grams dried ceps
65 grams dried morels
35 grams dried black trumpet mushrooms
500 grams Lacto Cep Water*
25 grams freeze-dried lingonberries
125 grams muscovado sugar
5 liters filtered water

Place the ingredients for the mushroom kelp and the master stock in separate rondeaus. Bring both pots to a boil, then cover and simmer on low heat overnight.

Strain the liquid in both pots. Carefully remove the thick pieces of kelp from the mushroom kelp pot and reserve them. With a superbag, squeeze the remaining solids from both pots for maximum extraction. Combine the strained stocks and reserved kelp in a pot and cook very slowly for 36 hours, or until the kelp becomes just tender. Remove from the heat and let cool, then transfer the broth and kelp to airtight containers. Reserve in the fridge.

Pine Dashi
1 liter Cold-Infused Dashi (left)
60 grams Dried Norwegian Spruce (page 350)

Combine the dashi and spruce in a vacuum bag, seal, and steam in a combi oven set to 60°C (100% fan) for 2 hours. Strain and let cool. Reserve in an airtight container in the fridge.

Yeast Broth
400 milliliters filtered water
60 grams Peaso (page 340)
20 grams Roasted Yeast (page 350)
12 grams freeze-dried gooseberries

Blend all the ingredients with an immersion blender until thoroughly homogenized, transfer to a 1-liter airtight container, and freeze.

Remove the frozen brick of yeast broth from the container and hang it in a cheesecloth-lined perforated gastro pan set over a deep gastro pan to catch the liquid as it thaws. Cover and let stand in the fridge for 2 to 3 days, until completely thawed. Do not press on the residual solids. Reduce the clarified broth immediately (see Yeast Broth Reduction, page 334) or vacuum seal and freeze.

Peaso Water
4 liters filtered water
600 grams Peaso (page 340)

Blend the water and peaso with an immersion blender to combine. Transfer to 1-liter airtight containers and freeze.

Remove the frozen bricks of peaso water from the containers and hang them in a cheesecloth-lined perforated gastro pan set over a deep gastro pan to catch the liquid as it thaws. Cover and let stand in the fridge for 2 to 3 days, until completely thawed. Do not press on the residual solids or you will cloud the liquid. Reserve the peaso water in an airtight container in the fridge.

Plum Kernel Water
500 grams plum kernel shells
1 liter filtered water

Combine the plum kernel shells and water in a vacuum bag and seal on 100% vacuum. Refrigerate for 1 day to infuse. Strain the liquid and discard the shells. Reserve the plum kernel water in an airtight container in the fridge or vacuum seal and freeze for longer storage.

Green Gooseberry Water
1 kilogram frozen green gooseberries
1 liter filtered water

Blend the gooseberries and water with an immersion blender for 45 to 60 seconds, transfer the purée to 1-liter airtight containers, and freeze.

Remove the frozen bricks of gooseberry purée from the containers and hang them in a cheesecloth-lined perforated gastro pan set over a deep gastro pan to catch the liquid as it thaws. Cover and let stand in the fridge for 2 to 3 days, until completely thawed and devoid of any further easily extractable liquid. Do not press on the residual solids or you will cloud the liquid. Reserve the gooseberry water in an airtight container in the fridge.

Ryeso Water
4 liters filtered water
600 grams Ryeso (page 340)

Blend the water and ryeso with an immersion blender to combine. Transfer to 1-liter airtight containers and freeze.

Remove the frozen bricks of ryeso water from the containers and hang them in a cheesecloth-lined perforated gastro pan set over a deep gastro pan to catch the liquid as it thaws. Cover and let stand in the fridge for 2 to 3 days, until completely thawed. Do not press on the residual solids or you will cloud the liquid. Reserve the ryeso water in an airtight container in the fridge.

Sweet Koji Water
800 milliliters filtered water
400 grams koji (any type; see page 335)

Blend the water and koji in a Thermomix on high speed for 1 minute. Transfer the mixture to 1-liter airtight containers and freeze.

Remove the frozen bricks of koji water from the containers and hang them in a cheesecloth-lined shallow perforated gastro tray set over a deep gastro tray to catch the liquid as it thaws. Cover and let stand in the fridge for 2 to 3 days, until completely thawed and devoid of any further easily extractable liquid. Do not press on the residual solids or you will cloud the koji water. Vacuum seal and freeze.

Ice-Clarified Tomato Water
1 kilogram vine-ripe tomatoes

Quarter the tomatoes and blitz them in a Thermomix for 45 seconds, until broken up and liquefied. Pour the tomato purée into 1-liter airtight containers and freeze.

Remove the frozen bricks of tomato purée from the containers and hang them in a cheesecloth-lined perforated gastro tray set over a deep gastro tray to catch the liquid as it thaws. Cover and let stand in the fridge for 2 to 3 days, until completely thawed and devoid of any further easily extractable liquid. Do not press on the residual solids or you will cloud the liquid. Vacuum seal the tomato water and freeze to prevent oxidation.

Smoked Tomato Water
1 liter Ice-Clarified Tomato Water (opposite)

Set up an offset cold smoker. Fill a smoking coil with wood dust and light the dust with a bit of white-hot charcoal. Pour the tomato water into a 1-liter container and place it on one of the top racks of the smoker. Smoke for at least 30 minutes, or until the desired flavor is achieved. Transfer to a clean airtight container and reserve in the fridge, or vacuum seal and freeze for future use.

Ice-Clarified Mirabelle Plum Juice
1 kilogram mirabelle plums
1 liter filtered water

In a large airtight container, massage the plums in the water until the flesh is completely broken up. Cover and transfer to the fridge to infuse overnight, then freeze.

Remove the frozen brick of plums from the container and hang it in a cheesecloth-lined perforated shallow gastro tray set over a deep gastro tray to catch the liquid as it thaws. Cover and let stand in the fridge for 2 to 3 days, until completely thawed and devoid of any further easily extractable liquid. Do not press on the residual solids or you will cloud the plum juice. Vacuum seal and freeze.

Ice-Clarified Mussel Juice
5 kilograms mussels
2 shallots, sliced
1.5 liters white wine

Wash any dirt from the mussels, scrubbing them if necessary, and remove any visible beards. Heat a large rondeau. Add the mussels, shallots, and wine to flash boil and steam the mussels. Cover the pot with a lid and agitate the pot to stir the mussels around. Lower the heat and cook until the mussels open, releasing their juices. Pull the pot off the stove, still covered, and let cool. Strain all the liquid through a fine-mesh nylon sieve, weigh it, and return it to the stove in a clean pot. Reduce the liquid to 66% of its starting weight, being sure to taste it as it reduces, as it can become bitter. Let cool, then transfer the reduced liquid to an airtight container and freeze.

Remove the frozen brick of mussel juice from the container and hang it in a perforated gastro pan lined with a dampened clean kitchen towel set over a deeper gastro pan. Cover and let stand in the fridge for 2 to 3 days, until completely thawed. Vacuum seal the mussel juice and freeze.

Ice-Clarified Red Gooseberry Water
1 kilogram frozen red gooseberries
1 liter filtered water

Blend the gooseberries and water with an immersion blender for 45 to 60 seconds, transfer the purée to 1-liter airtight containers, and freeze.

Remove the frozen bricks of gooseberry purée from the containers and hang them in a cheesecloth-lined perforated gastro pan over a deep gastro pan to catch the liquid as it thaws. Cover and let stand in the fridge for 2 to 3 days, until completely thawed and devoid of any further easily extractable liquid. Do not press on the residual solids or you will cloud the liquid. Reserve the gooseberry water in an airtight container in the fridge.

Japanese Quince Juice
100 grams Japanese quince, frozen

Defrost the quince. Using a wine press lined with cheesecloth, squeeze and press the quince to yield as much juice as possible. Reserve the juice in an airtight container in the fridge or vacuum seal and freeze.

Kiwi Juice
3 kilograms whole Danish kiwifruits, frozen

Defrost the kiwis in the fridge, then purée with a large immersion blender. Line a perforated gastro container with a shoyu bag and set it over a deep gastro container. Pour the puréed kiwi into the shoyu bag, fold the bag over itself, and press the bag to extract the juice. The shoyu bag will prevent particulates from clouding the juice, so press the bag well to yield as much juice as possible; compost the residual solids. Vacuum seal the kiwi juice and freeze.

Quince Juice
1 kilogram quince, frozen

Place the quince in a container and set aside to defrost. Chop the defrosted quince, reserving any liquid in the container, then juice them, pressing the resultant pulp for maximum yield. Combine the quince juice with the reserved liquid from the container. Strain through a fine-mesh nylon sieve into a pot. Bring the juice to a boil to separate out any impurities, then let cool. Strain the juice through a conical strainer lined with a dampened cloth to clarify it. Vacuum seal and freeze.

Red Currant Juice
1 kilogram red currants

Using a wine press lined with cheesecloth, squeeze and press the currants to yield as much juice as possible. Strain the juice through a fine-mesh nylon sieve, then vacuum seal and freeze.

White Currant Juice
1 kilogram white currants

Using a wine press lined with cheesecloth, squeeze and press the currants to yield as much juice as possible. Strain the juice through a fine-mesh nylon sieve, then vacuum seal and freeze.

Cold-Infused Jasmine Tea
7 grams jasmine tea leaves
1 liter cold filtered water

Combine the tea leaves and water in a 1-liter airtight container. Leave in the fridge to infuse overnight (8 to 12 hours). Strain the tea and reserve in an airtight container in the fridge.

Cold-Infused Oolong Tea
6 grams oolong tea leaves
1 liter cold filtered water

Combine the tea leaves and water in a 1-liter airtight container. Leave in the fridge to infuse overnight (8 to 12 hours). Strain the tea and reserve in an airtight container in the fridge.

Cold-Infused Tarry Lapsang Souchong Tea
6 grams Tarry Lapsang souchong tea leaves
1 liter cold filtered water

Combine the tea leaves and water in a 1-liter airtight container. Leave in the fridge to infuse overnight (8 to 12 hours). Strain the tea and reserve in an airtight container in the fridge.

Cold-Infused White Peony Tea
7 grams white peony tea leaves
1 liter cold filtered water

Combine the tea leaves and water in a 1-liter airtight container. Leave in the fridge to infuse overnight (8 to 12 hours). Strain the tea and reserve in an airtight container in the fridge.

Kombuchas

Apple Kombucha
1 liter unfiltered apple juice
100 milliliters finished apple kombucha (from a previous batch)
1 kombucha SCOBY

Pour the apple juice into a sanitized fermentation vessel and use a refractometer to measure its sugar content; it should sit between 9 and 14 °Bx. Add the finished kombucha as backslop to lower the pH. Add the SCOBY, then cover the vessel with a cloth and secure it with a rubber band. Ferment at room temperature or just above for 7 to 10 days, or until properly acidified (approximately 3.5 pH). Remove the SCOBY and reserve for reuse, then strain the kombucha. Vacuum seal and freeze to prevent further fermentation.

Birch Water Kombucha
200 grams birch wood
2 liters fresh birch water
Finished neutral kombucha (10% by weight)
1 kombucha SCOBY

Thoroughly rinse the birch wood to remove any dirt and debris. Place it in a pot with the birch water, then cook to reduce the birch water by half, stirring occasionally and removing any scum that forms on the surface with a fine-mesh nylon sieve. Remove the wood and strain the reduced liquid through a fine-mesh nylon sieve into a fresh pot. Continue to reduce the liquid until it reaches 14 °Bx as measured by a refractometer and then let cool. Weigh the liquid, transfer to a sanitized fermentation vessel, and add 10% (by weight) of finished kombucha. Add the SCOBY, then cover the vessel with a cloth and secure it with a rubber band. Ferment for about 4 days, until slightly sour (approximately 3.5 pH). Remove the SCOBY and reserve for reuse, then strain the kombucha. Vacuum seal and freeze to prevent further fermentation.

Citrus Seaweed Kombucha
200 grams citrus seaweed (*Flustra foliacea*)
Liquid nitrogen
180 grams sugar
1.82 liters filtered water
200 milliliters finished citrus seaweed kombucha (from a previous batch)
1 kombucha SCOBY

Freeze the seaweed with liquid nitrogen and blend it in a Blendtec to pulverize it. Transfer to a clean container and set aside. In a pot, combine the sugar with an equal amount (by weight) of the water; reserve the remaining water in a separate container. Bring to a boil to dissolve the sugar. Once the sugar has dissolved, pour the sugar water into the reserved water to cool it down, then pour all the liquid over the ground seaweed. Stir it around and allow it to infuse at room temperature for 30 minutes.

Strain the infusion through a fine-mesh nylon sieve, then through another fine-mesh nylon sieve lined with a moistened blue towel to catch the fine particulates. Transfer to a sanitized fermentation vessel. Add the finished kombucha as backslop to lower the pH. Add the SCOBY, then cover the vessel with a cloth and secure it with a rubber band. Ferment at 28°C for 7 to 10 days, or until properly acidified (approximately 3.5 pH). Remove the SCOBY and reserve for reuse, then strain the kombucha.

Vacuum seal and freeze to prevent further fermentation.

Cucumber Kombucha
600 grams sugar
4.4 liters strained cucumber juice (juiced with skin and seeds)
500 milliliters finished cucumber kombucha (from a previous batch)
1 kombucha SCOBY

In a pot, combine the sugar with an equal amount (by weight) of the cucumber juice and heat to dissolve the sugar; reserve the remaining cucumber juice in a sanitized fermentation vessel. Once the sugar has dissolved, pour the sweetened juice into the remaining cucumber juice to cool it down. Add the finished kombucha as backslop to lower the pH. Add the SCOBY, then cover the vessel with a cloth and secure it with a rubber band. Ferment at 28°C for 7 to 10 days, or until properly acidified (approximately 3.5 pH). Remove the SCOBY and reserve for reuse, then strain the kombucha. Vacuum seal and freeze to prevent further fermentation.

Söl Kombucha
150 grams dried Icelandic söl
Liquid nitrogen
5 liters filtered water
550 grams sugar
555 milliliters finished söl kombucha (from a previous batch)
1 kombucha SCOBY

Freeze the söl with liquid nitrogen to break it up into smaller pieces, increasing its surface area. In a pot, combine the sugar with an equal amount (by weight) of the water and heat to dissolve the sugar; reserve the remaining water in a separate container. Once the sugar has dissolved, pour the sugar water into the reserved water to cool it down. Add the söl to the water and sonicate the mixture for 7 minutes at 50% amplitude.

Strain the liquid into a sanitized fermentation vessel. Add the finished kombucha as backslop to lower the pH. Add the SCOBY, then cover the vessel with a cloth and secure it with a rubber band. Ferment at 28°C for 7 to 10 days, or until the kombucha reaches a pH of 3.5. Remove the SCOBY and reserve for reuse, then strain the kombucha. Vacuum seal and freeze to prevent further fermentation.

Elderflower Kombucha
600 grams fresh elderflower blossoms
600 grams sugar
4.4 liters filtered water
400 milliliters finished elderflower kombucha (from a previous batch)
1 kombucha SCOBY

Put the elderflower blossoms in a nonreactive heatproof container. Combine the sugar and water in a pot and bring to a boil to dissolve the sugar. Once the sugar has fully dissolved, pour the hot liquid over the elderflower blossoms and let cool to room

temperature. Cover the container and let stand in the fridge to infuse overnight.

Strain the elderflower syrup through a fine-mesh nylon sieve into a sanitized fermentation vessel, pressing on the blossoms to extract as much liquid as possible. Add the finished kombucha as backslop to lower the pH. Add the SCOBY, then cover the vessel with a cloth and secure it with a rubber band. Ferment at room temperature or just above for 7 to 10 days, or until properly acidified (approximately 3.5 pH). Remove the SCOBY and reserve for reuse, then strain the kombucha. Vacuum seal and freeze to prevent further fermentation.

Geranium Kombucha
200 grams rose geranium leaves
Liquid nitrogen
240 grams sugar
1.76 liters filtered water
200 milliliters finished geranium kombucha (from a previous batch)
1 kombucha SCOBY

Freeze the geranium leaves with liquid nitrogen, then blend them with a Blendtec to pulverize them. Transfer the leaves to a clean container and set aside. Combine the sugar and water in a pot and bring to a boil to dissolve the sugar. Once the sugar has dissolved, pour the sugar water over the geranium leaves and allow the mixture to steep as it cools to room temperature. Strain the liquid through a fine-mesh nylon sieve into a sanitized fermentation vessel. Add the finished kombucha as backslop to lower the pH. Add the SCOBY, then cover the vessel with a cloth and secure it with a rubber band. Ferment at 28°C for 7 to 10 days, or until properly acidified (approximately 3.5 pH). Remove the SCOBY and reserve for reuse, then strain the kombucha. Vacuum seal and freeze to prevent further fermentation.

Ginger Tea Kombucha
100 grams sliced peeled fresh ginger
1 liter filtered water
120 grams sugar
100 milliliters finished ginger tea kombucha (from a previous batch)
1 kombucha SCOBY

Place the ginger and water in a vacuum bag and seal it on 100% vacuum. Steam the mixture in a combi oven at 60°C (100% fan) for 1 hour. Let cool, then transfer the bag to the fridge to infuse overnight.

Strain the ginger tea, then transfer 120 milliliters of it to a pot; reserve the remaining tea in a sanitized fermentation vessel. Add the sugar to the pot and bring the tea to a boil to dissolve the sugar. Once the sugar has dissolved, let the sweetened tea cool to room temperature, then pour it into the remaining ginger tea. Add the finished kombucha as backslop to lower the pH. Add the SCOBY, then cover the vessel with a cloth and secure it with a rubber band. Ferment at 28°C for 7 to 10 days, or until properly acidified (approximately

3.5 pH). Remove the SCOBY and reserve for reuse, then strain the kombucha. Vacuum seal and freeze to prevent further fermentation.

Kiwi Kombucha
2.4 liters Kiwi Juice (page 331)
500 milliliters Cold-Infused White Peony Tea (page 331)
75 grams sugar
290 milliliters finished neutral kombucha
1 kombucha SCOBY

Combine the kiwi juice and tea in a sanitized fermentation vessel and measure the sugar content using a refractometer; it should be 14 °Bx. (Because the sweetness of the kiwi juice will vary, 75 grams of sugar is not an exact measurement; it will have to be adjusted batch to batch.)

In a pot, combine the sugar and a small portion of the kiwi-tea mixture and heat to dissolve the sugar. Pour the sweetened liquid into the fermentation vessel with the rest of the kiwi-tea mixture and let cool. Add the finished kombucha as backslop to lower the pH. Add the SCOBY, then cover the container with a cloth and secure it with a rubber band. Ferment at 28°C for 3 to 5 days, or until the kombucha reaches a pH of 3.5. Remove the SCOBY and reserve for reuse, then strain the kombucha. Vacuum seal and freeze to prevent further fermentation.

Lemon Verbena Kombucha
600 grams sugar
4.4 liters filtered water
50 grams dried lemon verbena leaves
500 milliliters finished lemon verbena kombucha (from a previous batch)
1 kombucha SCOBY

In a pot, combine the sugar and an equal amount (by weight) of the water; reserve the remaining water in a separate container. Bring to a boil to dissolve the sugar, then remove from the heat, add the lemon verbena leaves, and allow to infuse for 10 minutes. Stir in the reserved water and strain through a fine-mesh nylon sieve. Transfer the mixture to a sanitized fermentation vessel and let cool. Add the finished kombucha as backslop to lower the pH. Add the SCOBY, then cover the container with a cloth and secure it with a rubber band. Ferment at room temperature or just above for 7 to 9 days, or until properly acidified (approximately 3.5 pH). Remove the SCOBY and reserve for reuse, then strain the kombucha. Vacuum seal and freeze to prevent further fermentation.

Rose Kombucha
600 grams sugar
4.4 liters filtered water
700 grams spun rose pulp (reserved from making Rose Oil; see page 348)
500 milliliters finished rose kombucha (from a previous batch)
1 kombucha SCOBY

In a pot, combine the sugar with enough of the water to equal twice its

weight; reserve the remaining water in a container. Add the rose pulp to the pot and bring to a boil to dissolve the sugar. Once the sugar has dissolved, pour the sweetened mixture into the reserved water to cool it down immediately. Add the finished kombucha as backslop to lower the pH. Cover the container with a cloth and secure it with a rubber band. Steep at room temperature or just above for 24 hours.

Strain the liquid through a fine-mesh nylon sieve and skim off any residual oil, then transfer to a sanitized fermentation vessel. Add the SCOBY, then cover the vessel with a cloth and secure it with a rubber band. Ferment at room temperature or just above for 7 to 10 days, or until properly acidified (approximately 3.5 pH). Remove the SCOBY and reserve for reuse, then strain the kombucha. Vacuum seal and freeze to prevent further fermentation.

Saffron Kombucha
300 grams sugar
2.5 liters filtered water
3.75 grams saffron
275 milliliters finished saffron kombucha (from a previous batch)
1 kombucha SCOBY

Combine the sugar and water in a pot and heat to 60°C. Add the saffron to the liquid and let steep for 1 hour. Transfer the mixture to a sanitized fermentation vessel. Add the saffron kombucha as backslop to lower the pH. Add the SCOBY, then cover the vessel with a cloth and secure it with a rubber band. Ferment at room temperature or just above for 5 days, or until properly acidified (approximately 3.5 pH). Remove the SCOBY and reserve for reuse, then strain the kombucha. Vacuum seal and freeze to prevent further fermentation.

Sumac Kombucha
2.5 liters filtered water
250 grams wild sumac buds
250 grams sugar
250 milliliters finished sumac kombucha (from a previous batch)
1 kombucha SCOBY

Place the water and wild sumac buds in an airtight container and blend with an immersion blender for 1 minute. Cover and leave in the fridge to infuse for 4 hours. Strain the liquid through a fine-mesh nylon sieve, then through another fine-mesh nylon sieve lined with a moistened blue towel to catch the fine particulates.

Transfer about 375 milliliters of the strained liquid to a pot, add the sugar, and heat to dissolve the sugar; reserve the remaining sumac-infused water in a sanitized fermentation vessel. Once the sugar has dissolved, combine the sweetened liquid with the reserved sumac-infused water. Add the finished kombucha as backslop to lower the pH. Add the SCOBY, then cover the vessel

with a cloth and secure it with a rubber band. Ferment at 30°C for 7 to 10 days, or until the kombucha reaches a pH of 3.5. Remove the SCOBY and reserve for reuse, then strain the kombucha. Vacuum seal and freeze to prevent further fermentation.

Reductions and Syrup

Aronia Berry Reduction
1 liter aronia berry juice

Place the aronia berry juice in a pot and simmer to reduce it to a syrupy texture. Remove from the heat and let cool. Vacuum seal and freeze.

Celery Juice Reduction
5 heads celery, leaves removed

Juice the celery and strain the juice through a conical strainer, then through a fine-mesh nylon sieve. Bring to a boil in a large pot, then skim off the chlorophyll and reduce the juice slowly by 75%. Transfer the reduction to a 1-liter container and place it in a dehydrator set to 60°C. Reduce until syrupy (60 °Bx as measured by a refractometer). Let cool, then vacuum seal and freeze to prevent oxidation.

Cucumber Juice Reduction
5 cases cucumbers

Juice the cucumbers with their skin on and strain the juice through a conical strainer. Bring to a boil in a large pot, then skim off the chlorophyll and reduce the juice slowly until syrupy (approximately 60 °Bx as measured by a refractometer). Let cool, then vacuum seal and freeze to prevent oxidation.

Dashi Reduction
DASHI BASE
2 liters filtered water
30 grams kelp
80 grams katsuobushi

Combine the water and kelp in a pot and bring to a boil. Add the katsuobushi, turn off the heat, and allow to infuse for 10 minutes. Strain the liquid; this is your dashi base.

REDUCTION
800 milliliters Dashi Base
100 milliliters Mushroom Garum (page 338)
100 milliliters sake
10 grams muscovado sugar

Combine the dashi base, garum, sake, and sugar in a pot and heat to dissolve the sugar. Transfer to a 1-liter container and place it in a dehydrator set to 65°C. Reduce to a sugar content of 67 °Bx as measured by a refractometer. Let cool, then vacuum seal and freeze to prevent further oxidation.

Elderflower Syrup

750 milliliters filtered water
750 grams sugar
250 grams elderflower bouquets
80 grams lemon slices

Combine the water and sugar in a pot and bring to a boil to dissolve the sugar. Once all the sugar has dissolved, pour the hot liquid into a container over the elderflower—the flowers will float. Layer the lemon slices over the floating flowers and lay a sheet of plastic wrap over the top, in direct contact with the liquid. Let cool to room temperature, then transfer to the fridge to infuse for 2 weeks. Strain the syrup through a conical strainer, pressing on the pulp to maximize yield; reserve the pulp. Strain the syrup again through a conical strainer. Vacuum seal the finished syrup and reserved pulp separately and freeze to prevent oxidation.

Blueberry Reduction

1 kilogram blueberries

Blend the blueberries in a Thermomix until well puréed. Freeze the mixture in 1-liter containers, leaving room in the containers for expansion in the freezer. Once frozen, remove the solid bricks from their containers and place them in a cheesecloth-lined perforated gastro pan set over a deep gastro pan to catch the liquid as it thaws. Cover and let stand in the fridge for 2 to 3 days, until completely thawed. Wring out the thawed mass for maximum extraction. Transfer the liquid to 1-liter containers and place in a dehydrator set to 60°C. Reduce to a sugar content of 80 °Bx as measured by a refractometer. Let cool, then vacuum seal and freeze.

Fennel Juice Reduction

10 fennel bulbs

Juice the fennel, then strain the juice through a conical strainer into a large pot. Bring to a boil, then skim off the chlorophyll and continue reducing slowly until reduced by 75%. Transfer the liquid to a 1-liter container and place it in a dehydrator set to 60°C. Reduce until syrupy (55 °Bx as measured on a refractometer). Let cool, then vacuum seal and freeze to prevent oxidation.

Gooseberry Reduction

1 liter Green Gooseberry Water (page 330)

Place the gooseberry water in a pot and bring it to a simmer. Transfer the liquid to a 1-liter container and place it in a dehydrator set to 60°C. Reduce to a sugar content of 68 °Bx as measured by a refractometer. Let cool, then vacuum seal and freeze.

Peaso Water Reduction

1 liter Peaso Water (page 330)

Place the peaso water in a pot and bring it to a simmer. Weigh the liquid, then transfer to a 1-liter container and place in a dehydrator set to 60°C. Reduce to 8% of the liquid's initial weight (63 °Bx as measured by a refractometer). Let cool, then vacuum seal and freeze to prevent further oxidation.

Plum Reduction

20 small black plums, pitted

Blend the plums briefly in a Thermomix to purée, transfer to a 1-liter container, and freeze.

Remove the frozen brick of plum purée from the container and hang it in a cheesecloth-lined perforated gastro pan set over a deep gastro pan to catch the liquid as it thaws. Cover and let stand in the fridge for 2 to 3 days, until completely thawed. Bag the residual solids and spin in a centrifuge to maximize yield, then combine the spun juice with the rest of the plum juice. Transfer to 1-liter containers and place them in a dehydrator set to 60°C. Reduce to a sugar content of 50 °Bx as measured by a refractometer. Let cool, then vacuum seal and freeze.

Potato Stock Reduction

2 cases (about 20 kilograms) baking potatoes
Cold filtered water

Roughly chop the potatoes and transfer them to a pot. Add cold water to cover. Bring to a boil, reduce the heat to maintain a simmer, and cook for 2 hours, skimming any scum that rises to the surface. Carefully strain the liquid through a conical strainer and then through a fine-mesh nylon sieve. As you strain the liquid, try to not break apart the potatoes; otherwise, an excess of starch will be released into the stock. Discard the potatoes (or reserve for staff food) and reduce the strained stock by half. Let cool, then transfer to 1-liter containers and freeze.

Remove the frozen bricks of potato stock and hang them in a perforated gastro pan lined with dampened cloths set over a deep gastro pan to catch the liquid as it thaws. Cover and let stand in the fridge for 2 to 3 days, until completely thawed and devoid of any further easily extractable liquid. Do not press on the residual solids or you will cloud the liquid.

Pour the strained potato stock into a pot and bring to a simmer, then transfer to clean 1-liter containers and place them in a dehydrator set to 60°C. Reduce to a sugar content of 20 °Bx as measured by a refractometer. Let cool, then vacuum seal and freeze.

Ryeso Reduction

2 liters Ryeso Water (page 330)

Place the ryeso water in a pot and bring it to a boil. Transfer the liquid to 1-liter containers (filling them no more than 75% full) and place them in a dehydrator set to 60°C. Reduce to a sugar content of 64 °Bx as measured by a refractometer. Let cool, then vacuum seal and freeze to prevent further oxidation.

Sweet Koji Water Reduction

1 liter Sweet Koji Water (page 330)

Place the koji water in a pot and bring it to a simmer. Transfer the liquid to a 1-liter container and place in a dehydrator set to 60°C. Reduce to a sugar content of 63 °Bx as measured by a refractometer. Let cool, then vacuum seal and freeze.

Tomato Water Reduction

2 liters Ice-Clarified Tomato Water (page 330)

Place the tomato water in a pot and bring to a simmer. Transfer the liquid to 1-liter containers and place them in a dehydrator set to 60°C. Reduce to a sugar content of 63 °Bx as measured by a refractometer. Let cool, then vacuum seal and freeze to prevent oxidation.

White Wine Reduction

100 milliliters white wine

Bring the wine to a boil in a pot and reduce it to 30 milliliters. Let cool. Use immediately or vacuum seal and freeze.

Yeast Broth Reduction

400 milliliters filtered water
60 grams Peaso (page 340)
20 grams Roasted Yeast (page 350)
12 grams freeze-dried gooseberries

Blend all the ingredients with an immersion blender until thoroughly homogenized. Transfer the mixture to a 1-liter airtight container and freeze.

Remove the frozen brick of yeast broth from the container and hang it in a cheesecloth-lined perforated gastro pan set over a deep gastro pan to catch the liquid as it thaws. Cover and let stand in the fridge for 2 to 3 days, until completely drained. Weigh the strained liquid, transfer to a clean container, and place it in a dehydrator set to 60°C. Reduce to 8% of the liquid's initial weight (63 °Bx as measured by a refractometer). Let cool, then vacuum seal and freeze to prevent further oxidation.

Ferments

Barley Koji
1 kilogram pearl barley
Salt
Filtered water
1 pack koji tane (*Aspergillus oryzae* spores)

Soak the barley in an ample amount of lightly salted filtered water in the fridge overnight. Rinse the soaked barley in a conical strainer under running water until any excess starch has washed off and the water runs clear. Transfer the barley to a perforated gastro tray and steam in a combi oven set to 90°C (90% humidity, 80% fan) for 45 minutes. Remove the tray from the oven and place on a wire rack on a clean counter.

Line a clean perforated gastro tray with a damp, clean towel. Wearing gloves, use your hands to break up the barley into individual grains, transferring it to the lined gastro tray as you work. Let cool to 25°C.

Using a fine tea strainer with a handle, take a small amount of the koji tane and gently dust it over the barley as if you were dusting a cake with sugar. Once you have completed one pass, use gloved hands to turn the barley to mix it, then sprinkle another round of koji tane over the top. Still wearing gloves, mix the barley one more time and cover it with a clean, lightly dampened cloth. Place the tray on a speed rack in a chamber held at 30°C and 80% relative humidity for 24 hours.

After 24 hours have passed, you should see the first inklings of mold growth. Wearing gloves, mix the barley and furrow it into two rows. Cover with a freshly dampened cloth and let sit in the same conditions for another 24 hours. At this point, the barley should be fuzzy and set into a cake. The koji is now ready. Let it mature in the fridge for 2 days before use; for storage beyond that, transfer to an airtight container and freeze.

Note: This recipe can be adapted to make other varieties of koji, including but not limited to awamori koji (using *Aspergillus awamori* spores) and citric koji (using *Aspergillus luchuensis* spores). These can be used in other recipes calling for koji.

Øland Wheat Koji
1 kilogram polished Øland wheat
Filtered water
1 pack koji tane (*Aspergillus oryzae* spores)

Soak the wheat in an ample amount of filtered water in the fridge overnight. Rinse the soaked wheat in a conical strainer under running water until any excess starch has washed off and the water runs clear. Transfer the wheat to a perforated gastro tray and steam in a combi oven set to 100°C (90% humidity, 80% fan) for 45 minutes. Remove the tray from the oven and place on a wire rack on a clean counter.

Line a clean perforated gastro tray with a damp, clean towel. Wearing gloves, use your hands to break up the wheat into individual grains, transferring it to the lined gastro tray as you work. Let cool to 25°C.

Using a fine tea strainer with a handle, take a small amount of the koji tane and gently dust it over the wheat as if you were dusting a cake with sugar. Once you have completed one pass, use gloved hands to turn the wheat to mix it, then sprinkle another round of koji tane over the top. Still wearing gloves, mix the wheat one more time and cover it with a lightly dampened cloth. Place the tray on a speed rack in a chamber held at 30°C and 80% relative humidity for 24 hours.

After 24 hours have passed, you should see the first inklings of mold growth. Wearing gloves, mix the wheat and furrow it into two rows. Cover with a freshly dampened cloth and let sit in the same conditions for another 24 hours. At this point, the wheat should be fuzzy and set into a cake. The koji is now ready. Let it mature in the fridge for 2 days before use; for storage beyond that, transfer to an airtight container and freeze.

Rice Koji
5 kilograms polished sushi rice
Salt
Filtered water
1 pack koji tane (*Aspergillus oryzae* spores)

Soak the rice in an ample amount of lightly salted filtered water in the fridge overnight. Rinse the soaked rice in a conical strainer under running water until any excess starch has washed off and the water runs clear. Transfer the rice to a perforated gastro tray and steam in a combi oven set to 87°C (90% fan, 100% steam) for 45 minutes. Remove the tray from the oven and place on a wire rack on a clean counter.

Line a clean perforated gastro tray with a damp, clean towel. Wearing gloves, use your hands to break up the rice into individual grains, transferring it to the lined gastro tray as you work. Let cool to 25°C.

Using a fine tea strainer with a handle, take a small amount of the koji tane and gently dust it over the rice as if you were dusting a cake with sugar. Once you have completed one pass, use gloved hands to turn the rice to mix it, then sprinkle another round of koji tane over the top. Still wearing gloves, mix the rice one more time and bring it in from the sides of the tray so the rice is only sitting over the perforations in the tray to maximize airflow. Cover the rice with a clean, lightly dampened cloth and place the tray on a speed rack in a chamber held at 38°C and 80% relative humidity for 24 hours.

After 24 hours have passed, you should see the first inklings of mold growth. Wearing gloves, mix the rice and furrow it into two rows. Cover with a freshly dampened cloth and let sit in the same conditions for another 24 hours. At this point, the rice should be fuzzy and set into a cake. The koji is now ready. Let it mature in the fridge for 2 days before use; for storage beyond that, transfer to an airtight container and freeze.

Fallow Deer Bushi
200 grams salt
100 grams muscovado sugar
45 grams arctic thyme
2 kilograms fallow deer loin
Hay, for smoking
Liquid katsuobushi fungus (*Aspergillus repens*)
Filtered water

Mix the salt, sugar, and arctic thyme to make a cure; set aside while you clean the deer loin. Remove any silver skin or sinew from the loin and pat it dry. Weigh the cleaned loin and measure enough of the cure to equal 5% of that weight. Using gloved hands, massage the cure into the loin. Wrap in parchment paper, seal in a vacuum bag, and cure in the fridge for 6 hours.

Set up a hot smoker lit with hay. Remove the loin from the bag, wipe off the cure, and place the loin in the smoker. Smoke at 60° to 70°C for 2 hours, turning the loin twice during this process to ensure even smoking. The internal temperature of the loin should reach 65°C but should not exceed 70°C. Remove the loin from the smoker and place it in a dehydrator set to 50°C until completely dry.

Dilute the liquid katsuobushi fungus with water at a ratio of 1:9. Place the dilute fungus in an atomizer and spray each side of the loin with two even coats. Transfer the loin to a wire rack and place it in an incubation chamber held at 30°C and 75% relative humidity for 4 days, turning the loin once halfway through the process. When finished, the loin should be covered in a short, fuzzy, bluish-green mold.

Return the loin to the dehydrator and dry it at 50°C for 24 hours, or until completely devoid of moisture. Wrap the deer bushi in parchment, vacuum seal, and reserve at room temperature.

Fermented Wild Boar Belly
128 grams Barley Koji (left)
1 kilogram skin-off wild boar belly (use a center-cut piece to maximize fat-to-lean ratio)
28 grams salt
37 grams Japanese black garlic, peeled

With gloved hands, break up the barley koji into smaller pieces and place in a perforated gastro pan. Steam the koji in a combi oven set to 100°C (100% fan) for 15 minutes. Let cool to room temperature.

Cut the boar belly into smaller cubes, approximately 5 x 5 centimeters. Put the belly in a bowl and combine with the salt and black garlic. With gloved hands, mix the ingredients thoroughly, trying to mash up the garlic while mixing to form a thick paste, which should cover the cubes of boar belly. Add the koji to the bowl and mix by hand until the starch from the koji and the garlic form a starchy film on the bottom of the bowl. Transfer everything to a large vacuum bag and seal on 100% vacuum. Ferment in a chamber held at 28°C for 3 days, flipping the bag over each day, then transfer the bag to the fridge and chill completely. Reseal the bag (100% vacuum) and freeze.

Golden Trout Bushi
DOUGLAS FIR AND KELP PRALINE
280 grams sugar
120 grams Douglas fir needles
150 grams kelp sediment (reserved from making Roasted Kelp Oil, page 348)

TROUT BUSHI
1 golden trout
Salt
Hay and small Douglas fir branches, for smoking
Liquid katsuobushi fungus (*Aspergillus repens*)
Filtered water

Combine the sugar, fir needles, and kelp sediment in a pot and cook over medium-high heat until the sugar caramelizes to amber. Transfer the caramel to a nonstick tray and place in a dehydrator set to 50°C until completely dried. Blend the praline to a powder in a Thermomix and reserve.

Make the trout bushi: Break down the trout into fillets. Remove the pin bones and skin the fish. Cut the fillets in half lengthwise. Season each fillet on both sides with 1% salt and 10% praline by weight. Wrap the fish in parchment paper, vacuum seal in large vacuum bags, and cure in the fridge for 24 hours.

Set up a hot smoker lit with hay and Douglas fir. Remove the fish from the bag and brush off the cure. Place the fillets in the smoker and smoke at 60° to 70°C for 2 hours. Remove the fish from the smoker and dry the fillets in a dehydrator set to 50°C for 24 hours.

Dilute the liquid katsuobushi fungus with water at a ratio of 1:9. Place the dilute fungus in an atomizer and spray each side of the fillets with two even coats. Transfer the fish to wire racks and place them in a chamber held at 30°C and 75% relative humidity for 4 days, turning the fish once halfway through the process. When finished, the fish should be covered in a short, fuzzy, bluish-green mold.

Return the fish to the dehydrator and dry it at 50°C for 24 hours, or until completely devoid of moisture. Wrap the trout bushi in parchment, vacuum seal, and reserve at room temperature.

Nomite
100 grams Peaso (page 340)
90 grams nutritional yeast
10 grams Roasted Yeast (page 350)
700 milliliters filtered water
Celery Juice Reduction (page 333)
Roasted Kelp Salt (page 351)

Blend the peaso, nutritional yeast, roasted yeast, and water together in a Thermomix. Transfer the mixture to a 1-liter airtight container and freeze.

Remove the frozen mixture from the container and place it in a fine-mesh nylon sieve set over a deep container. Cover and let stand in the fridge for 2 to 3 days, until no further liquid remains in the pulp.

Transfer the liquid to a pot and bring it to a simmer. Pour the warmed liquid into a 1-liter container and place in a dehydrator set to 60°C. Reduce to a sugar content of 80 °Bx as measured by a refractometer. Remove from the dehydrator and season with 2.5% celery reduction and 0.5% kelp salt by weight. Let cool, then vacuum seal and freeze.

Rice Amazake
500 grams Rice Koji (page 335)
1 liter filtered water

Blend the rice koji and water in a Thermomix till homogenous. Place in a sanitized nonreactive fermentation vessel and secure a lid on top. Leave in a chamber held at 60°C to ferment overnight. Chill the amazake in the fridge, then use immediately or vacuum seal and freeze.

Brined Japanese Quince
1 kilogram Japanese quince
3 liters 6% salt brine

Place the quince and brine in a sous vide bag and seal on 100% vacuum. Leave the salted fruit in the fridge to rest for 1 month before using. Reserve in the bag in the fridge.

Brined Onion Cress
1 kilogram onion cress
8% salt brine

Wash the onion cress well and remove any large stems. Weigh the onion cress, place in a vacuum bag, and add twice its weight in 8% salt brine. Seal the bag on 100% vacuum and let rest in the fridge for 2 weeks before using. Reserve in the fridge.

Salted Air Onion Capers
1 kilogram air onion bulbs
80 grams salt

Place the air onion bulbs and salt in a sous vide bag and mix them around thoroughly before sealing the bag on 100% vacuum. Let rest in the fridge for 3 months before using. Reserve in the bag in the fridge.

Salted Black Currant Capers
1 kilogram unripe black currants
80 grams salt

Place the currants and salt in a sous vide bag and mix them around thoroughly before sealing the bag on 100% vacuum. Leave the salted currants in the fridge to rest for 3 months before using. Reserve in the bag in the fridge.

Salted Green Gooseberry Capers
1 kilogram green gooseberries
80 grams salt

Place the gooseberries and salt in a sous vide bag and mix them around thoroughly before sealing the bag on 100% vacuum. Leave the salted gooseberries in the fridge to rest for 3 months before using. Reserve in the bag in the fridge.

Salted Noble Fir Cones
5 noble fir cones
5 liters 8% salt brine

Place the noble fir cones in a large vacuum bag with the brine and seal. Leave them in the fridge to rest for a minimum of 1 month before using. Reserve in the bag in the fridge.

When ready to use the cones, remove them from the brine, rinse them lightly, and peel the individual scales from the cones, being sure to remove and discard the inner seed. Vacuum seal the peeled scales in the brine and reserve in the fridge.

Note: The brine can be used to make Noble Fir Salt (page 351).

Salted Unripe Plums
1 kilogram unripe plums
200 grams salt

Place the plums and salt in a sous vide bag and mix them around thoroughly before sealing the bag on 100% vacuum. Rest in the fridge for 3 months before using. Reserve in the fridge.

Salted Ramson Capers
1 kilogram ramson buds
Salt
Apple balsamic vinegar

Place the buds in a sous vide bag with enough salt to completely submerge them and seal. Leave the salted ramson buds in the fridge to rest for at least 3 weeks. Remove the buds from the bag and wash off any excess salt. Weigh them, then place in a new sous vide bag with twice their weight in vinegar. Vacuum seal and let rest in the fridge for 3 months before using. Reserve in the bag in the fridge.

Salted Sloeberries
1 kilogram unripe sloeberries
80 grams salt

Place the sloeberries and salt in a sous vide bag and mix them around thoroughly before sealing the bag on maximum. Leave the salted sloeberries in the fridge to rest for 3 months before using. Reserve in the bag in the fridge.

Garums

BBQ Duck Garum
1 kilogram duck carcasses
Mushroom-Kelp Broth (page 330), reduced by half
225 grams Barley Koji (page 335)
300 milliliters filtered water
240 grams salt

Grill the duck carcasses over medium heat on a charcoal BBQ, glazing them with the mushroom-kelp broth, until they've browned and caramelized. Chop the grilled duck bones into small pieces roughly 4 centimeters in diameter.

In a sanitized nonreactive fermentation vessel, blend the koji, water, and salt with an immersion blender, then add the duck bones and stir them around. Press a sheet of plastic wrap directly against the surface of the mixture and cover the vessel with a lid. Ferment in a chamber held at 60°C for 4 weeks. Every day for the first week, skim off any fat that rises to the surface and stir the garum, then skim and stir once a week after that. Cover again with the plastic wrap and lid after each skimming.

Strain the finished garum through a fine-mesh nylon sieve to remove any solids and skim off any residual fat. Vacuum seal and freeze to prevent oxidation.

Beef Garum
225 grams Barley Koji (page 335)
1 kilogram lean ground beef
300 milliliters filtered water
240 grams salt

Using gloved hands, break the koji into small pieces and transfer to a sanitized nonreactive fermentation vessel. Add the ground beef, water, and salt and blend with an immersion blender to combine, then press a sheet of plastic wrap directly against the surface of the mixture. Cover the vessel with a lid and ferment in a chamber held at 60°C for 10 weeks. Every day for the first week, skim off any fat that rises to the surface and stir the garum, then skim and stir once a week after that. Cover again with the plastic wrap and lid after each skimming. The mixture will separate and the solids will remain on the bottom of the vessel.

Strain the finished garum through a fine-mesh nylon sieve; reserve the solids to dehydrate into sediment (see page 349). Skim off any residual fat from the garum, vacuum seal, and freeze to prevent its flavor from changing.

Blue Mussel Garum
MUSSEL BROTH
10 kilograms blue mussels
2 liters filtered water
1 liter sake

Wash any dirt from the mussels, scrubbing them, if necessary, and remove any visible beards. Heat a large rondeau. Add the mussels, water, and sake to flash boil and steam the mussels. Cover the pot with a lid and agitate the pot to stir the mussels around. Lower the heat and cook until the mussels open, releasing their juices, then cook for 30 to 40 minutes. Pull the pot off the stove, still covered, and let cool. Strain the mussel broth through a fine-mesh nylon sieve and reserve; discard or compost the mussels.

GARUM
200 grams Barley Koji (page 335)
1 liter Mussel Broth
1 liter Cold-Infused Dashi (page 330)
110 grams salt (5% of the total weight)

Using gloved hands, break up the koji into small pieces and transfer to a sanitized fermentation vessel. Add the mussel broth, dashi, and salt and mix to combine. Press a sheet of plastic wrap directly against the surface of the mixture and place a lid on the container. Ferment in a chamber held at 60°C for 7 days, stirring the garum once as it ferments to combine all the ingredients.

Transfer the vessel to the fridge to cool and let rest for 7 days. Strain the finished garum through a fine-mesh nylon sieve, vacuum seal, and freeze to prevent further fermentation.

Chicken Wing Garum
2 kilograms chicken bones
Cold filtered water
3 kilograms chicken wings
450 grams Barley Koji (page 335)
480 grams salt

Put the chicken bones in a large pot and add cold water just to cover, about 3 liters. Bring to a boil, skimming away any impurities that float to the surface, then reduce the heat to maintain a simmer and cook the stock for 3 hours.

Place the chicken wings on a sheet pan lined with parchment paper and roast them in an oven set to 180°C (100% fan) for 40 to 50 minutes, tossing several times while cooking to ensure that they take on an even, dark brown color. Remove from the oven and let cool. Weigh out 2 kilograms of the roasted wings and use a cleaver to chop them into small pieces.

Strain the chicken stock through a fine-mesh sieve and let cool. Pulse the koji in a food processor just enough to break it up into small pieces. Put the chopped chicken wings, koji, salt, and 1.6 liters of the stock in a sanitized nonreactive fermentation vessel and stir to combine thoroughly. Scrape down the walls of the vessel with a rubber spatula and press a sheet of plastic wrap directly against the surface of the liquid. Cover the vessel with a lid and ferment in a chamber held at 60°C for 4 weeks. Every day for the first week, use a clean spoon or ladle to skim off as much fat as you can, then stir the garum and cover again. Skim and stir once a week for the remaining 3 weeks of fermentation.

Strain the finished garum through a fine-mesh sieve and then through a sieve lined with cheesecloth. Allow the garum to settle, then skim off any fat that floats to the surface. Vacuum seal and freeze to prevent oxidation.

Dryad Saddle Garum
1 kilogram dryad saddle mushrooms
200 grams Barley Koji (page 335)
300 milliliters filtered water
60 grams salt

Check each mushroom by cutting it open to ensure worms have not infested it, then chop the mushrooms in a Robot-Coupe until coarsely ground. Transfer to a sanitized nonreactive fermentation vessel and fold thoroughly with the koji, water, and salt. Wipe down the walls of the vessel, then press a sheet of plastic wrap directly against the top of the mixture. Cover with a cloth and secure it with a rubber band to allow the garum to breathe. Ferment in a chamber held at 30°C for 3 to 4 weeks. The finished garum should be pleasantly sour and deep in flavor. Strain the garum through a fine-mesh conical strainer, pressing the pulp with a ladle for maximum extraction. Vacuum seal and freeze.

Egg White Garum
595 grams Rice Koji (page 335)
2.9 kilograms egg whites
150 grams fine salt

Roast 40 grams of the koji until caramelized and let cool. Transfer to a sanitized nonreactive fermentation vessel and blend with an immersion blender. Add the remaining 555 grams koji, the egg whites, and the salt and blend with the immersion blender to combine. Press a sheet of plastic wrap directly against the surface of the mixture and cover the vessel with a lid. Ferment in a chamber held at 60°C for 5 weeks, stirring every few days. Strain the finished garum through a fine-mesh nylon sieve. Vacuum seal and freeze.

Grasshopper Garum
400 grams wax moth larvae
600 grams grasshoppers
225 grams Barley Koji (page 335)
300 grams filtered water
240 grams salt

Blend the insects with the koji in a Thermomix until well blended. Mix the insect purée, water, and salt together and transfer the mixture to a sanitized nonreactive fermentation vessel. Press a sheet of plastic wrap directly against the surface of the mixture and cover the vessel with a lid. Ferment in a chamber held at 60°C for 10 weeks. The mixture will separate and the solids will remain on the bottom of the vessel.

Blend the finished garum in a Thermomix on high speed until smooth, then pass it through a tamis lined with a fine-mesh nylon sieve. Vacuum seal and freeze to prevent oxidation.

Grilled Mushroom Garum

GRILLED MUSHROOMS
16.5 liters filtered water
9 kilograms maitake mushrooms
3 kilograms shiitake mushrooms
1 kilogram Mushroom-Kelp Broth (page 330), reduced by half

Bring the water to a boil. Place the maitakes and shiitakes in separate sanitized plastic buckets. Pour 12 liters of the boiling water over the maitakes. Pour the remaining 4.5 liters boiling water over the shiitakes. Fill two additional buckets with some rocks and place one on top of each mushroom bucket to weight the mushrooms down and keep them submerged. Transfer to the fridge and chill overnight.

Remove the maitakes and shiitakes from their soaking liquid, reserving the liquid from the buckets separately, and drain well. Transfer the mushrooms to a dehydrator set to its maximum temperature and dry until the mushrooms are no longer slicked with moisture on the surface. Grill the dried mushrooms over charcoal, taking care to develop good char without burning. Once color is achieved, glaze generously with the mushroom-kelp broth and return to the heat to cook in the glaze. When the glaze no longer runs, remove the mushrooms from the grill and let cool.

GARUM
5.5 kilograms Grilled Mushrooms
1.24 kilograms Barley Koji (page 335)
5 kilograms reserved maitake soaking liquid
1.7 kilograms reserved shiitake soaking liquid
676 grams salt

Combine all the ingredients in a large container and purée with a large immersion blender. Transfer to a sanitized nonreactive fermentation vessel and press a layer of plastic wrap directly against the surface of the mixture. Cover the vessel with an airtight lid. Ferment in a chamber held at 60°C for 5 weeks; do not stir. Strain the finished garum through a conical strainer and then through a fine-mesh nylon sieve. Vacuum seal and freeze.

King Crab Garum

1 kilogram king crab, in the shell
800 milliliters filtered water
230 grams koji (any type; see page 335)
126 grams salt
50 grams pumpkin seed pulp (reserved from making Pumpkin Seed Oil, page 348)
20 grams kelp

Place the crab in a perforated gastro pan and steam in a combi oven set to 100°C for 3 minutes. Remove it from the oven and let cool slightly. Using scissors, remove the crabmeat from the crab shell and cartilage.

Combine the crabmeat, water, koji, salt, and pumpkin seed pulp in a container and briefly blend with an immersion blender. The goal is to mix the ingredients and break them down slightly, not to purée them.

Transfer the mixture to a sanitized nonreactive fermentation vessel and add the kelp. Press a sheet of plastic wrap directly against the surface of the mixture and cover the vessel with a lid. Ferment in a chamber held at 60°C for 1 day, then remove the kelp and sonicate the mixture at 20% amplitude for 20 minutes. Cover the vessel and return it to the chamber. Ferment for another 4 days, sonicating the mixture at 20% amplitude for 5 minutes and returning it to the chamber each day. After the fourth day of sonicating, leave the garum in the chamber to age for 2 weeks.

Strain the finished garum through a fine-mesh nylon sieve. Vacuum seal and freeze to prevent oxidation.

Lobster Garum

225 grams Barley Koji (page 335)
1 kilogram cooked lobster meat
300 milliliters filtered water
240 grams salt

Using gloved hands, break up the koji into small pieces and transfer to a sanitized nonreactive fermentation vessel. Add the lobster meat, water, and salt and blend with an immersion blender to combine, then press a sheet of plastic wrap directly against the surface of the mixture. Cover the vessel with a lid and ferment in a chamber held at 60°C for 10 weeks. Every day for the first week, skim off any fat that rises to the surface, stir, and cover again. Skim and stir once a week for the remaining 9 weeks of fermentation. The mixture will separate and the solids will remain on the bottom of the vessel.

Strain the finished garum through a fine-mesh nylon sieve and skim off any residual fat. Vacuum seal and freeze to prevent the flavor of the garum from changing.

Maitake Garum

1 kilogram maitake mushrooms
200 grams Barley Koji (page 335)
300 milliliters filtered water
60 grams salt

Chop the mushrooms in a Robot-Coupe until coarsely ground. Transfer to a sanitized nonreactive fermentation vessel and fold thoroughly with the koji, water, and salt. Wipe down the walls of the vessel, then press a sheet of plastic wrap directly against the surface of the mixture. Cover the vessel with a cloth and secure it with a rubber band to allow the garum to breathe. Ferment in a chamber held at 30°C for 3 to 4 weeks. The finished garum should be pleasantly sour and deep in flavor.

Strain the finished garum through a fine-mesh conical strainer, pressing the pulp with a ladle for maximum extraction. Vacuum seal and freeze.

Mushroom Garum

2.5 kilograms cremini mushrooms
1.06 liters filtered water
202 grams salt
363 grams Rice Koji (page 335)

Rinse the mushrooms of any dirt and remove the very bottoms of their stems. Transfer to a sanitized nonreactive fermentation vessel. Combine the water and salt in a pot and bring to a boil to dissolve the salt. Pour the salted water over the mushrooms and use a large immersion blender to blend them into a paste, pitching in some of the koji bit by bit to evenly spread it throughout the paste. Once totally blended, press a sheet of plastic wrap directly against the surface of the mixture and cover the vessel with a lid. Ferment in a chamber held at 60°C for 5 weeks. Strain the finished garum through a fine-mesh nylon sieve, pressing the pulp lightly to maximize yield. Vacuum seal and freeze to prevent oxidation.

Oyster Garum

1 kilogram shucked oysters (both flesh and juice)
225 grams koji (see page 335)
800 milliliters filtered water
Salt

Measure the salinity of the oyster juices with a salt refractometer and mark this number down. Combine the oysters and their juice, koji, and water in a container and weigh the mixture; the target for salt in this recipe is 11% of that weight. Subtract the salinity content of the oyster juices and add salt to reach 11% of the total weight. Blend with an immersion blender to combine, then transfer to a sanitized nonreactive fermentation vessel. Press a sheet of plastic wrap directly against the surface of the mixture and cover the vessel with a lid. Ferment in a chamber held at 60°C for 2 weeks. Strain the finished garum, vacuum seal, and freeze to prevent oxidation.

Shrimp–Tarry Lapsang Souchong Garum

200 grams Øland Wheat Koji (page 335)
2 kilograms peeled Norwegian shrimp
110 grams salt
1.2 liters Cold-Infused Tarry Lapsang Souchong Tea (page 331)

Using gloved hands, break up the koji into smaller pieces and transfer to a sanitized fermentation vessel. Add the shrimp and salt.

Warm the tea in a pot until it reaches 65°C, then pour it over the solids in the fermentation vessel and stir. Place a lid on the vessel and steam in a combi oven set to 60°C (100% fan) for 1 hour to rapidly increase the temperature of the ingredients. Remove the lid and press a sheet of plastic wrap directly against the surface of the mixture, then replace the lid. Ferment in a chamber held at 60°C for 6 days, stirring twice during fermentation to combine all the ingredients.

Transfer the vessel to the fridge to cool and rest for 4 to 5 days. Strain the finished garum through a fine-mesh nylon sieve, vacuum seal, and freeze to prevent further fermentation.

Smoked Beef Garum
1 liter Beef Garum (page 337)

Set up an offset cold smoker lit with birch wood chips. Pour the garum into a 1-liter container and place it on one of the top racks of the smoker. Smoke for 30 minutes, or until the flavor becomes noticeably smoky. Vacuum seal and freeze.

Smoked Mushroom Garum
1 liter Mushroom Garum (opposite)

Set up an offset cold smoker lit with birch wood chips. Pour the garum into a 1-liter container and place it on one of the top racks of the smoker. Smoke for 3 to 4 hours, stirring every 30 minutes. Vacuum seal and freeze.

Spirulina Garum
200 grams spirulina
225 grams Barley Koji (page 335)
800 milliliters filtered water
144 grams salt

Blend all the ingredients together with an immersion blender, then transfer to a sanitized fermentation vessel. Press a sheet of plastic wrap directly against the surface of the mixture and cover the vessel with a lid. Ferment in a chamber held at 60°C for 10 weeks; do not stir. Strain the finished garum, vacuum seal, and freeze to prevent oxidation.

Squid Garum
CLARIFIED SQUID BROTH
3 extra-large Danish squid
Filtered water

Prepare each squid by gently pulling out its insides, being careful to keep the ink sac intact so as not to create a mess or stain the squid's flesh. Pull out the cuttlebone (the clear "backbone" that looks like plastic). Gently place your fingers under the flaps and go around the squid to remove them and some of the outer skin. Reserve the flaps and tentacles for staff food. Place your knife inside the hood and follow the natural seam in the squid to open it. Rinse the squid quickly and gently under cold water, then lay it flat on the cutting board so the inner side of the squid is facing up. Make an incision at the bottom end of the squid, about 2 centimeters up from the wing-shaped bottom edge. Cut 90% of the way through the squid—do not cut all the way through it. After making the cut, flip the squid over, grab the bottom part of the squid where you made the cut, and peel the skin and membrane off using gray towels. Use towels to wipe off any residual membrane or skin from the exterior and interior of the squid.

Cut 1 kilogram of the squid into 2-centimeter cubes and reserve in the fridge. Take the remaining cleaned squid, cut it into smaller pieces, and place in a Thermomix with water at a ratio of 1 part squid to 1.5 parts water. Blend on high for 1 minute, then turn the speed down to 6, set the temperature to 60°C, and blend for 30 minutes. Transfer the squid purée to a vacuum bag and submerge in ice to cool it rapidly. Vacuum seal the bag as much as possible without allowing the paste to escape the bag, then seal the bag in a second bag to prevent any loss if the first one splits open. Steam the double-bagged squid in a combi oven set to 100°C (100% steam) for 45 minutes. The proteins in the squid will coagulate and clarify the liquid.

Carefully cut open the vacuum bags and strain the clarified squid broth through a fine-mesh nylon sieve into a container set over ice. Let cool.

GARUM
200 grams Barley Koji (page 335)
1 kilogram reserved raw squid cubes
800 milliliters Clarified Squid Broth
100 grams salt

Using gloved hands, break up the koji into small pieces and transfer to a sanitized fermentation vessel. Add the squid, broth, and salt and mix. Press a sheet of plastic wrap directly against the surface of the mixture and place a lid on the vessel. Place the container in a chamber held at 60°C and ferment for 7 days, stirring once during fermentation to combine all the ingredients. Transfer the vessel to the fridge to cool and rest for 7 days. Strain the finished garum through a fine-mesh nylon sieve, vacuum seal, and freeze to prevent further fermentation.

Squirrel Garum
1 kilogram squirrel
225 grams Barley Koji (page 335)
300 milliliters filtered water
240 grams salt

Clean the squirrels of any entrails and discard them. Using a cleaver, chop the squirrels (bone in) into 10 or 12 small pieces and place in a sanitized nonreactive fermentation vessel. Using gloved hands, break up the koji into small pieces and add them to the fermentation vessel. Add the water and salt and blend with an immersion blender to combine. Press a sheet of plastic wrap directly against the surface of the mixture and cover the vessel with a lid. Ferment in a chamber held at 60°C for 2 weeks. The mixture will separate and the solids will remain on the bottom of the vessel. Strain the finished garum through a fine-mesh nylon sieve and skim off any residual fat. Vacuum seal and freeze to prevent oxidation.

Yeast Garum
725 grams nutritional yeast
75 grams Roasted Yeast (page 350)
250 grams Peaso (page 340)
225 grams Barley Koji (page 335)
1 liter filtered water
200 grams salt

Blend all the ingredients in a Thermomix for about 45 seconds, or until you have a smooth paste. Transfer the paste to a sanitized fermentation vessel and press a sheet of plastic wrap directly against the surface of the paste. Cover the vessel tightly with a lid and ferment in a chamber held at 60°C for 4 weeks, stirring once a week. The finished garum should be meaty, rich, sour, and full of umami. Purée the garum into a fine paste and pass it through a fine-mesh sieve lined with cheesecloth. Vacuum seal and freeze to prevent oxidation.

Misos and Shoyus

Elderflower Peaso
800 grams dried yellow split peas
Cold filtered water
1 kilogram Barley Koji (page 335)
Centrifuged elderflower pulp (reserved from making Elderflower Oil; see page 346)
100 grams salt, plus more if needed

Place the dried peas in a large container and add double their volume in cold water. Soak at room temperature for at least 4 hours to rehydrate them. Drain the peas, place them in a large pot, and add double their volume in fresh cold water. Bring to a boil, then reduce the heat to maintain a simmer and cook, stirring every 10 minutes and skimming away any foam that rises to the surface, for 45 to 60 minutes, until the peas are soft enough to crush between your thumb and forefinger without applying much pressure. Drain the peas and spread them out on a sheet pan. Let cool to room temperature.

Weigh the peas. You should have close to 1.5 kilograms, but this may vary. Add enough of the koji to equal 66.6% of the weight of the cooked peas. Grind the peas and koji, weigh the mixture, then add enough of the elderflower pulp to equal 5% of that weight and mix well with gloved hands. Check the texture and moisture content by squeezing a small handful of the mixture in your hand; it should easily form a compact ball. If the mixture crumbles, it's too dry, and you'll need to hydrate it; to do so, make a quick 4% brine by blending 4 grams salt into 100 milliliters water with an immersion blender or a whisk until the salt has completely dissolved, then add a bit of the brine at a time to the mixture until you've achieved the proper texture. Weigh the mixture, add enough salt to equal 4% of that weight, and mix thoroughly once more.

One handful at a time, transfer the peaso to a sanitized fermentation vessel, packing it in as tightly as possible. Start at the edges of the bucket, forcing any air out, then work your way toward the center. Punch the mixture down with your fists after each addition to ensure it's well packed. Smooth and flatten the top of the peaso, wipe down the sides of the vessel with a paper towel. and lightly sprinkle the surface with salt to help prevent mold growth. Press a sheet of plastic wrap directly against the surface of the peaso, making sure it reaches all the way to the edges. Wipe down the walls of the vessel again with a clean paper towel.

Find a flat dinner plate that fits snugly inside your fermentation vessel. Place the plate right-side up on top of the peaso and press it down with your hand. Place a heavy rock in a plastic bag to keep things sanitary and set it on top of the plate to weight it down. Cover the vessel with a clean kitchen towel or cheesecloth and secure it with a couple of large rubber bands. Ferment the peaso in a chamber held at 28°C for about 3 months.

The peaso is finished when the texture has softened significantly, the taste of salt has subsided slightly, and sweet, nutty tones have emerged through the perfumed floral notes of the elderflower pulp. It should have a mild acidity without being overly sour. Vacuum seal and freeze to prevent further fermentation.

Fresh Corn Miso
20 kilograms fresh corn
Koji Flour (page 350)
Salt

Clean the husks and silk from the corn and cut all the kernels off the cobs. Grind the kernels with a meat grinder into a large container. Begin adding koji flour until the wetness of the corn is absorbed by the koji and the mixture has the same consistency as a well-made peaso. Weigh the mixture and add 4% of that weight in salt. Mix thoroughly. Pack the miso into sanitized nonreactive fermentation vessels. Weight the miso down and cover according to the directions outlined in the peaso recipe (below). Ferment in a chamber held at 28°C for 2 months. Vacuum seal and freeze.

Peaso
800 grams dried yellow split peas
Cold filtered water
Kelp
1 kilogram Barley Koji (page 335)
100 grams salt, plus more if needed

Place the dried peas in a large container and add double their volume in water. Soak the peas at room temperature for at least 4 hours to rehydrate them. Drain the peas, place them in a large pot, and add double their volume in fresh cold water, measuring how much water you add. For every liter of water, add 23 grams of kelp. Bring to a boil, then reduce the heat to maintain a simmer and cook, stirring every 10 minutes and skimming away any foam that rises to the surface, for 45 to 60 minutes, until the peas are soft enough to crush between your thumb and forefinger without

applying much pressure. Drain the peas and spread them out on a sheet pan. Let cool to room temperature.

Remove the kelp, then weigh the peas. You should have close to 1.5 kilograms, but the weight can vary. Add enough of the koji to equal 66.6% of the weight of the cooked peas. Grind the peas and koji and mix well with gloved hands. Check the texture and moisture content by squeezing a small handful of the mixture in your hand; it should easily form a compact ball. If the mixture crumbles, it's too dry, and you'll need to hydrate it; to do so, make a quick 4% brine by blending 4 grams salt into 100 milliliters water with an immersion blender or a whisk until the salt has completely dissolved, then add a bit of the brine at a time to the mixture until you've achieved the proper texture. Weigh the mixture, add enough salt to equal 6.6% of that weight, and mix thoroughly once more.

One handful at a time, transfer the peaso to a sanitized fermentation vessel, packing it in as tightly as possible. Start at the edges of the bucket, forcing any air out, then work your way toward the center. Punch the mixture down with your fists after each addition to ensure it's well packed. Smooth and flatten the top of the peaso, wipe down the sides of the vessel with a paper towel, and lightly sprinkle the surface with salt to help prevent mold growth. Press a sheet of plastic wrap directly against the surface of the peaso, making sure it reaches all the way to the edges. Wipe down the walls of the vessel again with a clean paper towel.

Find a flat dinner plate that fits snugly inside your fermentation vessel. Place the plate right-side up on top of the peaso and press it down with your hand. Place a heavy rock in a plastic bag to keep things sanitary and set it on top of the plate to weight it down. Cover the vessel with a clean kitchen towel or cheesecloth and secure it with a couple of large rubber bands. Ferment the peaso in a chamber held at 28°C for about 3 months.

The peaso is finished when the texture has softened significantly, the taste of salt has subsided slightly, and sweet, nutty tones have emerged. It should have a mild acidity without being overly sour. Vacuum seal and freeze to prevent further fermentation.

Note: Peaso can be made with any variety of koji—barley, wheat, or rice (see page 335)—depending on the desired result.

Ryeso
1.8 kilograms rye bread
1.2 kilograms Barley Koji (page 335)
120 grams salt, plus more as needed
100 milliliters filtered water

Wearing gloves, cut the bread into pieces that will be easy for your food

processor to manage. Pulse the bread until it crumbles into a coarse meal, then transfer to a sanitized large bowl. Pulse the koji in the food processor, then add it to the rye crumbs along with the salt and thoroughly mix to combine the ingredients. Unlike when making peaso, where the texture is often spot-on from the start, dryness can be a problem when making miso from bread. You will almost certainly need to add moisture. Make a quick 4% brine by blending 4 grams of salt into the filtered water with an immersion blender or a whisk until the salt has completely dissolved. Add the brine to the bread mixture a little bit at a time until you can squeeze the mixture into a loose but firm ball in your hand.

Pack the ryeso mix tightly into a sanitized fermentation vessel. Smooth and level the top, wipe the walls of the vessel clean, and sprinkle the surface with additional salt. Find a flat dinner plate that fits snugly inside your fermentation vessel. Place the plate right-side up on top of the ryeso and press it down with your hand. Place a heavy rock in a plastic bag to keep things sanitary and set it on top of the plate to weight it down. Cover the bucket with a clean kitchen towel or cheesecloth and secure it with a couple of large rubber bands. Ferment in a chamber held at 28°C for 3 to 4 months. Vacuum seal and freeze.

Fava Rice Shoyu
600 grams dried fava beans
600 grams sushi rice
1.9 kilograms filtered water
Koji tane (*Aspergillus oryzae* spores)
365 grams salt

Soak the dried fava beans in double their volume of cold water for 4 hours at room temperature.

Meanwhile, spread the rice over a large sheet pan and toast in the oven set to 170°C for 1 hour, stirring every 15 minutes. The grains should be very dark. Remove the rice from the oven and let cool to room temperature. Crack the rice using a tabletop grain mill on its coarsest setting and set aside.

Drain the soaked beans and put them in a pot with double their volume in fresh cold water. Bring the water to a boil, then reduce the heat to maintain a bare simmer and cook, skimming off any foam that accumulates on the surface, for 45 to 60 minutes, until the beans are soft enough to crush between your thumb and forefinger with light pressure. Take care not to let the beans overcook to the point of mushiness, but even more important is not undercooking them; if the beans aren't soft enough, the koji's mycelium won't be able to penetrate their flesh and take hold. Drain the beans and let cool to body temperature.

Weigh out 1.125 kilograms of the cooked fava beans and place in a large bowl. Add 600 grams of the cracked rice and mix thoroughly. Line an inoculation tray with a clean, lightly dampened towel. Spread the fava bean mixture over the towel. Using a fine tea strainer with a handle, sift the koji spores over the mixture. Place the tray on a speed rack in a chamber held at 25°C for 24 hours, making sure it doesn't sit on the bottom of the chamber or too close to the heat source. Leave the chamber open slightly to allow fresh air in and heat out.

After 24 hours have passed, you should see the first inklings of mold growth. Wearing gloves, break up and turn the koji, then furrow it into three rows. Increase the heat in the chamber to 29°C and let the koji sit for another 24 hours, after which you'll see a fairly drastic color change.

Just before the koji is finished, bring 950 milliliters of the water to a boil, add the salt, and whisk to dissolve. Remove from the heat and add the remaining water to cool down the brine. Set aside until the temperature of the brine falls below 35°C.

Crumble the koji into a sanitized fermentation vessel. Pour the cooled brine over the koji and give it a good stir with a whisk; this is your moromi. Weigh the vessel with its contents and note that number on the side of the vessel. Press a sheet of plastic wrap directly against the surface of the moromi, then cover with either a loosely fitting lid left slightly ajar or with a breathable towel secured with a rubber band (either way, just ensure the mixture can vent). Place the vessel in a spot held at slightly cooler than normal room temperature, with normal humidity, and ferment for 4 months. Once a day for the first 2 weeks, stir the moromi well with a whisk. After that, stir once a week.

After 4 months, calculate how much water was lost to evaporation and add that amount of fresh cold water. Transfer the moromi to a mesh bag and use a small cider press to extract the liquid (as you would press fruits for their juice). Once you've extracted all the shoyu, strain it through a fine-mesh nylon sieve. Vacuum seal and freeze to prevent oxidation.

Kohlrabi Shoyu
2 kilograms moromi solids (reserved from making Nordic Shoyu, right)
1 kilogram kohlrabi, peeled and quartered
Filtered water

In a sanitized fermentation vessel, begin layering the moromi and kohlrabi quarters, ensuring that the kohlrabi is completely buried and encased in the moromi. Press a sheet of plastic wrap directly against the surface of the mixture and weight it down lightly with a plate. Leave in a chamber held at 28°C for 21 days to effectively pickle the kohlrabi in the moromi.

Remove the kohlrabi from the moromi (save the moromi; it can be reused for one more batch of kohlrabi shoyu) and dry it in a dehydrator set to 50°C for 10 to 12 hours. Coarsely chop the dried kohlrabi, weigh it, and blend with twice its weight in water using an immersion blender. Pour the mixture into 1-liter airtight containers and freeze.

Remove the frozen bricks of puréed kohlrabi from the containers and hang them in a cheesecloth-lined shallow perforated gastro tray set over a deep gastro tray to catch the liquid as it thaws. Cover and let stand in the fridge for 2 to 3 days, until completely thawed and devoid of any further easily extractable liquid. Do not press on the residual solids or you will cloud the shoyu. Vacuum seal the kohlrabi shoyu and freeze to prevent further fermentation.

Nordic Shoyu
600 grams dried yellow split peas
600 grams whole-grain wheat
Koji tane (*Aspergillus oryzae* spores)
1.9 kilograms filtered water
365 grams salt

Place the dried peas in a large container and add double their volume in cold water. Soak at room temperature for 4 hours to rehydrate.

While the peas are soaking, spread the wheat over a large sheet pan and roast it in an oven set to 170°C (100% fan) for 1 hour, stirring every 15 minutes. The grains should be very dark. Remove from the oven and let cool to room temperature, then crack the wheat using a tabletop grain mill on its coarsest setting. Set the cracked wheat aside.

Drain the soaked the peas and put them in a large pot. Cover again with double their volume in fresh cold water. Bring to a boil, then reduce the heat to maintain a bare simmer and cook, skimming any foam that accumulates on the surface, for 45 to 60 minutes, until the peas are soft enough to crush between your thumb and forefinger with light pressure. Take care not to let the peas overcook to the point of mushiness, but even more important is not undercooking them; if the peas aren't soft enough, the koji's mycelium won't be able to penetrate their flesh and take hold. Drain the peas and let cool to body temperature.

Weigh out 1.125 kilograms of cooked peas, place in a large bowl, and mix thoroughly with 600 grams of the cracked wheat. Line an inoculation tray with a clean, lightly dampened kitchen towel. Spread the pea mixture over the towel. Using a fine tea strainer, sift the koji spores over the mixture. Place the tray in a chamber held at 25°C for 24 hours, making sure it doesn't sit on the bottom of the chamber or too close to the heat source. Leave the chamber open slightly to allow fresh air in and heat out.

After 24 hours have passed, you should see the first inklings of mold growth. Wearing gloves, use your hands to break up and turn the koji, then furrow it into three rows. Increase the heat in the chamber to 29°C and let the koji sit for another 24 hours, after which you'll see a fairly drastic color change.

Just before the koji is finished, bring 950 milliliters of the water to a boil, add the salt, and whisk to dissolve. Remove from the heat and add the remaining water to cool down the brine. Set aside until the temperature of the brine falls below 35°C.

Crumble the koji into a sanitized fermentation vessel. Pour the cooled brine over the koji and give it a good stir with a whisk; this is your moromi. Weigh the vessel with its contents and note that number on the side of the vessel. Press a sheet of plastic wrap directly against the surface of the mixture, then cover the vessel with a breathable towel and secure it with a rubber band. Place the vessel in a spot held at slightly cooler than normal room temperature, with normal humidity, and ferment for 4 months. Once a day for the first 2 weeks, stir the moromi well with a whisk. After that, stir once a week.

After 4 months, calculate how much water was lost to evaporation and add that amount of fresh cold water. Transfer the moromi to a mesh bag and use a small cider press to extract the liquid (as you would press fruits for their juice). Once you've extracted all the shoyu, strain it through a fine-mesh nylon sieve. (Reserve the moromi solids to make Kohlrabi Shoyu, left.) Vacuum seal the Nordic shoyu and freeze to prevent oxidation.

Smoked Mussel Shoyu
SMOKED MUSSELS
200 grams Barley Koji (page 335)
800 milliliters filtered water
10 grams salt
5 grams Madagascar peppercorns (voatsiperifery)
10 kilograms blue mussels

Blend the koji, water, salt, and Madagascar pepper in a Thermomix till smooth and homogenous. Transfer this cure to a container and set aside.

Wash any dirt from the mussels, scrubbing them if necessary, and remove any visible beards. Heat a large rondeau. Add the mussels and enough water to steam open the shells. Cook until the mussels have opened, remove them from the pan, and let cool. Remove the meat from the shells, placing the mussels in an airtight container and discarding the shells. Weigh the mussels and pour an equal amount (by weight) of the cure over them; make sure they are fully submerged. Cure in the fridge for 1 hour.

Set up an offset cold smoker. Fill a smoking coil with wood dust and light it with a bit of white-hot charcoal. Set a wire rack over a gastro pan. Using gloved hands, remove the mussels from the cure and lay them out on the rack, allowing the cure to drip off. Transfer the gastro pan setup to the smoker. Smoke the mussels for 3½ hours, then transfer to a dehydrator set to 50°C and dry overnight.

SHOYU
400 milliliters Cold-Infused Dashi (page 330)
400 milliliters Fava Rice Shoyu (page 340)
80 grams dried Smoked Mussels

Combine all the ingredients in a vacuum bag and seal, then seal the first bag in a second bag to prevent any loss if the first one splits open. Steam in a combi oven set to 70°C (100% fan) for 3 hours. Remove the bag and shock in ice water, then transfer the bag (still sealed) to a gastro pan and leave in the fridge to infuse for 7 days. Strain the shoyu through a fine-mesh nylon sieve, vacuum seal, and freeze to prevent oxidation.

Smoked Seaweed Shoyu
120 grams kelp
1 liter Nordic Shoyu (page 341)
1 liter filtered water

Set up an offset cold smoker. Break the kelp into smaller pieces and place in a perforated gastro pan. Transfer the pan to the smoker and smoke the kelp for 1 hour. Combine the smoked kelp, shoyu, and water in a sanitized nonreactive fermentation vessel. Ferment in a chamber held at 60°C for 4 days. Strain the shoyu, vacuum seal, and freeze.

Black Pepper Tamari
1 kilogram Peaso (page 340)
10 grams black peppercorns, toasted
2.02 liters filtered water

Place the peaso in a large container. Grind the peppercorns into a powder and add it to the peaso. Add the water and use a large immersion blender to blend until homogenous. Transfer the mixture to 1-liter airtight containers and freeze.

Remove the frozen bricks of peaso mixture from the containers and hang them in a cheesecloth-lined perforated gastro tray set over a deep gastro tray to catch the liquid as it thaws. Cover and let stand in the fridge for 2 to 3 days, until completely thawed and devoid of any further easily extractable liquid. Do not press on the residual solids or you will cloud the tamari. Transfer the tamari to clean containers, place in a dehydrator set to 60°C, and reduce until syrupy (67 °Bx on the refractometer). Let cool, then vacuum seal and freeze.

Cep Tamari
500 grams dried ceps
4 liters hot filtered water
500 grams Peaso (page 340)

Combine the dried ceps and hot water in a sanitized container. Fill another sanitized container with rocks and place it in the first to keep the mushrooms submerged. Transfer to the fridge to soak overnight.

Add the peaso to the vessel with the mushrooms and their soaking liquid and purée with an immersion blender. Transfer the mixture to 1-liter airtight containers and freeze.

Remove the frozen bricks of purée from the containers and hang them in a cheesecloth-lined shallow perforated gastro tray set over a deep gastro tray to catch the liquid as it thaws. Cover and let stand in the fridge for 2 to 3 days, until completely thawed and devoid of any further easily extractable liquid. Do not press on the residual solids or you will cloud the tamari. Transfer the liquid to clean containers, place in a dehydrator set to 60°C, and reduce until syrupy (60 °Bx on the refractometer). Let cool, then vacuum seal and freeze.

Kimchi Tamari
KIMCHI PASTE
24 grams Dried Horseradish (page 350)
64 grams seeded dried pasilla chile
71 grams yellow mustard seeds
250 grams Lacto Green Gooseberries (page 345)
22 grams muscovado sugar

Grind the horseradish, pasilla chile, and mustard seed to a powder in a spice grinder. Transfer the mixture to a blender, add the gooseberries and sugar, and blend into a homogenous paste. If not using immediately, transfer the kimchi paste to an airtight container and reserve in the fridge until needed.

TAMARI
50 grams Kimchi Paste, plus more as needed
50 grams Peaso (page 340)
200 milliliters filtered water

Blend all the ingredients in a Thermomix on high speed until smooth. Transfer the purée to an airtight container and freeze. Remove the frozen brick of purée from the container and hang it in a fine-mesh nylon sieve set over a deep container to catch the liquid as it thaws. Cover and let stand in the fridge for 2 to 3 days, until completely thawed. Do not press the residual solids or you will cloud the tamari. Transfer the liquid to a clean container and place it in a dehydrator set to 60°C. Reduce the tamari to a sugar content of 48 °Bx as measured by a refractometer. Weigh the reduction and add additional kimchi paste to equal 5% of that weight. Stir the mixture well, then centrifuge for 10 minutes and strain the resulting liquid through a fine-mesh nylon sieve. Vacuum seal and freeze.

Red Pepper Tamari
500 grams red bell peppers, seeded
Peaso (page 340)
Filtered water
Fresh red bell pepper juice

Weigh the seeded peppers, chop them into pieces small enough to fit into the jug of a Thermomix, and blend until finely chopped. Add an equal weight of peaso and blend again to homogenize. Transfer the mixture to a sanitized fermentation

vessel. Press a sheet of plastic wrap directly against the surface of the mixture, then top with a plate and cover with a lid. Ferment in a chamber held at 60°C for 7 days. Weigh the pepper-peaso mixture, add twice its weight in water, and blend with an immersion blender. Transfer the mixture to 1-liter airtight containers and freeze.

Remove the frozen bricks of pepper-peaso mixture from the containers and hang them in a cheesecloth-lined perforated gastro tray set over a deep gastro tray to catch the liquid as it thaws. Cover and let stand in the fridge for 2 to 3 days, until completely thawed and devoid of any further easily extractable liquid. Do not press on the residual solids or you will cloud the tamari.

Transfer the tamari to clean containers, place in a dehydrator set to 60°C, and reduce until the liquid reaches 70 °Bx as measured by a refractometer. Season the tamari to taste with fresh red bell pepper juice and let cool. Vacuum seal and freeze.

Strawberry-Rhubarb Tamari
1.59 kilograms frozen strawberries
1.1 liters filtered water, plus more as needed
100 grams freeze-dried rhubarb
2.79 kilograms Peaso (page 340, made with rice koji)

In a large container, purée the strawberries with a large immersion blender. Heat the water to 60°C, then pour it over the puréed strawberries. Mix in the freeze-dried rhubarb so the rhubarb is well soaked. Add the rice peaso and blend with the immersion blender till well homogenized. Transfer the mixture to a sanitized fermentation vessel and press a sheet of plastic wrap directly against the surface, then top with a plate. Ferment in a chamber held at 60°C for 7 days.

Weigh the mixture, add twice its weight in filtered water, and blend with an immersion blender to combine. Transfer the mixture to 1-liter airtight containers and freeze.

Remove the frozen bricks of strawberry mixture from the containers and hang them in a cheesecloth-lined perforated gastro tray set over a deep gastro tray to catch the liquid as it thaws. Cover and let stand in the fridge for 2 to 3 days, until completely thawed and devoid of any further easily extractable liquid. Do not press on the residual solids or you will cloud the tamari.

Transfer the liquid to clean containers, place in a dehydrator set to 60°C, and reduce to a sugar content of 67 °Bx as measured by a refractometer. Let cool, then vacuum seal and freeze.

Vinegars and Pickled Goods

Aquavit-Seawater Vinegar
VINEGAR BASE
300 milliliters aquavit
600 milliliters seawater

Place the aquavit in a rondeau and bring it to a simmer, then carefully ignite the aquavit. Turn off the burner and leave the aquavit ablaze until all the alcohol burns off (use caution when burning off large quantities of high-proof alcohol). Strain the aquavit through a fine-mesh nylon sieve into another pot and let cool.

Strain the seawater through a fine-mesh nylon sieve into a separate pot and bring it to a boil. Remove the pot from the stove and strain the seawater through a fine-mesh nylon sieve to further remove any particulates or sand. Combine the aquavit and seawater; this is the vinegar base.

VINEGAR
850 milliliters Vinegar Base
42.5 grams muscovado sugar
170 milliliters apple balsamic vinegar
68 milliliters ethanol

Combine about 125 milliliters of the vinegar base and the sugar in a saucepan and heat to dissolve the sugar; reserve the remaining vinegar base in a sanitized fermentation vessel. Once the sugar has dissolved, pour the sweetened vinegar base into the fermentation vessel with the rest of the vinegar base and whisk to homogenize. Whisk in the apple balsamic vinegar and ethanol. Place an air stone in the vessel so that it rests on the bottom and run the hose out the top to an air pump. Cover the vessel with cheesecloth and secure it with a rubber band. Transfer the vessel to a chamber held at 28°C and turn on the pump. Ferment for 10 to 14 days, or until you can't taste the alcohol anymore and the vinegar has a pH of approximately 3.2. Strain the vinegar through cheesecloth, vacuum seal, and freeze to prevent further fermentation.

Butternut Squash Vinegar
4 kilograms butternut squash, halved and seeded
Apple balsamic vinegar
Ethanol (96% ABV)

Cut the squash into manageable pieces, leaving the skin on. Wearing gloves, put the squash through a juicer. Strain the juice through a fine-mesh sieve and weigh it. Pour the juice into a sanitized fermentation vessel and add 20% of its weight in vinegar. Weigh the mixture and add 8% of the total weight in ethanol. Place an air stone in the vessel so that it rests on the bottom and run the hose out the top to an air pump. Cover the vessel with cheesecloth and secure it with a rubber band. Transfer to a chamber held at 28°C and turn on the pump. Ferment for 10 to 14 days. Strain the squash vinegar through cheesecloth, vacuum seal, and freeze to prevent further fermentation.

Celery Vinegar
Celery stalks
Apple balsamic vinegar
Ethanol (96% ABV)

Run the celery through a juicer and strain the juice through a fine-mesh nylon sieve. Weigh the juice. In a sanitized nonreactive fermentation vessel, combine the celery juice with 20% of its weight in vinegar. Weigh the mixture and add 8% of the total weight in ethanol. Add an air stone to the vessel so that it rests on the bottom and run the hose out the top to an air pump. Cover the vessel with cheesecloth and secure it with a rubber band. Transfer the vessel to a chamber held at 28°C and turn on the pump. Ferment for 14 days, until the desired flavor is achieved. Strain the celery vinegar (if necessary), vacuum seal, and reserve in the fridge or freezer.

Cep and Birch Bark Vinegar
60 grams carrots, sautéed
60 grams white onions, sautéed
220 grams birch bark
150 grams dried ceps
4 bay leaves
4 allspice berries
4 garlic cloves
2 liters filtered water
Apple balsamic vinegar
Ethanol (96% ABV)

Combine the carrots, onions, birch bark, ceps, bay leaves, allspice, garlic, and water in a sous vide bag and vacuum seal on maximum. Steam in a combi oven set to 90°C (100% fan, 100% steam) for 12 hours. Strain the stock through a fine-mesh nylon sieve, pressing the solids for maximum extraction, and let cool to room temperature.

Weigh the stock. In a sanitized nonreactive fermentation vessel, mix the stock with 20% of its weight in vinegar. Weigh the mixture and add 8% of the total weight in ethanol. Place an air stone in the vessel so it rests on the bottom and run the hose out the top to an air pump. Cover the vessel with cheesecloth and secure it with a rubber band. Transfer the vessel to a chamber held at 28°C and turn on the pump. Ferment for 20 days. Strain the vinegar, vacuum seal, and freeze.

Cherry Vinegar
Sweet cherries, stemmed
Apple balsamic vinegar
Ethanol (96% ABV)

Cut the cherries in half and remove the pits. Using a wine press lined with cheesecloth, squeeze and press the cherries to yield as much juice as possible. Strain the juice through a fine-mesh nylon sieve and weigh it. In a sanitized nonreactive fermentation vessel, mix the cherry juice with 20% of its weight in vinegar. Weigh the mixture and add 8% of that weight in ethanol. Add an air stone to the vessel so that it rests on the bottom and run the hose out the top to an air pump. Cover the vessel with cheesecloth and secure it with a rubber band. Transfer the vessel to a chamber held at 28°C and turn on the pump. Ferment for 14 days, until the desired flavor is achieved. Strain the cherry vinegar (if necessary), vacuum seal, and reserve in the fridge or freezer.

Double Algae Vinegar
80 grams kelp
500 milliliters filtered water
100 milliliters apple balsamic vinegar
48 milliliters ethanol (96% ABV)

Set up an offset cold smoker. Break 40 grams of the kelp into smaller pieces and place in a perforated gastro pan. Transfer the pan to the smoker and smoke the kelp for 1 hour. Place the smoked kelp, remaining 40 grams unsmoked kelp, and water in a vacuum bag and seal on 100% vacuum. Steam in a combi oven set to 60°C (100% fan, 100% humidity) for 1 hour. Strain the contents of the bag through a fine-mesh nylon sieve and let cool to room temperature, then transfer to a sanitized fermentation vessel and add the vinegar and ethanol. Place an air stone in the liquid so that it rests on the bottom of the vessel and run the hose out the top to an air pump. Cover the vessel with cheesecloth and secure it with a rubber band. Transfer to a chamber held at 22°C and turn on the pump. Ferment for about 2 weeks, until properly acidified. Strain the algae vinegar, vacuum seal, and freeze.

Elderberry Balsamic Vinegar
1.15 kilograms sugar
1.15 liters plus 1.7 liters filtered water
500 grams elderflower blossoms, stemmed
1 packet liquid saison yeast
1 liter apple balsamic vinegar
600 grams ripe elderberries, stemmed

Put the sugar and 1.15 liters of the water in a large pot and bring to a boil to dissolve the sugar. Meanwhile, put the elderflowers in an airtight container. Once the sugar has dissolved, pour the liquid over the elderflowers and let cool to room temperature. Place a couple of sheets of plastic wrap in direct contact with the surface of the liquid—the elderflowers tend to float and the plastic will help keep them submerged—then cover and leave in the fridge to infuse for 2 weeks.

Strain the elderflower syrup through a fine-mesh sieve into a sanitized 5-liter fermentation vessel, pressing on the elderflowers for maximum extraction. Add the remaining 1.7 liters water, which will bring the sugar content down to 30 °Bx (from a starting point of 50 °Bx) as measured by a refractometer. Add the yeast and stir with a clean spoon. Cover the vessel with a lid, ensuring that it's airtight, then fill the airlock with water and insert it into the rubber stopper. Transfer the vessel to a chamber held at slightly cooler than room temperature—about 18°C is ideal—and ferment for 3 to 5 days. We want a good amount of residual sweetness left in the elderberry wine and an alcohol level of 8% to 10% ABV. If you're using a refractometer, take an initial reading, then test again after the third day of fermentation.

Once you've reached the desired alcohol content, add the apple cider vinegar and elderberries. Cover the vessel with cheesecloth and secure it with a rubber band. Ferment at room temperature for 3 to 4 months, stirring every few days with a clean spoon, as the berries tend to float.

Strain the vinegar through a fine-mesh sieve, pressing the berries against the sides of the sieve for maximum extraction, then strain again through cheesecloth. Using a funnel, transfer the vinegar to a small oak barrel and cap the hole. Leave the barrel in a cool room or basement, ideally around 18°C. The humidity of the environment will affect the rate of evaporation within the barrel; the drier the room, the faster it will evaporate. Store the elderberry vinegar in the barrel; it can be used immediately but will gain complexity as it ages.

Lemon Thyme Vinegar
Lemon thyme flower buds
Apple balsamic vinegar

Vacuum seal the lemon thyme buds with twice their weight in vinegar. Age in the fridge for at least 6 months before using. Reserve in the fridge.

Oregano Vinegar
Oregano flower buds
Apple balsamic vinegar

Vacuum seal the oregano buds with twice their weight in vinegar. Age in the fridge for at least 6 months before using. Reserve in the fridge.

Pine Vinegar
60 grams Douglas fir needles
200 milliliters white wine vinegar

Blend the fir needles and vinegar together in a Thermomix on full speed for 45 seconds, then strain immediately through a fine-mesh nylon sieve. Vacuum seal and reserve in the fridge.

Quince Vinegar
Quince Juice (page 331)
Apple balsamic vinegar
Ethanol (96% ABV)

In a sanitized nonreactive fermentation vessel, mix the quince juice with 20% of its weight in vinegar. Weigh the mixture and add 8% of that weight in ethanol. Place an air stone in the vessel so it rests on the bottom and run the hose out the top to an air pump. Cover the vessel with

a cheesecloth and secure it with a rubber band. Transfer the vessel to a chamber held at 28°C and turn on the pump. Ferment for 14 days, until the desired flavor is achieved. Strain the vinegar (if necessary), vacuum seal, and reserve in the fridge or freezer.

Smoked Kelp Vinegar
VINEGAR BASE
280 grams kelp
1 liter Cold-Infused Dashi (page 330)
1 liter Cold-Infused Tarry Lapsang Souchong Tea (page 331)

Set up an offset cold smoker. Break the kelp into smaller pieces and place in a perforated gastro container. Transfer the pan to the smoker and smoke the kelp for 1 hour. Transfer the smoked kelp to a pot and pour in the dashi and tea. Heat to a gentle simmer, then turn off the heat and let the vinegar base cool to room temperature, 45 minutes to 1 hour.

VINEGAR
1 liter vinegar base
200 milliliters apple balsamic vinegar
80 milliliters ethanol (96% ABV)

In a sanitized fermentation vessel, whisk together the cooled vinegar base, apple balsamic vinegar, and ethanol. Place an air stone in the vessel so that it rests on the bottom and run the hose out the top to an air pump. Cover the vessel with cheesecloth and secure it with a rubber band. Transfer the vessel to a chamber held at 28°C and turn on the pump. Ferment for 10 to 14 days, or until you can't taste the alcohol anymore and the vinegar has a pH of approximately 3.2. Strain the vinegar through cheesecloth. Vacuum seal and freeze to prevent further fermentation.

Whisky Vinegar
1.5 liters plus 350 milliliters 80-proof whisky
400 milliliters unpasteurized apple cider vinegar
Filtered water

Heat a tall, deep pot till very hot but not smoking. Add 500 milliliters of the whisky to flash-boil it. Exercising extreme caution, use a grill lighter to ignite the boiling whisky and let the alcohol burn off. Once the flames have subsided, add 500 milliliters more whisky and repeat the process; repeat again with another 500 milliliters of the whisky. Once the initial 1.5 liters of whisky has burned off, add enough filtered water to the pot to bring the total volume of liquid up to 1.25 liters. Add the remaining 350 milliliters whisky and the vinegar.

Transfer the mixture to a sanitized fermentation vessel, place an air stone in the vessel so that it rests on the bottom, and run the hose out the top to an air pump. Cover the vessel with cheesecloth and secure it with a rubber band. Transfer the vessel to a chamber held at 28°C and turn on the pump. Ferment for 14 days, tasting frequently toward the end of this time frame, until the desired flavor

is achieved. Strain the whisky vinegar (if necessary), vacuum seal, and reserve in the fridge or freezer.

Pickled Black Currant Shoots
1 kilogram black currant shoots
2 liters apple balsamic vinegar

Vacuum seal the black currant shoots with the vinegar. Age in the fridge for at least 6 months before using. Reserve in the bag in the fridge.

Pickled Elderflower
1 kilogram elderflower blossoms (smaller stems attached)
2 liters apple balsamic vinegar

Vacuum seal the elderflower blossoms with the vinegar. Age in the fridge for at least 6 months before using. Reserve in the bag in the fridge.

Pickled Rose Petals
1 kilogram beach rose petals
2 liters apple balsamic vinegar

Vacuum seal the rose petals with the vinegar. Age in the fridge for at least 6 months before using. Reserve in the bag in the fridge.

Pickled Chanterelles
500 grams button chanterelles
1 liter Butternut Squash Vinegar (page 343)

Clean and gently wash the chanterelles of any dirt, then allow them to dry on clean towels in the fridge. Transfer the chanterelles to a vacuum bag, add the vinegar, and seal on 100% vacuum. Age in the fridge for a minimum of 1 month before using. Reserve in the bag in the fridge. Cut the mushrooms into small dice before use.

Lacto Fermentations

Lacto Ceps and Lacto Cep Water
2 kilograms frozen ceps
40 grams fine salt

For lacto ceps: Place the mushrooms and salt in a sous vide bag and mix them around thoroughly before sealing the bag on 100% vacuum. Place the bag in a chamber held at 28°C and ferment for 5 days, or until the mushrooms have let out much of their liquid, yellowed, and soured. Should the bag overinflate during fermentation, cut it open to vent the gas, then carefully reseal it and continue fermenting. Strain the contents of the bag through a fine-mesh sieve and reserve the liquid. Transfer the mushrooms to a new bag, vacuum seal, and freeze; use in applications calling for lacto ceps.

For lacto cep water: Transfer the reserved mushroom liquid to an airtight container and freeze.

Remove the frozen brick of mushroom liquid from the container and hang it in a cheesecloth-lined perforated gastro tray set over a deeper gastro tray to catch the liquid as it thaws. Cover and let stand in the fridge for 2 to 3 days, until completely thawed. Vacuum seal the lacto cep water and freeze to prevent oxidation or further fermentation.

Lacto Cherries and Lacto Cherry Juice
1 kilogram sweet wild cherries, stemmed
20 grams fine salt

Place the cherries and salt in a vacuum bag and shake them around to ensure they're evenly coated. Seal the bag on 100% vacuum. Place the bag in a chamber held at 28°C and ferment for 5 days, or until the cherries have soured. Should the bag overinflate during fermentation, cut it open to vent the gas, then carefully reseal it and continue fermenting. Strain the liquid from the bag through a fine-mesh nylon sieve, vacuum seal, and freeze to prevent further fermentation. Transfer the cherries to a separate bag, vacuum seal, and freeze to prevent further fermentation.

Lacto Green Gooseberries and Lacto Green Gooseberry Juice
1 kilogram green gooseberries
20 grams fine salt

Place the gooseberries and salt in a vacuum bag and shake them around to ensure they're evenly coated. Seal the bag on 100% vacuum. Place the bag in a chamber held at 28°C and ferment for 5 days, or until the gooseberries have soured. Should the bag overinflate during fermentation, cut it open to vent the gas, then carefully reseal it and continue fermenting. Strain the liquid from the bag through a fine-mesh nylon sieve, vacuum seal, and freeze to prevent further fermentation. Transfer the gooseberries to a separate bag, vacuum seal, and freeze to prevent further fermentation.

Lacto Green Strawberries and Lacto Green Strawberry Juice
2 kilograms green strawberries, tops removed
40 grams fine salt

Place the strawberries and salt in a vacuum bag and mix them around thoroughly before sealing the bag on 100% vacuum. Place the bag in a chamber held at 28°C and ferment for 5 to 8 days, or until the strawberries have soured and let out a bit of their juice. Should the bag overinflate during fermentation, cut it open to vent the gas, then carefully reseal it and continue fermenting. Vacuum seal and reserve in the fridge.

Lacto Koji Water
1 kilogram koji (any type—see page 335)
2 liters filtered water
60 grams fine salt

In two batches, blend the koji and water in a Thermomix on high speed for 1 minute. Mix the batches of blended koji water together to ensure a homogenous finished product. Add the salt and whisk briefly to incorporate. Transfer the salted koji water to a vacuum bag and seal on 100% vacuum. Ferment in a chamber held at 28°C for 2 to 3 days, until the pH drops to 4.5 or below. The finished mixture should be sweet, sour, and fruity—if it tastes vinegary or alcoholic, it has fermented too far. Pour the fermented koji water into 1-liter airtight containers and freeze.

Remove the frozen bricks of koji water from the containers and hang them in a cheesecloth-lined perforated shallow gastro tray set over a deep gastro tray to catch the liquid as it thaws. Cover and let stand in the fridge for 2 to 3 days, until completely thawed and devoid of any further easily extractable liquid. Do not press on the residual solids or you will cloud the liquid. Vacuum seal the koji water and freeze to prevent further fermentation.

Lacto Plums and Lacto Plum Juice
2 kilograms plums, halved and pitted
40 grams fine salt

Place the plums and salt in a vacuum bag and mix them around thoroughly before sealing the bag on 100% vacuum. Place the bag in a chamber held at 28°C and ferment for 5 days, or until the plums have softened, soured, and released some juice. Strain the liquid from the bag through a fine-mesh nylon sieve. Vacuum seal the lacto plum juice and freeze to prevent further fermentation. The plums can be frozen on sheet trays, then vacuum sealed and reserved in the freezer.

Note: Once defrosted, the skins of the frozen plums can be dried and blended into a powder (see page 349).

Note: The same process can be used to make lacto mirabelle plums; no need to halve or pit the mirabelles before combining with the salt.

Lacto Red Gooseberries and Lacto Red Gooseberry Juice
1 kilogram ripe red gooseberries
20 grams fine salt

Place the gooseberries and salt in a vacuum bag and shake them around to ensure they're evenly coated. Seal the bag on 100% vacuum. Place the bag in a chamber held at 28°C and ferment for 5 days, or until the gooseberries have soured. The berries should have their sweetness diminished but taste pleasantly of lactic acid. Should the bag overinflate during fermentation, cut it open to vent the gas, then carefully reseal it and continue fermenting. Strain the liquid from the bag through a fine-mesh nylon sieve, vacuum seal, and freeze to prevent

further fermentation. Transfer the berries to a separate bag, vacuum seal, and freeze to prevent further fermentation.

Oils and Butters

Ancho Chile Oil
200 grams ancho chiles, stemmed
1 kilogram grapeseed oil

Blend the chiles and oil in a Thermomix on high for 1 minute, then turn the speed down to 6, set the temperature to 80°C, and blend for 9 minutes. Transfer the blended oil to an airtight container and leave in the fridge to infuse overnight.

Transfer the infused oil to a fine-mesh nylon sieve set over a container, cover, and let stand in the fridge for 24 hours. Compost the pulp; vacuum seal the oil and freeze to prevent oxidation.

Árbol Chile Oil
100 grams árbol chiles, stemmed
1 kilogram grapeseed oil

Blend the chiles and oil in a Thermomix on high for 1 minute, then turn the speed down to 6, set the temperature to 80°C, and blend for 9 minutes. Transfer the blended oil to an airtight container and leave in the fridge to infuse overnight.

Transfer the infused oil to a fine-mesh nylon sieve set over a container, cover, and let stand in the fridge for 24 hours. Compost the pulp; vacuum seal the oil and freeze to prevent oxidation.

Black Currant Leaf Oil
600 grams young black currant leaves
400 grams grapeseed oil

Blend the black currant leaves and oil in a Thermomix on maximum speed for 7 minutes. As the timer goes off, immediately transfer the mixture to a gastro container set over another gastro container filled with ice to cool it down rapidly. Once cool, stir the mixture, divide it evenly among 700-gram vacuum bags, and seal on 100% vacuum. Leave in the fridge to infuse overnight. Spin the bags in a centrifuge to separate the oil from the solids. Strain the oil through a fine-mesh nylon sieve and compost the pulp. Vacuum seal the oil and freeze to prevent oxidation.

Black Currant Wood Oil
1 kilogram young black currant wood twigs
2 kilograms grapeseed oil

Use a wood chipper to break the black currant wood into small pieces, or crush it in a mortar and pestle or with a hammer against a hard surface like a cutting board. Immediately place it in a vacuum bag, pour in the oil, and seal, then seal the bag in a second bag to prevent any loss if the first one splits open. Steam in a combi oven set to 60°C

(100% fan) for a minimum of 4 hours or up to overnight. Let cool, then transfer the bag to the fridge and leave to infuse overnight. Strain the oil and compost the wood. Vacuum seal and freeze to prevent oxidation.

Burning Embers Marigold Oil
400 grams red marigold (*Tagetes linnaeus* 'Burning Embers') flowers
800 grams grapeseed oil

Blend the marigolds and oil in a Thermomix at 70°C for 7 minutes. Pour into a container set over ice and let cool, then transfer to the fridge to infuse overnight. Strain the oil through a fine-mesh nylon sieve and set aside. Vacuum seal the pulp in 700-gram bags and spin in a centrifuge to maximize yield. Strain off the oil and mix it with the rest of the flavored oil to homogenize. Vacuum seal and freeze to prevent oxidation.

Celery Leaf Oil
1 kilogram celery leaves
Grapeseed oil

Bring a large pot of water to a boil. Blanch the celery leaves for 5 to 6 minutes, or until tender, then remove with a spider and shock in ice water. Remove the cooled celery leaves from the ice water, wring them out, and place on racks in a dehydrator set at 50°C to dry overnight.

Weigh the dried celery leaves and transfer to a Thermomix. Add three times their weight in oil and blend for 7 minutes. Transfer the blended oil to an airtight container and leave in the fridge to infuse overnight.

Transfer the infused oil to a fine-mesh nylon sieve set over a clean container, cover, and let stand in the fridge for 24 hours. Vacuum seal the oil and freeze to prevent oxidation.

Cep Oil
1 kilogram frozen ceps
2 kilograms grapeseed oil

Vacuum seal the ceps and oil. Steam in a combi oven set to 80°C (100% fan, 100% steam) for 8 hours. Let cool, then transfer the bag to the fridge to infuse overnight. Strain the oil, vacuum seal, and freeze to prevent oxidation. Vacuum seal the ceps and freeze for another use.

Chamomile Oil
300 grams pineappleweed (wild chamomile, *Matricaria discoidea*) buds and leaves (a few tender stems are okay)
600 grams grapeseed oil

Blend the chamomile and oil in a Thermomix on high speed for 7 minutes. Transfer to a container set over another container filled with ice to cool, then leave in the fridge to infuse overnight. Strain the oil through a fine-mesh nylon sieve and set aside. Vacuum seal the pulp and spin in a centrifuge to maximize

yield. Strain off the oil and mix it with the rest of the flavored oil to homogenize. Vacuum seal and freeze to prevent oxidation.

Douglas Fir Oil
450 grams Douglas fir needles
100 grams fresh parsley leaves
Liquid nitrogen
1 kilogram grapeseed oil

Freeze the pine needles and parsley leaves with liquid nitrogen, then transfer to a Thermomix. Add the oil and blend on high speed for 1 minute. Transfer the blended oil to vacuum bags, seal, and spin in a centrifuge at 4000g for 10 minutes. Strain the oil through a fine-mesh nylon sieve; discard the solids. Vacuum seal and freeze to prevent oxidation.

Dried Rose Oil
500 grams dried rose petals
1 kilogram grapeseed oil

Blend the dried rose petals in a Thermomix on high speed for 30 seconds to yield a fine powder. Add the oil and blend on high speed for 6 minutes. Transfer the blended oil to an airtight container and leave in the fridge to infuse overnight. Pour the infused oil into a container lined with a fishnet, cover, and let stand in the fridge for 24 hours. Compost the pulp; vacuum seal the oil and freeze to prevent oxidation.

Elderflower Oil
750 grams elderflower blossoms
750 grams grapeseed oil

Blend the elderflower blossoms and oil in a Thermomix for 7 minutes. Transfer the blended oil to a container set over ice to cool, then cover and leave in the fridge to infuse overnight. Pour the infused oil into a container lined with a fishnet, cover, and let stand in the fridge for 24 hours. Strain the oil and set aside. Vacuum seal the pulp and spin in a centrifuge to maximize yield. Strain off the oil and mix it with the rest of the infused oil to homogenize. Vacuum seal and freeze to prevent oxidation.

Fresh Barley Koji Oil
1 kilogram Barley Koji (page 335)
2 kilograms grapeseed oil

Using gloved hands, crumble the koji into individual grains. Combine the koji and oil in a pot, bring to a boil, reduce the heat to maintain a simmer, and cook overnight. Let cool to room temperature, then strain the oil through a fine-mesh nylon sieve, squeezing the sediment to maximize yield and flavor; compost the sediment. Vacuum seal the koji oil and freeze.

Fresh Mustard Seed Oil
1 kilogram yellow mustard seeds

Preheat a nut press. In a sauté pan, slowly toast the mustard seeds over the course of 10 minutes, until toasted and fragrant. Take your time with this process—if you go too quickly, you run the risk of burning the seeds, which will yield a bitter oil. Transfer the seeds to the preheated nut press and run them through. The yield is not substantial with mustard seeds, but the oil should be deep and nutty in flavor. Compost the resulting solids. Vacuum seal the oil and freeze to prevent oxidation.

Geranium Oil
300 grams fresh rose geranium leaves
Liquid nitrogen
600 grams grapeseed oil

Freeze the geranium leaves with liquid nitrogen, transfer to a Thermomix, and blend on high speed for 10 seconds, resulting in a fine powder. Add the oil and blend on high speed for 5 minutes. Transfer the blended oil to a container set over another container filled with ice to cool it down as quickly as possible. Cover and leave in the fridge to infuse overnight. Strain the oil through a fine-mesh nylon sieve and set aside. Vacuum seal the pulp in a 700-gram bag and spin in a centrifuge to maximize yield. Strain off the oil and mix it with the rest of the flavored oil to homogenize. Vacuum seal the oil and freeze to prevent oxidation.

Hazelnut Oil
1 kilogram Piedmont hazelnuts

Preheat a nut press. Spread the hazelnuts over a sheet pan and toast in an oven set to 160°C (100% fan) for 5 minutes. Transfer the warm hazelnuts to the nut press and run them through to extract their oil. Reserve the pulp for another application. Transfer the oil to an airtight container and leave in the fridge to infuse overnight. Strain the oil through a fine-mesh nylon sieve, vacuum seal, and freeze to prevent oxidation.

Hazelnut and Lobster Garum Oil
200 grams hazelnuts
60 grams Lobster Garum (page 338)

Preheat a nut press. Toss the nuts in the garum on a sheet pan and toast in the oven at 160°C (100% fan) for 8 to 10 minutes, until the nuts color slightly and the garum cooks in. Transfer the hazelnuts to the nut press and run them through. The oil coming out should taste well seasoned and umami rich. If it tastes underseasoned at the beginning of the pressing process, fold a bit more garum through the unpressed nuts and continue. Vacuum seal the oil and sediment and freeze to prevent oxidation.

Horseradish Oil

1 kilogram fresh horseradish
2 kilograms grapeseed oil

Finely grate the horseradish with a box grater directly into the oil to prevent oxidization. Vacuum seal the mixture in a large sous vide bag and let rest in the fridge overnight. Strain the oil, pressing on the pulp for maximum extraction. Vacuum seal and freeze to prevent oxidation.

Kanzuri Oil

250 grams kanzuri paste
750 grams grapeseed oil

Set up a barbecue grill for smoking. Seal the kanzuri paste in a vacuum bag and spin in a centrifuge to separate the solids from the liquid. Pour off the liquid and reserve for another use. Transfer the kanzuri pulp to a tamis and smoke it lightly over the grill for 3 weeks.

Once sufficiently smoked and dried, transfer the kanzuri pulp to a Thermomix, add the oil, and blend on high for 5 minutes. Pour the blended oil into a nonstick pan and slowly simmer for 3 hours. Return the mixture to the Thermomix and blend on high for 5 minutes. Transfer to an airtight container and let cool, then leave in the fridge to infuse overnight. Strain the oil, vacuum seal, and freeze.

Koji Oil

500 grams Dried Koji (page 350)
1 kilogram grapeseed oil

Blend the dried koji and oil in a Thermomix on high speed for 6 minutes. Transfer the blended oil to an airtight container and leave in the fridge to infuse overnight. Transfer the oil to a fine-mesh nylon sieve set over a container, cover, and let stand in the fridge for 24 hours. Compost the pulp; vacuum seal the oil and freeze to prevent oxidation.

Note: Any variety of dried koji can be used for this oil.

Konini Oil

500 grams konini grains
1 kilogram grapeseed oil

Spread the konini over a sheet pan and roast in the oven at 180°C for 1 hour, or until deeply browned and nutty, turning the grains every 15 minutes to ensure even roasting. Let cool, then transfer the grains to a Thermomix and blend on maximum for 15 seconds. Add the oil and blend on maximum for 6 minutes more. Transfer the blended oil to an airtight container and leave in the fridge to infuse overnight. Pour the oil into a fine-mesh nylon strainer set over a container, cover, and let stand in the fridge for 24 hours. Discard the pulp; vacuum seal the oil and freeze.

Lemon Thyme Oil

10 bunches lemon thyme
Liquid nitrogen
Grapeseed oil, chilled in the fridge

Dunk the lemon thyme into liquid nitrogen to freeze it. Working quickly, without letting the lemon thyme thaw, roughly pick the leaves off the stems; discard the stems. Weigh the frozen leaves, transfer to a Thermomix, and add twice their weight in chilled oil. Blend on full speed for 3 minutes. Pour the blended oil into a vacuum bag set over ice and let chill until ice cold. Seal the bag on maximum and leave in the fridge to infuse overnight.

Strain the oil through a fine-mesh nylon sieve and set aside in the fridge. Vacuum seal the pulp in a sous vide bag and spin in a centrifuge to maximize yield. Strain off the oil and mix it with the rest of the flavored oil to homogenize. Vacuum seal and freeze to prevent further oxidation.

Lemon Verbena Oil

600 grams lemon verbena leaves
Liquid nitrogen
1.2 kilograms grapeseed oil

Freeze the lemon verbena with liquid nitrogen, transfer to a Blendtec blender, and blend on high speed for 45 seconds, resulting in a fine powder. Combine the lemon verbena powder and the oil in a plastic container set over ice and sonicate at 100% amplitude for 6 minutes, moving the container continuously to ensure even sonication. Transfer the mixture to a vacuum bag and seal on 100% vacuum. Leave in the fridge to infuse overnight. Strain the oil through a fine-mesh nylon sieve and set aside. Vacuum seal the pulp in 700-gram bags and spin in a centrifuge to maximize yield. Strain off the oil and mix it with the rest of the flavored oil to homogenize. Vacuum seal and freeze to prevent oxidation.

Lovage Oil

1 kilogram lovage leaves
Grapeseed oil

Bring a large pot of water to a boil. Blanch the lovage for 5 to 6 minutes, or until tender, then remove with a spider and shock in ice water. Once cool, remove the lovage from the water, wring the leaves out, and place on racks in a dehydrator set to 50°C to dry overnight.

Weigh the dried lovage and transfer to a Thermomix. Add three times its weight in oil and blend for 7 minutes. Transfer the blended oil to an airtight container and leave in the fridge to infuse overnight.

Transfer the oil to a fine-mesh nylon sieve set over a container, cover, and let stand in the fridge for 24 hours. Vacuum seal and freeze to prevent oxidation.

Maitake Oil

1 kilogram maitake mushrooms
500 grams grapeseed oil

Blend the mushrooms and oil in a Thermomix for 7 minutes. Transfer to a rondeau and slowly cook over low heat to caramelize the mushrooms, which will separate from the oil. Cover the mixture with a cartouche, transfer to an oven set to 80°C, and cook for 2 days, stirring often. Let cool, then transfer to a fine-mesh nylon sieve set over a container and let stand in the fridge overnight. Vacuum seal and freeze. Vacuum seal the mushrooms separately and freeze for another use.

Marigold Oil

250 grams marigold (*Tagetes minuta*) leaves
500 grams grapeseed oil

Blend the marigold leaves and oil in a Thermomix on maximum for 30 seconds, then turn down the speed to 7 and blend for an additional 6 minutes 30 seconds. Transfer the blended oil to a gastro pan set over ice to cool it down rapidly. Vacuum seal and leave in the fridge to infuse overnight. Strain the oil through a fine-mesh nylon sieve and set aside. Vacuum seal the pulp and spin it in a centrifuge to maximize yield. Strain off the oil and mix it with the rest of the flavored oil to homogenize. Vacuum seal and freeze to prevent oxidation.

Meadowsweet Oil

100 grams dried meadowsweet
300 grams grapeseed oil

Combine the meadowsweet and oil in a vacuum bag, seal, and steam in a combi oven set to 60°C (100% fan) for 8 hours. Set the bag in a bowl of ice water and let cool, then transfer to the fridge to infuse overnight. Strain the oil through a fine-mesh nylon sieve. Vacuum seal and freeze to prevent oxidation.

Morita Chile Oil

100 grams morita chiles, stemmed
1 kilogram grapeseed oil

Blend the chiles and oil in a Thermomix on high speed for 1 minute, then turn the speed down to 6, set the temperature to 80°C, and blend for 9 minutes. Transfer the blended oil to a container and leave in the fridge to infuse overnight. Transfer the oil to a fine-mesh nylon sieve set over a container, cover, and let stand in the fridge for 24 hours. Compost the pulp; vacuum seal the oil and freeze to prevent oxidation.

Parsley Oil

300 grams fresh parsley leaves
600 grams grapeseed oil

Blend the parsley leaves and oil in a Thermomix on high speed for 7 minutes. Transfer the blended oil to a container set over ice to cool it down rapidly, then cover and leave in the fridge to infuse overnight. Strain the oil through a fine-mesh nylon sieve and set aside. Vacuum seal the pulp in 700-gram bags and spin in a centrifuge to maximize yield. Strain off the oil and mix it with the rest of the flavored oil to homogenize. Vacuum seal and freeze to prevent oxidation.

Pheasant-Spice Oil
6 pheasants (1.6 kilograms)
Butter
6 bay leaves
20 grams juniper berries
20 grams black peppercorns
4 pieces pasilla chile, seeded
3 liters grapeseed oil

Break the pheasants down into 8 pieces each and smear a bit of butter on each piece. Place the pheasant pieces on a wire rack set over a parchment-lined gastro pan and roast in an oven set to 200°C (100% fan) for 12 minutes. Reduce the oven temperature to 170°C (70% fan) and roast for an additional 20 minutes, until golden brown and crisped. Remove from the oven and let cool.

Transfer the cooled pheasant pieces to a large rondeau and add the bay leaves, juniper berries, pepper, pasilla chile, and oil. Heat over medium heat (setting 6 on an induction burner) to bring the mixture to a temperature of 100° to 110°C, then cook at this temperature for 4 hours (start the timer as soon as the oil comes to temperature). Transfer the oil to 1-liter airtight containers and let cool, then leave in the fridge to infuse overnight. Strain the infused oil first through a conical strainer and then through a fine-mesh nylon sieve. Vacuum seal and freeze to prevent oxidation.

Pumpkin Seed Oil
1 kilogram pumpkin seeds

Preheat a nut press. Spread the pumpkin seeds over a sheet pan and toast in an oven set to 160°C (100% fan) for 8 to 10 minutes, stirring them once. Transfer the seeds to the nut press and run them through to extract their oil. Compost the solids; vacuum seal the oil and freeze to prevent oxidation.

Roasted Kelp Oil
500 grams kelp
Grapeseed oil

Place the kelp in a dehydrator set to 60°C and dry overnight.

Transfer the dried kelp to a Thermomix and blend on high speed for 30 seconds to result in a fine powder, then add twice its weight in oil and blend for an additional minute. Transfer the mixture to a rondeau, heat to 160°C, and cook, stirring continuously, for 15 minutes (start the timer only after the oil has come to temperature). Lower the oil temperature to 150°C and cook for 1 hour, stirring every 5 minutes. Drop the temperature down to 140°C and

cook for 1 hour, stirring every 5 minutes. Continue this process, dropping the oil temperature by 10°C every hour until you reach 80°C, then leave the oil to cook at 80°C overnight.

Bring the oil temperature back up to 130°C and cook for 15 minutes, then drop the temperature to 120°C and cook for 1 hour. Remove from the heat and let cool a bit. Blend the mixture in a Thermomix on full speed for 5 minutes. Strain the oil, reserving the sediment. Vacuum seal the sediment and oil in separate bags and freeze.

Note: The sediment can be used for Golden Trout Bushi (page 336).

Roasted Yeast Oil
500 grams Roasted Yeast (page 350)
1 kilogram grapeseed oil

Place the roasted yeast in a Thermomix and briefly blend it to yield a fine powder. Add the oil and blend on high speed for 7 minutes. Transfer the blended oil to an airtight container and leave in the fridge to infuse overnight. Pour the oil into a fine-mesh nylon sieve set over a container, cover, and let stand in the fridge for 24 hours. Compost the pulp; vacuum seal the oil and freeze to prevent oxidation.

Rose Oil
750 grams wild beach rose petals
750 grams grapeseed oil

Blend the rose petals and oil in a Thermomix on high speed for 7 minutes. Transfer the blended oil to a container set over ice to cool it down rapidly. Divide the oil among medium vacuum bags, seal, and leave in the fridge to infuse overnight. Spin the pulp in a centrifuge to separate the oil from the solids and maximize yield. Strain off the oil, reserving the pulp. Vacuum seal the oil and the rose pulp in separate bags and freeze to prevent oxidation.

Rhubarb Root Oil
1 kilogram rhubarb roots
Grapeseed oil

Wash the rhubarb roots thoroughly with a pressure washer, then transfer to a large bucket of water and wash again as you use a turning knife to carve away their exterior. Once peeled, slice the rhubarb roots into 3-millimeter-thick slices and dry them in a dehydrator set to 45°C until completely devoid of water.

Weigh the dried roots, transfer to a sous vide bag, and add 3 times their weight in oil. Seal and leave in the fridge to infuse for 8 to 12 hours. Strain the oil through a fine-mesh nylon sieve into an airtight container; cover and reserve in the fridge. Transfer the roots to a clean sous vide bag with twice their weight in oil, seal, and leave in the fridge to infuse for 8 to 12 hours. Strain and reserve the

infused oil as you did for the first batch. Repeat the infusion process once more with an equal weight of oil, then strain the oil and discard or compost the roots.

Combine the three batches of infused oil to homogenize, then vacuum seal and freeze.

Smoked Koji Oil
250 grams Koji Oil (page 347)

Set up an offset cold smoker. Fill a smoking coil with wood dust and light it with a bit of white-hot charcoal. Place the koji oil in a 1-liter container, filling it no more than one-third full. Place the container on a rack in the smoker. Smoke the koji oil for a minimum of 2 hours or up to 4 hours. Vacuum seal and freeze to prevent oxidation.

Söl Oil
1 kilogram dried Icelandic söl
Liquid nitrogen
1.8 kilograms grapeseed oil

Place the söl in a dry container and pour liquid nitrogen over it to break it into smaller pieces, increasing its surface area. Transfer the broken-down söl to a Thermomix, add the oil, and blend on high speed for 7 minutes. Transfer the mixture to an airtight container and leave in the fridge to infuse overnight.

Taste the infused oil; you may have to blend it again if it isn't flavorsome enough. Transfer the oil to a fine-mesh nylon sieve set over a nonreactive container and place a weight on top to press the oil. Let stand in the fridge overnight. Vacuum seal the oil and freeze to prevent oxidation.

Spruce Wood Oil
100 grams thin spruce branches
300 grams grapeseed oil

Hammer the spruce branches with a mallet to split open the wood, revealing the aromatic flesh inside. Immediately place the wood in a vacuum bag, pour in the oil, and seal on 100% vacuum, then seal the bag in a second bag to prevent any loss if the first one splits open. Steam in a combi oven set to 60°C for a minimum of 4 hours. Remove from the oven and let cool, then transfer the bag to the fridge to infuse overnight. Strain the oil and compost the wood. Vacuum seal and freeze to prevent oxidation.

Note: Ensure that you pick the spruce wood in the late spring when green shoots are growing on the branches.

Sunflower Seed and Beef Garum Oil
200 grams sunflower seeds
60 grams Beef Garum (page 337), plus more if needed

Preheat a nut press. Toss the sunflower seeds in the garum and spread them over a sheet pan. Cook in an oven set at 160°C (100% fan) for 8 to 10 minutes, until the seeds color slightly and the garum cooks in. Transfer the seeds to the nut press and run them through to extract their oil. The oil coming out should taste well seasoned and umami rich. If it tastes underseasoned at the beginning of the pressing process, fold a bit more garum in through the unpressed seeds and continue. Vacuum seal the oil and sediment and freeze to prevent oxidation.

Toasted Hay Oil
100 grams Toasted Hay (page 351)
800 grams grapeseed oil

Blend the toasted hay and oil in a Thermomix on high speed for 7 minutes. Transfer the mixture to an airtight container and leave in the fridge to infuse overnight. Vacuum seal the infused oil mixture and spin in a centrifuge to separate the oil and pulp. Strain the oil through a fine-mesh nylon sieve, vacuum seal, and freeze to prevent oxidation.

Walnut Oil
1 kilogram walnuts

Bring three large pots of water to a boil and set up an ice bath next to the stove. Blanch and shock the walnuts three times, each time in a fresh pot of water. Drain them well and transfer them to a parchment-lined sheet pan. Place in an oven set to 80°C and dehydrate overnight, or until the nuts are completely dried. Preheat a nut press for 15 minutes. As the press is heating up, coarsely chop the dried walnuts so they'll fit into the press. Feed the chopped nuts into the press to extract the oil. Collect the oil in an airtight container and let settle in the fridge overnight. Strain the oil through a fine-mesh nylon sieve, holding back as much cloudy sediment in the container as possible. Vacuum seal and freeze to prevent oxidation.

Brown Butter
10 kilograms butter, cubed

Heat the butter in a pot over low heat (power 1 or 2 on an induction cooktop) until it splits, bubbles, and caramelizes to a nutty, rich brown. Whisk the contents of the pot often to reincorporate the solids, which will yield an evenly browned final product. Be careful not to scorch the butter and be aware that it will continue to brown after you turn the heat off. Remove from the heat and let cool to room temperature, then strain through a conical strainer. Transfer to an airtight container and reserve in the fridge.

Fresh Barley Koji Butter
2 kilograms butter
1 kilogram fresh Barley Koji (page 335)

The barley koji for this recipe cannot be frozen—it must be fresh. Using

gloved hands, crumble the fresh koji into individual grains. Combine the koji and butter in a pot, bring to a boil, reduce the heat to maintain a simmer, and cook for 8 hours. Let cool to room temperature, then strain the butter through a fine-mesh nylon sieve, squeezing the sediment to maximize yield and flavor; compost the sediment. Vacuum seal the koji butter and freeze.

Smoked Butter, Clarified Smoked Butter, and Smoked Butter Whey
5 kilograms butter, cut into 2-centimeter cubes

For smoked butter: Set up an offset cold smoker. Fill a smoking coil with wood dust and light the dust with a bit of white-hot charcoal. Place the butter in a perforated gastro pan and set the pan on one of the top racks of the smoker. Smoke the butter for 30 minutes, then check to make sure it smells rich and smoky; if so, remove from the smoker. Transfer the smoked butter to a clean airtight container and reserve in the fridge, or use to make smoked butter whey.

For clarified smoked butter and whey: Heat the smoked butter in a pot over low heat (power 1 on an induction cooktop) until it splits to yield clarified smoked butter and smoked butter whey. Carefully pour off the clarified butter from the whey and reserve the two in separate airtight containers in the fridge.

Powders and Dried Goods

Beef Garum Sediment
Beef garum solids (reserved from making Beef Garum; see page 337)

Dry the beef garum solids in a dehydrator set to 60°C overnight or until well dried. Reserve in an airtight container at room temperature.

Dried Douglas Fir Powder
500 grams Douglas fir needles

Dry the fir needles in a dehydrator set to 50°C until completely devoid of moisture. Transfer to a Thermomix and blend on maximum to yield a powder. Pass the powder through a fine-mesh nylon sieve and reserve in an airtight container at room temperature.

Dried Tomato Powder
100 grams cherry tomatoes

Slice the tomatoes in half, transfer to a dehydrator, cut-side up, and dry at 60°C until completely desiccated. Blitz in a Thermomix to yield a fine powder and pass the powder through a fine-mesh nylon sieve. Reserve in an airtight container at room temperature.

Freeze-Dried Gooseberry Powder
500 grams freeze-dried green gooseberries

Place the gooseberries in a dehydrator set to 50°C and dry overnight. Transfer the dried gooseberries to a Thermomix and blitz to yield a fine powder. Pass the powder through a fine-mesh nylon sieve and reserve in an airtight container at room temperature.

Lacto Plum Skin Powder
25 frozen Lacto Plums (page 345)

Peel the plums while still frozen; reserve the flesh for another application. Transfer the plum peels to a perforated dehydrator tray and dry at 65°C until completely devoid of moisture. Transfer the dried skins to a Thermomix and blitz into a powder. Pass the powder through a fine-mesh nylon sieve and reserve in an airtight container at room temperature.
   Note: This same process can be applied to lacto mirabelle plum skins (see page 345).

Dried Bluefoot Mushrooms
1 kilogram bluefoot mushrooms

Cut the mushrooms in half and lay them out on a tray in a single layer. Dry in the oven or in a dehydrator set to 60°C until dry. Let cool, then transfer to an airtight container and reserve at room temperature.

Dried Carrot Flowers
1 kilogram carrot flowers

Lay the carrot flowers out on a tray in a single layer and dry in the oven or in a dehydrator set to 45°C until dry. Let cool, then transfer to an airtight container and reserve at room temperature.

Dried Cucumber
1 case (about 5 kilograms) cucumbers

Cut the cucumbers lengthwise into eighths. Lay them skin-side down on a dehydrator tray and dry at 50°C until completely devoid of moisture. Transfer to an airtight container or vacuum seal at 60% vacuum and reserve at room temperature.

Dried Ginger, Dried Ginger Skins, and Ginger Powder
1 kilogram fresh ginger

For dried ginger and dried ginger skins: Peel the ginger and reserve the skins. Use a mandoline to thinly slice the peeled ginger and transfer it to a dehydrator set to 60°C. Lay the ginger skins on dehydrator trays and add them to the dehydrator. Dry until the flesh and the skins are completely devoid of moisture. Reserve the dried ginger skins in an airtight container at room temperature.

Reserve the dried ginger in a separate airtight container or use to make ginger powder.

For ginger powder: Blitz the dried ginger in a Thermomix to yield a fine powder. Pass through a fine-mesh nylon sieve and reserve in an airtight container at room temperature.

Dried Horseradish and Horseradish Powder
1 kilogram fresh horseradish

For dried horseradish: Peel the horseradish and thinly slice with a mandoline. Transfer to a dehydrator set to 60°C and dry until completely devoid of water. Reserve the dried horseradish in an airtight container at room temperature, or use to make horseradish powder.

For horseradish powder: Blitz the dried horseradish in a Thermomix to yield a fine powder. Pass the powder through a fine-mesh nylon sieve and reserve in an airtight container at room temperature.

Dried Japanese Quince
10 Japanese quince

Cut the quince into eighths. Dry them in a dehydrator set to 60°C until completely devoid of moisture. Reserve in an airtight container at room temperature.

Dried Koji and Koji Flour
1 kilogram koji (any variety—see page 335)

For dried koji: Crumble the koji onto dehydrator mats and dry it at 45°C for 24 hours, or until completely devoid of moisture. Reserve the dried koji in an airtight container at room temperature, or use to make koji flour.

For koji flour: Blitz the dried koji in a Thermomix to yield a fine powder. Pass the powder through a fine-mesh nylon sieve and reserve the koji flour in an airtight container at room temperature.

Dried Norwegian Spruce
1 kilogram fresh Norwegian spruce branches with needles

Break down the spruce into smaller branches, place them in a gastro container, and dry in an oven set to 60°C for 12 hours. Strip the needles from the branches and discard the bare branches. Vacuum seal the dried needles at 80% vacuum and reserve at room temperature.

Dried Oyster Mushrooms
1 kilogram oyster mushrooms

Tear the mushrooms into smaller pieces and discard any inedible stems. Lay the mushroom pieces out on a tray in one layer and dry in the oven or in a dehydrator set to 60°C until completely dried. Transfer to an airtight container and reserve at room temperature.

Dried Samphire
500 grams samphire

Rinse the samphire to remove any sand and transfer it to a dehydrator tray. Dry at 50°C until completely devoid of moisture. Transfer to a Thermomix and blitz into a powder. Transfer to an airtight container or vacuum seal at 60% vacuum and reserve at room temperature.

Dried Sea Lettuce
500 grams fresh sea lettuce

Thoroughly wash the sea lettuce in cold water to ensure it's free of sand and dirt. Pat it dry and transfer it to a dehydrator set to 50°C; dry overnight. Reserve in an airtight container at room temperature.

Dried Strawberries
250 grams strawberries, leaf caps trimmed
Koji Oil (page 347)

Toss the strawberries in koji oil and transfer them to a dehydrator set to 60°C. Dry, turning them occasionally to ensure even dehydration, until completely desiccated. Reserve in an airtight container at room temperature.

Roasted Kelp, Roasted Kelp Powder, and Roasted Kelp Flour
250 grams kelp

For roasted kelp: Spread the kelp over sheet pans and roast in an oven set to 160°C (100% fan) for 45 minutes, until aromatically toasted and deeply browned. Remove from the oven and let cool. Break up the roasted kelp and reserve in an airtight container at room temperature, or use to make roasted kelp powder.

For kelp powder and kelp flour: Blitz the roasted kelp in a Thermomix to yield a fine powder. Reserve the kelp powder in an airtight container at room temperature, or pass the powder through a fine-mesh nylon sieve and reserve the kelp flour in an airtight container at room temperature.

Roasted Yeast
1 kilogram fresh biodynamic baker's yeast

Crumble the yeast onto metal sheet pans and roast in an oven set to 160°C (dry heat) for 45 to 60 minutes, or until the yeast is no longer moist inside. Let cool. Transfer to an airtight container or vacuum seal at 60% vacuum and reserve at room temperature.

Semi-Dried Mulberries
20 ripe mulberries
Koji Oil (page 347)

Brush the mulberries with koji oil. Dry the berries in a dehydrator set to 60°C for approximately 6 hours (depending on size), turning them every 2 hours, brushing them with a bit of koji oil as

you do, to ensure even dehydration and a nice final shape as the berries set. They should be just slightly less chewy than a good sultana raisin when they're done. Vacuum seal at 85% vacuum and freeze.

Semi-Dried Tomatoes
20 ripe yet firm cherry tomatoes
Koji Oil (page 347)

Bring a pot of unsalted water to a boil and set a bowl of ice water nearby. Lightly score an X into the bottom of each tomato. Quickly blanch and shock the tomatoes. Remove them from the ice water and peel them. Pat the peeled tomatoes dry and brush them with koji oil. Place on dehydrator trays and dry in a dehydrator set to 60°C for approximately 8 hours (depending on size), turning them every 2 hours, brushing them with the koji oil as you do, to ensure even dehydration and a nice final shape as the tomatoes set. They should be just slightly less chewy than a good sultana raisin when they're done. Vacuum seal at 85% vacuum and freeze.

Semi-Dried Red Currants
500 grams red currants on the vine
Koji Oil (page 347)

Dress the red currants (still on the vine) with a bit of koji oil. Place on a dehydrator mat and dry in a dehydrator set to 60°C for 2 to 3 hours, or until semi-dried and slightly chewy. Vacuum seal at 85% vacuum and freeze.

Salts

Cold-Infused Kelp Salt
1 liter Cold-Infused Dashi (page 330)

Bring the dashi to a boil, then skim off any scum on the surface and transfer the liquid to 1-liter containers, filling them about 75% full. Place the containers in a dehydrator set to 65°C and dry until 95% devoid of moisture. Use an offset spatula to scrape the resulting salt from the containers. Vacuum seal the salt on 80% vacuum and freeze.

Kelp Salt
1 kilogram filtered water
23 grams kelp

Vacuum seal the water and kelp and steam in a combi oven at 60°C (100% fan) for 1 hour. Strain the liquid and transfer it to 1-liter containers. Place in the oven and dry at 90°C until completely devoid of moisture. Chip the resulting salt off the bottom of the container and reserve in a dry airtight container at room temperature.

Noble Fir Salt
800 grams brine from Salted Noble Fir Cones (page 336)

Strain the brine and transfer it to a 1-liter container. Place the container in a dehydrator set to 60°C and dry until completely desiccated. Chip the resulting salt off the bottom of the container in small chunks, then crush the crystals using a mortar and pestle. Reserve in a dry airtight container at room temperature.

Pine Salt
50 grams Douglas fir needles
Liquid nitrogen
50 grams ground flake sea salt

Put the fir needles in a mortar and freeze with liquid nitrogen. Use the pestle to grind the frozen needles into a fine powder and then combine with the salt. Reserve in a dry airtight container in the freezer.

Roasted Kelp Salt
40 grams Roasted Kelp (opposite)
1 liter filtered water
60 grams fresh kelp

Vacuum seal the roasted kelp and water. Steam in a combi oven set to 60°C for 1 hour. Strain the liquid through a fine-mesh nylon sieve into an airtight container and let cool. Add the fresh raw kelp, cover, and leave in the fridge to infuse for 12 hours.

Strain the infused liquid through a fine-mesh nylon sieve into a clean 1-liter container. Place in a dehydrator set to 65°C and dry until 95% devoid of moisture. Chip the resulting salt off the bottom of the container in small chunks and reserve in a dry airtight container at room temperature.

Miscellaneous

Aronia Kelp
250 grams kelp (thick center-cut pieces only)
2 liters aronia berry juice, plus 1.5 liters to refresh
1 liter filtered water
70 grams muscovado sugar
30 grams dried ceps
25 grams dried morels
20 grams freeze-dried lingonberries
10 grams roasted juniper wood
8 grams loose quince tea
Spruce Wood Oil (page 348)

In a large pot, combine the kelp, 2 liters of the aronia juice, the water, sugar, ceps, morels, lingonberries, juniper wood, and quince tea. Bring to a boil, then reduce the heat to barely maintain a simmer and cook for 24 hours. Add the remaining 1.5 liters aronia juice to refresh, cover the pot with plastic wrap, and simmer for another 48 hours. Uncover the pot and simmer for another 24 hours, until the liquid has a nappé consistency.

Remove the kelp from the braising liquid and transfer it to parchment-lined sheet trays. Brush the kelp with spruce wood oil and let air-dry at room temperature, turning it every 3 hours, until no longer wet to the touch; this may take 1 to 2 days total. Layer the kelp in airtight containers with parchment squares between each layer and reserve in the freezer.

Black Apples
10 Gala apples

Peel and core the apples. Place them in a vacuum bag in a single layer and seal on 100% vacuum. Leave the bag in a chamber held at 60°C for 2 months. Reserve the black apples (still in the bag) in the freezer.

Black Chestnuts
100 chestnuts

Place the nuts in a vacuum bag and seal. Place the bag in a gastro pan and leave in a chamber held at 60°C for 3 weeks. Reserve the black chestnuts (still in the bag) in the freezer.

Note: Ensure that the chestnuts are not too far along in the season; otherwise, they can be quite starchy, which can affect the strength of the chestnut flavor.

Black Koji Grains
100 grams Barley Koji (page 335)

Break up the koji into individual grains and place them in a single layer over the bottom of an airtight plastic container. Leave in a chamber held at 60°C for 48 hours, until the koji has colored slightly and become sweet and flavored of dark fruit. Transfer to a clean airtight container and reserve in the fridge.

Black Pears
10 Conference pears

Peel and core the pears. Place them in a vacuum bag in a single layer and seal on 100% vacuum. Leave the bag in a chamber held at 60°C for 2 months. Remove the pears from the bag and transfer them to a parchment-lined dehydrator tray. Dry in a dehydrator set to 35°C for 1 week, until shriveled, tacky, and pasty. Vacuum seal and freeze.

Grilled Lemon Thyme
1 bunch lemon thyme
Clarified Smoked Butter (page 349)

Lightly dress the lemon thyme with clarified butter, transfer it to a large tamis, and gently grill over hot coals until smoky, slightly charred, and crisp. Transfer the grilled lemon thyme to a paper towel–lined container to absorb any excess fat and reserve in a low-temperature dehydrator.

Preserved Mixed Mushrooms
Ethanol spray (60% ABV)
10 kilograms mixed mushrooms (cauliflower, chanterelles, ceps, etc.)
Cep Oil (page 346)

Sanitize canning jars by running them through the dishwasher, then spraying their interiors with 60% ethanol spray; let dry. Meanwhile, sort the mushrooms by variety and size. Check for any mold and remove it where necessary. Clean the mushrooms with a paring knife and wash them if necessary. Cut up larger mushrooms if needed so they'll fit inside the jars. Tightly pack the mushrooms into the sanitized jars without breaking or crushing them, filling the jars all the way up to the top. Pour cep oil over the mushrooms up to the beginning of the neck of each jar. Seal the jars and place them in a combi oven set to 130°C (forced steam) for 1 hour 20 minutes. Carefully remove them from the oven and let cool to room temperature. Reserve the cooled jars in the fridge.

Preserved Truffles
Ethanol spray (60% ABV)
1 kilogram black winter truffles
1 kilogram canned truffle juice
Apple balsamic vinegar

Sanitize canning jars by running them through the dishwasher, then spraying the interiors with ethanol spray; let dry. Clean the truffles of any mold and brush them to remove any dirt. Pack them into the sanitized jars as tightly as possible and set aside.

Pour the truffle juice into a separate container and measure its pH. While stirring continuously, add vinegar in a slow, steady stream and continually measure the pH of the mixture until it drops to 4.3. Pour the vinegared truffle juice over the truffles in the jars, leaving 1.5 centimeters of headroom. Close the jars, ensure they are sealed, and place it in a combi oven set to 100°C (100% steam) for 30 minutes. Turn the oven off and leave the jars in the oven for another 30 minutes. Remove from the oven and let cool to room temperature before transferring the jars to the fridge for longer-term storage. When taking truffles from the jar, be sure to use a sterile utensil. The juice left in the jar can be used to preserve another batch of truffles; reserve it in the jar in the fridge.

Toasted Hay
100 grams hay

Place the hay in a deep gastro pan and set a perforated gastro pan on top to keep the hay contained but still allow air to circulate. Toast the hay in an oven set to 200°C (100% fan) for 45 to 60 minutes, or until it smells toasty. Carefully remove and let cool. Reserve in an airtight container at room temperature.

Acknowledgments

This book is not meant to be a "twenty-year yearbook." To catalog all that has transpired at Noma over the course of the past twenty years would require many more volumes. It is impossible to encapsulate the importance of every individual who has helped to progress Noma from where we started to where we are now—the farmers, foragers, fishmongers, and hunters we work with; the artisans using calloused hands to create our plates and glassware; the keen-eyed florists and designers continually connecting our ceilinged interior with nature; our kitchen team bringing the dreams of the test kitchen to life; our front-of-house team welcoming our guests with a genuine hug of comfort and familiarity; our office, which finds a way to convert logistical hypotheticals into reality. This book is meant to show where the kitchen is right now—how our new surroundings have shaped our interpretation of what it means to dine at Noma. This can and will change as time goes on (as all things must), but for now we wanted to focus on the food; it is a cookbook, after all.

Over the last twenty years, an incredible array of talented people have come through the doors of Noma. Industry leaders, the best craftspeople, creative masterminds. To properly acknowledge everyone who has played a part in the formation of what Noma is today would be virtually impossible. Rather, try to imagine this book as a giant puzzle. And each puzzle is made up of all the different people who have been involved in the restaurant since we opened in 2003. Some have been a bigger piece than others, but they are all a part of the whole. We are the sum of our collective parts.

These short paragraphs of acknowledgment are meant for a specific group of people who were and who continue to be involved with the day-to-day creativity at Noma:

Our first pastry chef, Mette Ryde, who set the standard for that department. The first-ever sous-chef hired at Noma, Søren Ledet—I distinctly remember working on a dish of roots with pork crackling with you many years ago.

Torsten Vildgaard. Ten years of working together side by side in the test kitchen. What a ride we've had together. If anyone was ever a part of when the nucleus exploded into a planet, Torsten was, along with his faithful sous-chef, Søren Westh. Wow, did we work a lot in those days, pulling our hair out trying to figure out what this whole thing would consist of.

Sam Nutter, who today lives in France as a full-time jujitsu master—what a creative mind. Lars Williams, who was first in charge of the banqueting but clearly has his head screwed on in a completely different way from others—analytical, curious. I've had some of my most mind-blowing experiences at Noma with Lars. There's one specific moment that is burned into my memory and remains one of my most cherished memories. Thank you for that, Lars, and thank you for everything.

David Zilber, who took over from Lars. How do you fill the shoes of a giant? With another giant. Simply the most curious and smartest person you can imagine.

Thank you for all those hours of trying to grow mold on stuff. Thank you for the fermentation book. And for that wonderful journey around the world together.

Rosio Sanchez. The most mind-blowing mind and all-around fantastic human being. She's the best of the best. She's the real deal. Creativity, action, tenacity, self-awareness. What an individual.

After Rosio came Malcolm Livingston II from NYC. At the time, he was exactly what we all needed. A different energy, a different approach, a different way of looking at things. It was the first time we had hired anyone as a sous-chef who hadn't spent time in a kitchen. I'm extremely proud to call Malcolm my friend today, and forever grateful for all the mind-bending hours trying to figure out the right texture for an ice cream or a mousse.

Thomas Frebel. We cannot speak about Noma without speaking about Thomas Frebel. He could have easily been a coauthor of this book. I would dare say that everything in the past fifteen years that has been on the menu or has been a creative thought has been influenced by Thomas in some way. But you don't hear about Thomas because he doesn't care about receiving credit. He's not only my creative partner but also my business partner at the restaurant today. I'm so grateful for you, Thomas. Thank you.

At this point our test kitchen really started developing. Arielle Johnson came through the doors with her scientific mind, her completely different approach to how we had previously operated. To be a student again. Wow. A true Noma legend.

We've had people who virtually learned to chop at the restaurant suddenly become a part of our creative team. Nate French from Boston, who started out in our kitchen completely green, barely knowing anything but never quitting and ultimately becoming one of the main pillars of our creative process. The go-to person whenever a piece of meat needs to be cooked perfectly. Let Nate do that; he'll figure it out.

There's Stu. Good old Stuey. The wild man from northern England who is gifted with some of the most natural and skilled cooking abilities I've come across. When he finds his moments of inner peace, he is an extraordinary, unstoppable force. He also has an incredible filter for bullshit. Always make sure you run things past Stu.

Riccardo. A big human being. Literally. He takes up a lot of space in the kitchen, but his refinement and technique are exceptionally exquisite. Poetic, even.

Mirek, the most tender jelly bean of a person disguised as a big Australian man. He's been a constant force between the kitchen and the test kitchen. Always helping with the creativity and expanding himself and the idea of what he thinks he can do. He's a pure joy.

These are some of the people who have contributed creatively in some way or another. But the truth is, there are so many more to talk about.

Luke Kolpin in the back kitchen keeping us all sane. Giving us all a burst of positive energy. The same could be said about Ali Sonko. Noma wouldn't be the same without you, Ali. You have to live till you're 100.

The Sock Monster, Ben Ing, for his calmness and team spirit.

Dan Giusti, a born leader and a born revolutionary.

And who can forget Matt Orlando? The first-ever head chef at Noma. He turned everything around when he came to Copenhagen. He set the tone of our kitchen when he became head chef—a lasting spirit that carried on long after he left to open Amass.

And of course, a huge thank-you to my coauthors, Mette Søberg and Junichi Takahashi. The two constant forces in the past five years of creativity. A decade we've been working together, and the creative energy that we collectively construct constantly feels fresh and new. I'm proud to share this book with you.

I could *easily* write another book about all of these people and so many more who have been critical to Noma in all departments, but again, this is a cookbook. James, Annegret, Annika, Mads, Gitte, Peter, Ben, Lau, Arve, Risa, Simon, Astrid, Claus, Kristian Byrge, Ali Food Snob, Ben Mervis, Pablo Soto, Kenneth Foong, Devin, Sebastian, Jacob Møller, Christian Puglisi, Kim Rossen, Kat Bont, Victor, Trevor, Jason, Sune Østergaard . . .

I want to finish by saying that the last twenty years of my life have been the most mind-boggling, most mind-blowing, toughest, most difficult, most exhilarating, and most every other possible adjective imaginable—sometimes all in one day. What gives me the power and the motivation to push forward is being around all of these people and experiencing the energy of doing something together.

A huge thank-you to the wizards of editing and efficiency at Artisan, specifically our publisher, Lia Ronnen, and her team: Martha Holmberg, Jane Treuhaft, Nancy Murray, Ivy McFadden, and Zach Greenwald. To Andrea Trabucco-Campos and his team of design gurus at Gretel. To Christine Rudolph for making our seasons come alive, and to Ditte Isager, our master photographer, for capturing this entire book and so many other memories over the years at Noma.

And finally, to the love of my life, Nadine Levy Redzepi, and our three daughters, Arwen, Gente, and Ro, thank you for being there and for all of us doing it together as a family. I love you all. And to my twin brother, Kenneth, thank you for being a part of all this craziness. Thank you all so much.

—René Redzepi

The time I spent at Marque in Australia and the people I met there mean a lot to me; had it not been for you, I'm not sure I would have had the confidence to start in the kitchen at Noma. And I cannot even begin to describe how grateful I am that I started at Noma. It has really meant the world to me and continues to make me happy and motivated every single day. All the people I've been so lucky to work with at Noma, you are amazing, and I'm extremely thankful to have some of you as my dearest friends. And René, thank you so much for every single day; you are the biggest inspiration, and I am forever grateful that you saw the potential in me nine years ago. I cannot wait to explore the future with you and the rest of the Noma family.

My dearest Bjørn and Mads, you are always on my side, and I cannot thank you enough for your love and support.

—Mette Søberg

I would like to extend my deepest gratitude to René, to past and present members of our test kitchen, and to the Noma team.

Before working at Noma, I had no knowledge of Nordic cuisine. The strong impression I got from when I dined at Noma for the first time is still burnt into my memory. Right after the meal I asked if I could work there. Back then, I could not even imagine that I would eventually become a part of the test kitchen—the core of creation at Noma.

Working at Noma these past ten years has been the greatest challenge and inspiration of my career and my life. René's energy, passion, and creativity inspire me to push myself further and have made me grow tremendously both professionally and personally.

Also to my family, friends, and former colleagues in Japan as well as my greatest inspiration, Chef Masao Saisu.

—Junichi Takahashi

Recipe Index

Noma Gastronomique

René Redzepi is the chef and co-owner of Noma in Copenhagen, five times recognized as the world's best restaurant. In 2021, Noma was awarded its third Michelin Star. Redzepi has been featured in publications from the *New York Times* to *Wired* and profiled in two feature-length documentaries and countless national and international media outlets. His first book, *Noma: Time and Place in Nordic Cuisine*, is an IACP and James Beard Award winner, and *The Noma Guide to Fermentation* is a *New York Times* bestseller. He lives in Copenhagen with his wife, Nadine Levy Redzepi, their three children, and their dog, Ponzu. Find him on Instagram at @reneredzepinoma and @nomacph.

Mette Søberg has been cooking in restaurants since 2010, first in Copenhagen and then later in Sydney at Marque, under the mentorship of Mark Best. She returned to Copenhagen in 2013 and immediately joined Noma, where two years later she became a member of the test kitchen, developing dishes for Noma's menus. In 2018, when Noma moved to its current location, she rose to the position of head of research and development. Mette lives with her fiancé, Bjørn, and their new baby, Mads. Find her on Instagram at @mette_soberg.

Junichi Takahashi is a chef from Miyagi Prefecture in Japan who has been cooking for twenty years in restaurants around Japan and Europe. He has been an integral member of the Noma team since 2012 and has been developing dishes for Noma's menus since 2016. Jun is not only known for his innovation and creativity but also for delivering satisfying dishes that are rich with umami and deeply rooted in tradition and craftsmanship. Find him on Instagram at @ryoriya.

Alex Telinde, Alice Arnoux, Aline Vlaemynck, André Andersen, Andrea Bano, Andreea Gintaru, Besa Rexhepi, Charlie Leonard Sims, Christina Rasmussen, Christos Giachos, Cristina Megias Torrego, Cúán Greene, Cynthia Hulé, Dahliane Caure, Daniel Cardenas del Rio, Daniel Craig Martin, Daniella Rebelo, David Jørgensen, Davide Nicotra, Diego Gutierrez, Dite Pauliukaite, Edoardo Fiaschi, Ewa Woronowska, Francesco Cavaleri, Furqan Meerza, Gilliann Szucs, Gintarė Galinskė, Giovanni Moncada, Hiro Nakamichi, Hugh Allen, Jack Blackwell, Jacob Lund Vestergaard, Jaime Lynn White, Jarjusey Sonko, Javier Rodriguez, Jeppe Adrian Thomsen, Jeppe Jung, Jesper Mørk, Jessica Natali, Jocelyn Ueng, Jose Ulises Montero Lombera, Joseph Bechameil, Kasper Herand, Kasper Pedersen, Keshet David, Kevin Jeung, Kristian Rise, Lamin Sonko, Lana Isabelle Pham, Lasse Bech Jacobsen, Lenk Szabolcs, Line Deth Hesselholt, Line Kleppe, Lorenzo Tirelli, Loui Skou Andersen,